A publication of
The Archbishop Torkom Manoogian
Educational and Cultural Fund

By order of
His Grace Bishop Khajag Barsamian, Primate
Diocese of the Armenian Church of America
630 Second Avenue, New York, NY 10016

Commentary on the Divine Liturgy

by Xosrov Anjewac'i

Translated with an introduction by S. Peter Cowe

Armenian Church Classics

St. Vartan Press
A Publication of the Department of Religious Education

Library of Congress Cataloging-in-Publication Data

Khosrov, Andzewats'i, 10th cent.
    [Meknut'iwn aghɔt'its' Pataragin. English]
    Commentary on the Divine Liturgy / Xosrov Anjewac'i ; translated with
an introduction by S. Peter Cowe.
            p.   cm.
    Translation of Meknut'iwn aghɔt'its' Pataragin.
    "A Publication of the Department of Religious Education, Diocese of the
Armenian Church of America."
    Includes bibliographical references and index.
    ISBN 0-934728-23-2
    1. Lord's Supper—Liturgy—Early works to 1800. 2. Mass—Liturgy—
Early works to 1800. I. Cowe, S. Peter. II. Title.
BX127.K4813   1991   91-42684
                                                                            CIP

Dedicated
to
Archbishop Tiran Nersoyan
(1904-1989)

Table of Contents

Preface

Avidly studied, copied and imitated over long centuries, this seminal reflection on the liturgy by Xosrov, bishop of Anjewac'ik' still retains much of its original vigour, lucidity and ethical profundity. As the earliest detailed source for the Armenian anaphora which became standard, its historical importance is paramount and its contribution to comparative liturgiology immense. Moreover, it has much to offer the contemporary movement towards liturgical renewal in the Armenian Church in delineating the central eucharistic themes and expounding their integration in the rite and in the transformation of the worshipping community.

Known primarily as the father of an illustrious son, Xosrov's scanty biographical data are discussed in the introduction along with questions of his theology, style and subsequent influence. The Armenian text reproduced is that of the unique Venice edition of 1869. Transliterations follow the Hübschmann-Meillet-Benveniste system.

1

Biographical Sketch of the Author

Comparative silence enshrouds the lives of most early and medieval Armenian writers, even the most famous. *Horror vacui* with regard to the latter has generated many folk tales and legends, the stories becoming ever more embellished as the figures grew in stature and reverence.[1] With the establishment of monastic academies from the end of the tenth century in Hałbat and Sanahin and subsequently, for example, at Glajor and Tat'ew and the regularization of studies at such institutions, it became conventional for pupils to write their mentor's *vita* in an appropriately panegyrical style. Indeed, Xosrov's youngest son, the renowned mystical poet Grigor Narekac'i is one of the first to be so honored.[2]

However, it often happens that most of what is known about a writer derives from the writings themselves. Here too one must rely on incidental references, since it was considered highly improper for an author to draw undue attention to himself and hence autobiography scarcely exists as a genre in this period.[3] Xosrov was probably born around the turn of the tenth century, if not slightly earlier, since it is stated that he was already aged in 954. As such, he would have been a near contemporary of Catholicos Anania Mokac'i who is the source of this information.[4] Moreover, as the hierarch died in 965, having outlived Xosrov by some time, Xosrov's death must be set within a decade of that reference.[5] Perhaps he grew up in the region of Vaspurakan, center of his later activity, and in a family with noble connections which would account for his extensive education. It is also implied by his marriage to a cousin of Anania,[6] founder of the prestigious monastery of Narek. Among other accomplishments he must have attained a certain familiarity with Greek, as well as a broad grounding in theology, amply displayed in the present commentary.

It is uncertain how he spent his middle years. The only extant data relate to the birth of his three sons Sahak, Yovhannēs and Grigor. The first in all likelihood gained much of his schooling from his father and was old enough to copy this commentary at the latter's dictation in 950.[7] The younger two studied with Anania at Narek whom Yovhannēs succeeded as abbot.

It seems that sometime after their mother's death,[8] the catholicos elevated Xosrov to the see of Anjewac'ik' with his seat at Hogeac' Vank'.[9] Certainly, in his previous office as abbot of neighboring Varag, Anania Mokac'i would have had occasion to observe Xosrov's character and achievements. Even after a bitter dispute found them on opposing sides, the hierarch singled out his adversary's attributes of modesty and learning.[10] In light of this last quality it is tempting to identify our author with the Xosrov *gitnakan*[11] (scholar) who assisted the catholicos at the beginning of his rule in his relations with Sahak, schismatic catholicos of Albania. The parallelism becomes all the more striking granted the paucity of attestations of the name at this period.[12] However,

4

since his namesake is cited in a list of vardapets, if the identification were accepted, one would have to posit the writer's having occupied that ecclesiastical rank for some years before his elevation to the episcopate.[13]

A major factor in the disharmony between the two catholicoi was their differing interpretation of the Council of Chalcedon (451) and its Christological definition.[14] During the latter part of the sixth century a similar schism had been occasioned over the same issue and the inner-Armenian debate on the subject continued throughout the following century from which the party rejecting the council emerged victorious.[15] This had also been the cause of a schism between Armenia and Georgia in 608. However, it appears that by the mid ninth century greater tolerance again prevailed, so much so that at the council of Širakavan of 862 a non-confrontational stance was adopted[16] which further encouraged intermarriage between the two confessional communities, following the lead of the Bagratid royal house.[17]

As in the sixth century manifestation of the debate, a major role was played by the metropolitan of Siwnik'.[18] The contemporary incumbent, Yakob, attempted to propagate his views by a vigorous letter-writing campaign to other prelates. Moreover, the historian Step'annos Ōrbēlean records a rumor circulating at the time that he was responsible for setting Xosrov against the catholicos,[19] although this cannot be verified by other evidence. Anania himself makes no mention of the connection, despite his detailed treatment of his dispute with the bishop of Anjewac'ik'. Nevertheless, the central issue relating to the prerogatives of the catholicos over those of the bishop was also contended by Yakob and both bishops died under the hierarch's ban. So closely were they associated by the mid thirteenth century that Kirakos' account actually confuses them at one point, suggesting that Xosrov

5

had taken refuge from the hierarch in a fortress of Siwnik'.[20]

Byzantine expansion and reconquest which continued throughout the tenth century, often under generals of Caucasian origin, added a further dimension to the theological discussion. Gradually Byzantine Armenia was regained (e.g. Melitene in 934, Amida in 941) and then began the annexation of provinces of Greater Armenia starting with Tarōn in 968. Consequently, there was much pro-Byzantine and specifically pro-Chalcedonian sentiment at this period in certain circles of Vaspurakan. This is probably the context in which we are to view Xosrov's proposals. The first of these aspires to phonetic authenticity, arguing that Armenian loanwords from Greek such as kirakē (Sunday, i.e. κυριακή) ought to be pronounced with the more emphatically trilled 'r' sound of the original rather than the softer enunciation of the Armenian letter re by which it had been represented.[21]

The form in which Armenian sources have preserved the second proposal suggests it is to be regarded as an etymological eccentricity with bizarre consequences for male coiffure. According to Anania, Xosrov derived the term ktrič (brave; bold youth) from the verb ktrem ('cut') and manuk[23] ('youth, young man') from manem ('twist, weave'). He thereby elaborated the principle that youths should have their hair cut until their beard grew, after which they were to let their hair grow in plats down their back. Kirakos, once again, seems to attest a garbled version of the same account,[24] substituting the term patani ('adolescent') for manuk and reversing the order. According to this version, youths should not cut their hair until it formed a wall (pat) along their back. Once cut, they should then be called ktrič.

However, it is possible that behind this quaint etymological literalism and solecistic hairstyling lies a reference to monastic tonsure. Far from issuing ordinances applying to the whole male population of his diocese, perhaps the bishop enjoined the practice of monks letting their hair grow after being tonsured. Regulations varied with time, but in the tenth and eleventh centuries tonsure involved the complete shaving of the head.[25] Whether monks later continued to have their hair cut or let it grow is unclear. Certainly, this became later custom in imitation of the Old Testament nazirite vow and was even adopted as the custom for secular clergy by the eighteenth century. The topicality of male hair length in the contemporary debate with Byzantium is underlined by the issue's appearance in Catholicos Xač'ik's reply to a letter from the metropolitan of Sebastia.

More significant theologically was Xosrov's query of the need to bless crosses before permitting them to be venerated by the faithful. This issue marked an obvious liturgical divergence between Byzantine and Armenian practice which recurs in much of the doctrinal correspondence between the two churches.[26] In addition to Catholicos Xač'ik's letter mentioned above, it featured, for example, in the letter of an Armenian Chalcedonian theologian Theopistēs at the beginning of the twelfth century.[27] Although Catholicos Anania does not consider it of such magnitude as to defend it in his brief encyclical,[28] Połos Tarōnac'i explicates the Armenian reasoning in his reply to Theopistēs. Significantly, he stresses the analogy between the cross and church building, both of which should be purified by scripture readings, cleansed by water and wine and anointed with oil in token of the Spirit's indwelling. Otherwise, he contends, reverence paid to it would resemble idolatry, focusing on the subject itself.[29]

In this connection, Połos notes that the T'ondrakite sectarians reject the sanctity of both the cross and its sanctuary,[30] as had been done in Armenia by another heretical sect, the Paulicians.[31] In his refutation of their iconoclasm Catholicos Yovhannēs

Ōjnec'i outlines the difference between Christian and pagan cult objects, underscoring the efficacy of unction in bestowing the seal of the Spirit[32] upon the former. The T'ondrakites' rejection of the cross was explicitly condemned in Anania Narekac'i's extensive denunciation of the heretical movement.[33]

Nevertheless, it was rather Xosrov's theory of the canonical equality between the episcopate and catholicate that exercised all the hierarch's attention and ingenuity of argument.[34] In turn, it is likely that Xosrov's consideration of the question was provoked by Anania's forceful attempts to conclude the schism in Siwnik' and Albania by securing submission from the offending prelates. Thus, when Sahak, catholicos of Albania, consecrated his relative Gagik to succeed him, Anania declared it invalid and referred to the Council of Part'aw in 709 where the then Armenian catholicos, Ełia Arčišec'i, had a regulation approved that no candidate be elevated to the other catholicate without consecration by his Armenian counterpart.[35] Similarly, Anania censured Metropolitan Yakob's annual reception of holy oil (miwṙon) from Albania rather than directly from himself, since Siwnik' fell within the Armenian jurisdiction.[36]

Xosrov's basic argument was that consecration to the catholicate involved merely a repetition of the episcopal rite,[37] and could not confer a higher degree; rather the distinction between bishop and the ranks of archbishop, metropolitan and patriarch was administrative, not sacramental. This certainly reflects Byzantine theory and (for the most part)[38] practice whereby episcopal candidates for higher office are installed without any further rite of consecration. Tacitly it also raises the issue of the catholicos' sole prerogative to consecrate bishops, a right also enjoyed by his Syrian (jacobite) counterpart,[39] which went beyond the injunctions of the Nicene canons.[40] In view of the centrifugal forces of contemporary Armenian politics, creating separate kingdoms in Vaspurakan and later in Siwnik', which seemed to be mirrored in the ecclesiastical realm, Xosrov's interpretation must have appeared as insubordination which might be construed as legitimizing such separatist tendencies. Its threat to established church order may also have fuelled suspicions of cryptic sectarian sentiments.

Catholicos Anania had commented on the widespread sympathy for Chalcedonian Christology in different parts of the country at this time.[41] That is well illustrated by the fate of Step'annos who succeeded to the throne after the Council of Ani deposed his predecessor for too overt Byzantine sympathies.[42] He decided to pursue the latter to the south-west where he had found asylum with the Arcrunid king Abusahl-Hamazasp only to be imprisoned there until his death in 972. Granted Xosrov's self-avowed openness to adopt such tenets of other churches as he deemed to be correct,[43] and the background of the innovations he wished to introduce into Armenia, it has been proposed that Xosrov was himself of Chalcedonian persuasion and influenced his son Grigor in the same direction.[44] Since the question impinges directly on the thought of his commentary, it is appropriate to reserve discussion until that is passed in review.

Such, then, is the scanty information that has been preserved concerning the activities and attitudes of the controversial bishop of Anjewac'ik'. However, even these meagre data suffice to convince us we are dealing with a man of uncommon ability and independence of judgement, unwilling to accept the status quo without analysis and justification, even at great personal cost. As his commentary exercised a major impact on the subsequent development of the genre, so his canonical inquiries encouraged greater coherence between theory and practice, particularly with respect

9

to the status of the catholicos.[45]

In view of its intrinsic importance as one of the few prime sources for Xosrov's life, albeit composed in a spirit of controversy, the catholicos' statement on Xosrov's anathematization is reproduced in full below:

> *The Reason for Anathematizing Xosrov, Bishop of Anjewac'ik' by the Lord Anania, Catholicos of the Armenians*
>
> The words of the divine oracles now stir us unwillingly to settle an account which has come to maturation during our days. Previously it was said, "Listen, all nations of the earth" (Ps 48:2), and in the same vein it says, "Listen, elders, and tell your children, if ever your times should witness the same evil which deceptive Satan has dictated and insinuated upon the pernicious tongues of the upright." In this way the supernatural voice anticipated the current situation. Nine hundred years ago the Holy Spirit predicted this through the divinely-inspired Paul who boasted his stewardship of God's mysteries in the verse, "Are you putting Christ to the test who speaks to you through me?" Indeed, this was no test, but the complete truth, since all his Spirit-inspired teachings have been realized and fulfilled, some in his lifetime, others in our days.
>
> That text applies to us which states "in the last times some will fall from faith and contemplate demonic error." And again, "Liars will arise among you to entice their followers to pursue fictitious fables. They will not cease attacking the word of

right doctrine established by God, trained by constant practice in devising fiction opposed to the truth. They are absolutely perverse and always unjust; disobedient, vicious, ungrateful children, unable to gainsay the father of faith, they turned their backs on the divine plan.

They arose from us, but were not of our number. Although their external appearance resembled ours in the flesh and they sprouted from the good and grew under its nourishment, in substance they adhered to evil counsel and sucked its lethal milk which does not feed (*pararē*) the palate, but envelops (*parurē*) the soul. Far from being a syrup sweet to the taste, it is noisome and insufferably bitter, full of the deadly poisons of the tare-scattering serpent.

In ancient times he professed his teaching to the tender, naïve, twin orifices of auricular vaults and convinced them by wily deceit it was the radiance of divinization with flattering speech. Then he brought about their loss of what they already possessed and removal from the bosom of their divinely-planted domicile. The same evil deceit has surreptitiously slunk into the children of rebellion and made them say disgraceful things, draw inappropriate comparisons and speak what is unseemly.

In the year 403 [of the Armenian era = A.D. 954] the fourteenth of my office, one of our bishops called Xosrov, to whom I had entrusted the see of Anjewac'ik', began to attract attention. He was a modest man, learned and advanced in hoary old age. Suddenly, as if enticed by an evil spirit, without any provocation he began to employ a more emphatic pronunciation, calling Sunday (Kirakē) kiwïrakē and Jerusalem (Erusałēm) Eïusałēm etc. as in Greek.

Subsequently, he came up with other ridiculous nonsense. He ordered boys' heads to be shaved until their beard grew in accordance with the term "brave" (ktričٛ) and thereafter to let their hair grow long in plats (manil) to the shank in accordance with the term "youth" (manuk). This continued for a time and then he introduced the refuse of his inanity into the church.

With regard to the cross of Christ, he stated that crosses blessed by priests and those unblessed share the same veneration and hence he concluded blessing was superfluous. We overlooked these foibles. However, he then started to propagate a new schism and infiltrate it into God's church. He averred that angels and archangels enjoyed equal honor and glory and consequently the patriarch and bishop shared equal glory and honor, citing as analogy the rubric "they call this person from the office of psalmodist to that of deacon and that person from the diaconate to the office of priesthood." So far one can rise in office. Yet when they call this person from the priesthood to the episcopal throne, this is no longer an office; for he has been elevated to a throne. When they call that person from the episcopacy to the patriarchal throne, there is no further nomenclature. There is therefore one throne and one dignity for the patriarch and bishop. Moreover, the second calling he maintained was dissolution of the first rather than the conferral of the additional honor of the patriarchate.

He continued to expound similar views to the same effect, and although I pleaded with him many times to turn from those specious, unorthodox arguments, even imploring him with tears, he refused to be guided. Thus, I was compelled at God's command to strike with the fiery sword and set his portion with the hypocrites. He bore this as his viaticum to the world to come with perdition in store, as he did not relent until his last breath. Hence, we were constrained to write this as an enduring testament to future generations to beware of such futile pursuits and rightly consider the implications for the next life; for "sufficient unto the day is the evil thereof."

Notes

1) In general, the tenth century historian Step'annos Taronec'i is the first source of such literary biography. For a series of medieval reviews of Armenian genres see Anasyan, *Matenagitut'yun*, vol. 1, 1959, pp. xliii-lxxvi.

2) See Yovsep'eanc', *Yišatakarank'*, coll. 141-146.

3) The one striking exception is provided by the seventh century mathematician Anania Širakac'i whose fairly brief account is basically an apologia for his scholarly interests and standards.

4) See Anania Mokac'i, "Letters", p. 276.

5) N. Bogharian tentatively suggests his death occurred in 963 (*Hay grołner*, p. 141). Consequently, the date of 972 first

recorded by Č'amč'ean is to be rejected (*AnjB*, vol. 2, p. 535).

6)   His son's biographer identifies Xosrov's wife more precisely as the daughter of Anania's paternal uncle (see Yovsep'eanc', *Yišatakarank'*, col. 141).

7)   On this see his brother Grigor's colophon on p. 231.

8)   See Bogharian, *Hay grołner*, p. 141 and *AnjB* vol. 2, p. 535. For the relation of this event to Grigor's birth see M. Abełyan, *Hayoc' hin grakanut'yan patmut'yun* [History of Ancient Armenian Literature] vol. 1, Erevan, Armenian Academy of Sciences: 1944, p. 519.

9)   On this monastery see J.-M. Thierry, "Monastères arméniens du Vaspurakan", *REA* (1967), pp. 167-168.

10)   For the context see his encyclical on pp. 11-13.

11)   In the encyclical mentioned above the catholicos refers to Xosrov by the variant of the same epithet (*gitnawor*).

12)   *AnjB*, vol. 2, pp. 529-538.

13)   The consecration must have taken place between Anania's accession in 941 and Xosrov's production of the present work in 950.

14)   For an overview see A. Gillmeier, S.J., *Christ in Christian Tradition*, vol. 1, *From the Apostolic Age to Chalcedon*, London, Mowbray: 1965 (second, revised ed. 1975).

15)   For a recent study of certain aspects of the problem see Cowe, "Job Fragment" and "The Significance of the Persian War (572-592) in the *Narratio de rebus Armeniae*", *Mus* 104 (1991), pp. 265-276.

16)   On the council and the authenticity of its acts see Fr. K. Maksoudian, "The Chalcedonian Issue and the Early Bagratids: The Council of Širakavan", *REA* 21 (1988-1989), pp. 333-344 and esp. p. 338 which cites the relevant articles.

17)   Intermarriage is referred to by Anania as one of the irregu-

larities he aspired to reform at the outset of his catholicate. See "Letters", p. 130. On the importance of Anania's work see F. Macler, "Anania Mokatsi, écrivain arménien du xe siècle", *RHR* cl (1930), pp. 5-15. See also D. M. Girard, "Anania Mogatzi. Episode de la lutte religieuse en Arménie (943-965)", *RHE* vii (1906), pp. 19 ff..

18) For the earlier phase of the debate see G. Garitte, *La narratio de rebus Armeniae*, CSCO subsidia 4, Louvain, 1952, §86, p. 38 and the notes to that passage.

19) Step'annos ōrbelēan, *Patmut'iwn nahangin sisakan* [History of the Province of Siwnik'] Tiflis, Alaneanc': 1910, p. 277.

20) Kirakos, *Patmut'iwn*, pp. 48-49.

21) For the contrast in pronunciation between the letters řa and ře see A. Meillet, *Altarmenisches Elementarbuch*, Heidelberg, Winters: 1913, p. 13. Several Greek borrowings in Armenian do in fact maintain continuity with the original in the way Xosrov proposes e.g. the diaconal admonition in the liturgy přōsxumē (πρόσχωμεν 'let us attend') and for others see *NBH* vol. 2, 1837, p. 661.

22) G. B. Jahukyan (ed.) *Žamanakakic' hayoc' leʒvi bac'atrakan bařaran* [Explanatory Dictionary of Contemporary Armenian] vol. 3, Erevan, Armenian Academy of Science: 1974, p. 215.

23) *ArmB*, vol. 3, 1977, pp. 255-256.

24) Kirakos, *Patmut'iwn*, p. 48.

25) See N. F. Robinson, *Monasticism in the Orthodox Churches*, London, Cope and Fenwick: 1916, p. 35 and M. Wawryk, *Initiatio Monastica in Liturgia Byzantina* OCA 180, Rome, 1968, pp. 84-93. In his reply to the metropolitan of Sebastia Catholicos Xač'ik charges his correspondent with treating long hair in men as a veritable criterion for Chistianity, alleging that others were branded as Saracens. In support of his own

position he cites St. Paul's pronouncement (1 Cor 11:14) and St. John Chrysostom's comments *ad loc.* See K. Šahnazareanc' (ed.), *Tiezerakan Patmut'iwn Step'annos vardapeti Tarōnec'woy* [Universal History of the vardapet Step'annos Tarōnec'i] Paris, Thunot: 1859, p. 229. I am indebted to Bishop Kallistos of Diokleia for guidance on Byzantine practice on this and other respects.

26) For Armenian justification of the practice see Conybeare, *Rituale*, pp. 51-53 and for the condemnation of Greek usage see Movsēs Erznkac'i, *Patasxanik'* (1975), p. 35. A prayer of blessing over icons and crosses seems to have been introduced in the seventeenth century, but previously St. John of Damascus' judgement prevailed on both icons and crosses that the representation is sanctified by the name of God or the saint inscribed upon it (*On Icons*, 2, 14: P. B. Kotter (ed.), *Die Schriften des Joannes von Damaskos*, vol. 3, Berlin, de Gruyter: 1975, p. 108). Nevertheless, Catholicos Anania regards this proposal as extra-ecclesial.

27) See K. Šahnazareanc' (ed.), *Tiezerakan Patmut'iwn Step'annos vardapeti Tarōnec'woy* Paris, Thunot: 1859, p. 229 and *T'ułt' eranelwoyn Pōłosi Tarōnac'woy* [Letter of the Blessed Pōłos Tarōnac'i] Constantinople, 1752, p. 174.

28) See pp. 10-13.

29) Conybeare, *Rituale*, pp. 174-176. The rite of blessing is expressly enjoined in canons 27-28 of the Council of Duin of 720.

See Ōjnec'i, *Matenagrut'iwnk'*, p. 43. For an English translation of the service see Conybeare, *Rituale*, pp. 39-51.

30) Pōłos Tarōnac'i, *Tułt'* p. 260.

31) For a classic study of this movement see N. G. Garsoïan, *The Paulician Heresy: A Study of the Origin and Development of Paulicianism in Armenia and the Eastern Provinces of the*

Byzantine Empire. The Hague, Mouton, 1967. It is likely that this body exercised an influence on the doctrinal development of the later sect.

32) Ōjnec'i, *Matenagrut'iwnk'*, pp. 52-56.

33) Unfortunately, Anania Narekac'i's treatise is no longer extant but was described in detail in a letter of Grigor. The material is presented by Nersessian in *Tondrakian Movement*, pp. 57-58.

34) His reply took the form of two closely argued epistles. See Anania Mokac'i, "Letters", pp. 277-288.

35) Ibid., p. 138. There Anania traces the arrangement to St. Gregory the Illuminator. On the council of 709 see Mxit'areanc', *Patmut'iwn Žoḷovoc'*, p. 90.

36) Anania Mokac'i, "Letters", p. 130. Canon five of the Council of Part'aw in 768 had denied bishops the prerogative of blessing the *miwṙon*. See Mxit'areanc', *Patmut'iwn Žoḷovoc'*, p. 97.

37) This situation also obtained in the Jacobite church (Hage, *Syrisch-jakobitische Kirche*, p. 15).

38) The one exception to this was provided by the Patriarchate of Moscow where such a rite of consecration was practised in the initial period after attaining autocephalous status until the Moscow Council of 1666-7. The Byzantine rite of installation may be found in I. Habert, *Archieratikon*, Paris, 1643, pp. 430 ff. See further Beck, *Kirche*, pp. 60-62.

39) See Hage, *Syrisch-jakobitische Kirche*, p. 16.

40) According to canon six, no episcopal consecration may take place without a metropolitan's authorization, while canon four stipulates as many bishops as possible from the jurisdiction should participate in the ceremony and at very least three (Hakobyan, *Kanonagirk'*, pp. 119, 120-121 and *Pēdalion*, Athens, 1908, pp. 133-134.

41) This may have been a factor in determining Anania to transfer the seat of the catholicate from Aɫt'amar to Argina in the vicinity of Kars, contemporary center of the Bagratid realm.

42) The charge focused on his insertion of icons (regarded as characteristic of Byzantine church art) into the cathedral at Argina. For the background to this see A. S. Sahakyan, "Miǰnadaryan patkerapaštut'yan haykakan tarberakě" [The Armenian Variant to the Medieval Veneration of Images] *PBH* (1987) no. 2, pp. 150-159.

43) Xosrov Anjewac'i, *Meknut'iwn žamakargut'ean* [Commentary on the Office] Constantinople, 1840, p. 199.

44) Mécérian, *Livre de prières*, pp. 21-25.

45) The later rite of catholicosal consecration was influenced by Lambronac'i's translation of the western ritual in the 1180's and diverges from the episcopal rite notably by anointing of the head. In later Armenian tradition this has been viewed as bearing an affinity to royal coronation. See A. Tēr-Mik'ayelean, *Hayastaneayc' aṙak'elakan uɫɫap'aṙ surb ekeɫec'in ew iwr surb kargě* [The Holy Orthodox Apostolic Church of Armenia and Its Holy Order] Vaɫaršapat, Mother See Press: 1897, p. 37. However, this feature was probably borrowed from the western form of episcopal consecration which in turn had been influenced by the rite of royal unction. See C. Walter, *Studies in Byzantine Iconography*, London, Variorum: 1977, p. 67.

Xosrov and the Shape of the
Armenian Liturgy

In the early centuries of our era Armenia found itself in an intimate cultural and religious continuum with Parthian Iran. The origins of Christian communities on its territory are not well documented, yet extant material allows us to postulate two main missionary thrusts from the eastern Roman Empire. Syrian centers like Edessa to the south marked one of these axes; the other matrix was formed by Cappadocia to the west. Both had a significant influence on the development of the Armenian church in the fourth and fifth centuries, their relative importance varying according to geographical locality and political ascendancy.

Thus, the Cappadocian metropolis, Caesarea, was the locus for the consecration of the first bishop, St. Gregory the Illuminator, in late summer 314.[1] Moreover, the chief Armenian bishop continued to be consecrated there until the time of Gregory's great-great grandson, St. Nersēs, whose program of charitable activity was probably inspired by the initiatives of Eustathius, incumbent of the intervening see of Sebaste.[2] However, with the partition of

19

387 A.D. most of the territory fell under Iranian hegemony, where Syriac became the primary liturgical language, as the historian Łazar P'arpec'i reports.[3]

The invention of an indigenous alphabet at the beginning of the fifth century offered the possibility of conducting divine worship fully in Armenian.[4] Once again Nersēs' son Sahak turned west in selecting a model. The original Armenian liturgy was appropriately an early form of the local Cappadocian anaphora which seems to have been redacted by St. Basil, with whose name it was subsequently associated.[5] The antiquity of the Armenian formulation is indicated by its agreements with the Egyptian redaction over against the Byzantine and Syrian forms which reveal a number of secondary traits (assimilation to scripture, clarificatory additions, redundancy of expression).[6] Consequently, it is a valuable witness in reconstructing the early Greek text. The widespread utilization of this liturgy within the Armenian realm in the fifth century is well illustrated by a lengthy and very accurate citation from the main eucharistic prayer attributed to P'awstos, whose epic histories tend to reflect a southern Syrian-related provenance.[7] In medieval manuscripts this anaphora was attributed to St. Gregory the Illuminator, indicating an awareness of its priority in Armenian usage.

Towards the end of the fifth century four further anaphorae were translated from Greek, all of which appear to have Cappadocian affinities to different degrees. Two of these appear to be variant recensions of the same basic liturgy of St. Basil. One bearing St. Sahak's name[8] clearly preserves a very early text form, while the other, imputed to St. Cyril of Alexandria, may be compared with the later Constantinopolitan formulation of that liturgy.[9] The third is known by the name of St. Basil's close associate, St. Gregory of Nazianzus, and indeed several striking paral-

20

lels with the latter's writings have been discovered, though these fall short of firm proof.[10] However, it was the final translation which the manuscripts assign to St. Athanasius[11] that gradually supplanted the liturgy of St. Gregory,[12] ultimately to become the sole eucharistic rite in Armenian usage. Hence, despite Xosrov's familiarity with other anaphorae,[13] this is the only one he selects for commentary.

Nevertheless, Armenians were exposed to several other rites during the Middle Ages, some of which left their impression on the principal ordo. One of the earliest of these was an anaphora original to Jerusalem which was ascribed to St. James, the brother of the Lord and first bishop of the city.[14] Once more the Armenian text is of great significance for the textual investigation of the formulary, since it evinces a structure at once divergent from the Greek and Syriac redactions which survive and at various points is reckoned simpler and more original. It has been suggested that it represents the eucharist of the "Julianist" Syrian church[15] with which the Armenian church was in communion at one point.[16] It appears to have influenced part of the prothesis of the later Armenian rite.[17]

Subsequently, the developed Byzantine form of the liturgy of St. Basil was rendered,[18] presumably for use by Armenian Chalcedonian parishes which grew in number during the eleventh and twelfth centuries.[19] It has been represented as a careful accomodation of the fifth century translation to the later Greek version rather than a completely new undertaking and this is supported by several doublet readings.[20] The same community also translated the lenten rite of the presanctified gifts (also attributed to St. Basil)[21] and the liturgy of St. John Chrysostom.[22]

Similarly, in token of the growing rapport between the Crusaders and the Armenian kingdom of Cilicia where both king

21

and catholicos accepted papal supremacy (temporarily) in 1198/9, the archbishop of Tarson, Nersēs Lambronac'i, produced a rendition of the Roman missal in conjunction with a wider project of translating liturgical and canonical texts employed by the Latins.[23] It is the source of the *Confiteor*, the priest's confessional formula during the preparation which entered the Armenian rite in the thirteenth century.[24] Probably the same century saw the translation in Cilicia of the final anaphora attributed to St. Ignatius of Antioch from a Syriac exemplar.[25]

It appears that the energetic catholicos Grigor Anawarzec'i (1293-1307), who was in favor of a permanent union with Rome, took the initiative of collecting the various anaphorae into a liturgical corpus.[26] This became the model for some of our extant witnesses such as the important collection at Lyon, copied in 1314.[27] Its significance resides not only in its comprehensive contents, but also its early date, as the overwhelming majority of Armenian missals derives from the seventeenth century and hence preserves the text in its almost contemporary form. Subsequently, the volume of copying abates as the number of printed editions becomes more plentiful.[28] Investigation of the missal's direct tradition takes us back once more to the thirteenth century in codices such as M9292[29] penned in 1297 at the monastery Xorin Anapat and M6473 of the following year from Hawuc' Tař.[30]

Consequently, since Xosrov's commentary was composed in the mid tenth century, it provides us with a valuable indirect perspective on a much more primitive form of the rite, especially as his approach is to quote a textual *lemma* in full before interpreting it. At the same time, his work has undergone its own transmission history in the course of which certain scribes sought to enhance its topicality by inserting passages from other commentators on portions of the liturgy not represented here, as well as other extraneous material. In the sole diplomatic edition so far produced[31] these are furnished from two later codices in the apparatus[32] to a base manuscript of 1336 from the Mxit'arist library in Venice. The secondary character of some of these can be determined by various criteria such as duplication of treatment, divergent understanding of the same segment and lack of harmony with the surrounding context. However, this cannot always be convincingly established as, for example, in certain instances where the interpolation evinces one of the commentator's characteristic themes.

Xosrov constantly draws analogies from a subject's conduct with regard to earthly monarchs to that of the worshipper before the heavenly counterpart. Two of the paragraphs in question utilize the figure in a lively, vivid manner reminiscent of the author and hence re-open the issue of their authenticity[33] and the possibility of omission on the part of the copyists of the base manuscript and its examplars. Obviously the collation sample is too narrow and excludes several older witnesses such as M2273 which was commissioned by the priest Step'annos of the famous monastery of Xoranašat in 1252, a year after its founder's death. Thus a comprehensive investigation of the manuscript tradition would both resolve such textual problems and improve the commentary's utility in plotting the evolution of the eucharistic rite.

Clearly, where the current evidence is in agreement, we can be reasonably sure this represents the liturgical form with which Xosrov was familiar and, as we have said, can apply this towards a history of the evolution of the rite. However, one can only proceed with a number of caveats. Granted the textual diversity among later missals at a time when a greater degree of uniformity in the rite had been achieved, it is likely that in the tenth century the level of divergence was much higher and the theoretical possibility of local variants must be acknowledged of which Xosrov's would be but one (i.e. that current in Vaspurakan).[34]

The brevity of the text Xosrov comments on is immediately apparent from comparison with our contemporary *textus receptus*. What we may deduce from this is not always so patent. Where Nersēs Lambronac'i lends support in his liturgical commentary of c. 1176/7[35] we are probably justified in concluding the unit under discussion is of later origin, particularly as his work is not dependent on that of his predecessor. However, as Nersēs' formular already evinces the overall structure of the present text, his agreement with Xosrov in the non-representation of specific hymns or prayers is rather limited.

Hence we must broach the question of the comprehensiveness of Xosrov's treatment. The developed eucharistic rite may broadly be divided into four main sections,[36] preparation, synaxis, holy sacrifice, blessing and dismissal, of which only the third is dealt with primarily in this commentary. Nevertheless, apart from inherent probability, the author himself implies a benediction formula in discussing the dismissal of catechumens in §16:

> At this point, "*Bless, Lord*", is said, as at the dismissal of the people . . . Thus the prayer is completed with a blessing . . .

With regard to the precise form it took, one might surmise with Gat'rčean the conclusion offered by Nersēs:[37]

Priest:	Be blessed by the grace of the Holy Spirit, go in peace and the Lord be with all.
People:	Amen.

The blessing may have been omitted not only for its brevity and comprehensibility, but also because the preceding prayer of thanksgiving provided a natural conclusion to his work with its trinitarian doxology, the conventional cadence of medieval Armenian texts.

It is much more difficult to discern Xosrov's acquaintance with rites of preparation. In Byzantium their elaboration occurred in the eighth century[38] and by Nersēs' time the process was also far advanced in Armenia. At all events, one must beware of interpreting the commentator's silence on the subject as a complete negation of the existence of this feature in his period.[39]

Although published separately, Xosrov's commentary on the liturgy of the hours[40] and eucharist were conceived as one undertaking as is revealed by the fact that the former is prefaced by an introduction and an afterword is appended to the latter. His previous discussion of the liturgy of the word in connection with the midday hour (*čašu žam*) accounts for the rather abrupt opening of his treatment of the preanaphoral rites in the second part of his work. If Xosrov is our first detailed source for the contents and disposition of the Armenian anaphora, he is anticipated in this capacity by Catholicos Yovhannēs Ojnec'i (c. 650-728)[41] and Step'annos Siwnec'i (c. 680-735)[42] with regard to the breviary.

Just as the codex Barberini 336[43] of the eighth century preserves the *enarxis* of the liturgy of St. John Chrysostom in almost its present shape, so from the description provided by these contemporary Armenian commentators the principal contours of the present structure are easily discernible. The *textus receptus* still maintains the blessing of the catechumens, albeit in a modified way,[44] and thus marks the division between the two services.[45] Moreover, the *čašu žam* preserves its integrity as an office outside a eucharistic context[46] and in this more conservative form betrays an even closer resemblance to the early evidence. In the rendering of the appropriate section of Ojnec'i's writing on Sunday usage below the following elements clearly emerge:

1) Responsory of the resurrection (Ps 93, 1-5)[47]
2) Trisagion[48]
3) Času psalm[49]
4) Lection from the prophets
5) Mesedi (prokeimenon)
6) Apostle
7) Alleluia
8) Gospel[50]
9) Creed

The Significance of the Prayers of the Third Hour on Sunday

First of all what is the significance of gathering in the narthex of the church at the third hour? It indicates our re-assembly by the heavenly Chief-Shepherd after being scattered by the alien [i.e. the Devil]. Then the beginning of the office[52] "The Lord is King. He is robed in majesty" (1) [demonstrates that] we are united with our King who took flesh from the Virgin and raised us to [join] the praises of the incorporeal ones. In the angelic throng as they sing verse upon verse they become one with the supernal hosts. Subsequently the One who was crucified for us at this hour in a sacrifice acceptable to the Father is united with those on high at the trisagion (2). Together with Him we approach as a reasonable sacrifice to our heavenly Father.

Then it introduces wondrous mysteries and

traditions hidden from the many. When the holy Gospel is borne aloft with the eye of the Spirit we see the Son of God seated upon it as on a throne high and exalted [Isa 6:1] according to Isaiah's vision and exclaim in a loud voice, looking straight up at the One who has called us to the one living light by the *trisagion* no longer to trip and fall as [the Devil] fell and cast down Adam.

Then there follows the suffusion of the Holy Spirit like incense issuing from the Father, wafting everyone upwards from where they had fallen. Emboldened by this they encircle the royal table, emitting the fragrant confession of the *trisagion* in company with the seraphim in honor of the immortal crucified One. Fired by the divine coals and called to adoption by the heavenly Father, they sing "a hymn in Sion and new prayers in Jerusalem" (3). Consonant with this, Isaiah proclaims aloud, filling the universe with fragrant knowledge. He announces the epiphany of the Son of God from the Virgin in the words, "Behold, a virgin shall conceive and bear a son and his name shall be called Emmanuel," [Isa 7:14] adding, "He bears our infirmities" [Isa 53:4]. This is the sense the church looks to in reading Isaiah. Confirmed by prophetic preaching, the choir sings a new song called a *misidi* (5)[53] which in Greek means the singing of anthems. Thus by intoning the prophetic words together with the prophets and reading the apostolic writings (6) with the apostles, they are nourished by the bread which came down from heaven. The

27

recitation of these songs of ascent in church moves every listener to wrapped attention. The Alleluia (7) is a signal to prepare oneself to encounter the dread, marvellous sound emanating from above, looking steadfastly towards the east. This is because it is not the voice of a messenger or angels, but the Lord Himself saying, "I left the Father and came to the world" [Jhn 8:42]. That is why they stand in utter silence, attending upon the Lord's words. (8)

After the completion of the Gospel, they confess the holy faith aloud [in the creed] presented to the Church by the holy Fathers at Nicaea (9) to dispel completely the Devil's wickedness and under the preaching of the apostles bring the whole universe to obedience to Christ Jesus our Lord, to whom be glory for ever. Amen.

In his afterword to this commentary[54] Xosrov discloses valuable information about his motivation in writing and his intended readership. Since his elevation to the episcopacy he had observed ignorance of the deeper spiritual significance of the liturgy and office on the part of ecclesiastics as well as indifference to the moral demands their priestly and intercessory ministry laid upon them.[55] The condition was so widespread that he could not hope to accomplish much by archpastoral visitation and personal admonition and hence was compelled to commit his message to writing in order to achieve the optimum impact.[56] His reference to people hearing the work being read, coupled with exhortations to consult patristic authorities for a more profound exposition of certain passages implies that the book was designed in the first instance for classes in the monastic academies.[57] Once the students graduated as *vardapets* they would be sent to parishes on preaching missions where their teaching would enlighten the local clergy. In order to raise their level of awareness and commitment the author states his emphasis on elucidating the text of the diaconal proclamations[58] and priestly prayers "on which salvation depends".

Consequently, much less mention is made of the role of the clerks (*dpirk'*) whose function is to provide psalmody and respond to exclamations from the sanctuary.[59] Similarly, although we know from Nersēs Lambronac'i that the people played a much more active part in hymnody than in recent practice, this too is only intermittently referred to e. g. the petitionary response "Remember, Lord, and have mercy" (§113) and other responses "It is worthy and right (§51) and "We give you thanks, Lord" (§165). Indeed, only two hymn texts are listed, viz. the *sanctus* (§§64-68), hymn of blessing (§§97-98) along with the Our Father (§§137-144). As in the case of the dismissal, there is at least one instance of Xosrov's familiarity with a hymn he neglects to cite. There is hence an awkward transition from §162 in which the deacon calls for pre-communion psalmody to §163 in which he exhorts post-communion thanksgiving. The omitted unit, as we learn from Nersēs, is the hymn of praise *Kristos patarageal baŝxi* [Christ sacrificed is shared . . .] which is of early origin, as we shall see, although its present form is attributed to Catholicos Nersēs Šnorhali (c. 1102-1173).[60] At the same time, comparison with Lambronac'i's commentary indicates that the elaboration of the hymnography included in the *textus receptus* was one of the final processes in the growth of the rite.

In order to clarify this general development, a brief analysis of the later structure is offered, utilizing a modified format of Nersoyan's schema. The units to which Xosrov testifies appear in

29

italics, while those first extant in Nersēs are designated by the symbol (N).[61] Certain variations in formulation within those units are discussed in the notes to the appropriate passage.[62]

Prayers after the Lections
Litany after the lections §§1-5
Prayers after the lections §§6-15
Last blessing of the synaxis §16

After the two initial petitions witnessed by Xosrov, Nersēs cites a series of subsidiary requests ("the angel of peace, remission and forgiveness of our transgressions" etc.) which appears a composite of elements of different litanies of the Byzantine rite,[63] combined with a petition for the protection of the cross which is characteristically Armenian[64] and overtly anti-Paulician.[65] The originality of the situation presented by Xosrov is suggested not only by its brevity and date of attestation, but also by the symmetry it exhibits at the offertory. There too two diaconal petitions are said during the priest's secret prayer. Moreover, as the Armenian prayer of offertory directly concerns the oblation rather than the preparation of the ministers, as found in other oriental rites,[66] the prayer after the lections in some way fulfills that function. Its themes of sacrifice and thanksgiving focus our attention on the impending eucharistic celebration.

The late fourth century *Apostolic Constitutions* refer to the dismissal of four categories of worshippers by the bishop at the end of the liturgy of the word, viz. catechumens, energumenoi, illuminandi and penitents.[67] Although by Xosrov's time the prayer for the second group had already attained the all-embracing form of the *textus receptus*, the author shows awareness of its earlier formulation and function (§§13-15). It originally sought the purification of those possessed by unclean spirits and their

30

reintegration into the community of faith. He also indicates that, at least in his region, it was normal for the homily to follow at this point before the great entrance.

Holy Sacrifice
The Great Entrance
Dismissal of catechumens §17
Hymn of the Great Entrance (N:538)
Bidding of the Great Entrance (N:538)
Prayer of the Great Entrance (N:539)
Hagiody
Responsory before the Cherubicon
Cherubicon (N:539)
Responsory of the Great Entrance

This section illustrates the developments the Armenian liturgy underwent in the eleventh and twelfth centuries. Consonant with Xosrov's textual occupation, rubrics are only alluded to where these impinge directly upon the meaning of the concomitant litanies and prayers, and indeed they may not have been very well developed at this time. This is then the context for his fairly brief reference to the solemn transference of the gifts to the altar (§17). From this we may observe the conservativeness of Armenian tradition in preserving the very simple, functional aspect of the act, conducted apparently completely in silence, as described by Theodore of Mopsuestia (†426).[68]

Unfortunately, there seems to be no early indication of exactly what form the transference would have taken, but there are grounds for supposing it was similar to current practice. Catholicos Yovhannēs ōjnec'i's eighth canon at the Synod of Duin in 720[69] enjoins strict fidelity to the custom of utilizing unleavened bread and unmixed wine at the eucharist, an injunction he traces back to St. Gregory himself. Another canon list affords further information on the duties of the deacons, who still retain the service of conveying the gifts to the altar in the Armenian rite:

> They themselves are soberly to prepare the bread
> for the sacrifice with psalms and remove the holy
> sacrifice to the altar . . .[70]

As the typical Armenian church plan involved a central sanctuary flanked by two side chapels, the elements would probably have been placed in the small chamber to the north of the altar in readiness for the entrance. That they were brought from the nave level is confirmed by the reference to their ascending the altar. Moveover, the location of the altar steps at the sides rather than in front of the *bema* seems to presuppose this sort of movement. At some point, as at Byzantium, the transference became increasingly ritualized, the movement being entirely confined to the sanctuary where the gifts were kept in a niche on the north wall.[71] Granted the brief distance and time involved in performing that act, it lacked the potential for ceremonial elaboration it was accorded in Constantinople.

That indeed is the source of the main additions evinced by Nersēs, the prayer of the great entrance (*Nemo dignus*) said by the priest in secret and the Cherubic Hymn which punctuates the deacons' movement.[72] The hymn of the great entrance (*Marmin tērunakan* . . . The body of the Lord) also occurs in the Chaldaean rite and is secondary here.[73] Similarly, bearing in mind the comparative lateness of the hymnic embellishment of the liturgy and the silence on its existence by both commentators, we are perhaps justified in viewing the hagiody as an Armenian reworking of the Cherubicon theme. The absence of the responsory of the great entrance (Ps 23:7-10) from both commentaries is perplexing since

32

this dialogue on the entry of the gifts which developed in Constantinople during the sixth century seems to have fallen into desuetude there by the tenth century.[74] The circumstances of its reception into the *textus receptus* have yet to be investigated.

Laying of the Gifts
Litany of the offertory §18-31
Prayer of the offertory §32-39[75]

Kiss of Peace
Greeting
Bidding for the kiss of peace §§40-41[76]
Hymn of the kiss of peace (N:542)

Once again we note the secondary character of the hymn *K'ristos i mēǰmer yaytnec'aw* (Christ has appeared in our midst). It is underscored by the regularity of the octosyllabic meter and the employment throughout of rhyme, a feature first exploited at length by Prince Grigor Magistros (†1059).[77] Characteristically, Xosrov expatiates on the moral and religious qualities the celebrant and people should exhibit in order to prepare themselves for the anaphora.

Prologue
Responsory before the eucharist §§42-51
Preface §§52-63

Anamnesis
Sanctus §§64-68
Anamnesis §§69-98
Hymn to the Father (early 14th cent.)
Hymn of Blessing (N:545)

Prayer of Humble Access §§99-101
Epiclesis
Hymn to the Son (early 14th cent.)
Prayer of the Epiclesis §§102-105

This section represents the ancient eucharistic core and rightfully occupies most of our commentator's attention as he explicates the many biblical events of salvation history and outlines their implications for his readers. There have been few later additions to this portion apart from hymns to the three persons of the trinity[78] which contrast with the prayers which, while referring to the Son's incarnation and the Spirit's sanctification of the gifts, are always addressed directly to the Father.

Diptychs
Hymn to the Holy Spirit (early 14th cent.)
Intercessions §§106-112, 116-126[79]
Litany of Intercessions §§113-115, 127-132
Dominical Prayer
Litany before the Lord's Prayer (N:549)
Prayer of the Paternal Name §§133-136
Lord's Prayer §§137-144
Embolis §§145-147

Xosrov's division of the prayers and litanies into two units most probably reflects the layout of the service books with which he was familiar. Nevertheless, functionally they are very similar in commending the wellbeing of the world and the church in their diverse conditions and aspects by commemoration through the sacrifice and in fact duplicate several of the same categories. The cohesion of the first prayer (§§106-112) is sustained by the literary device of repeating the opening "hereby" (*sovaw*) as opposed to the role of the imperative "remember" (*yišea*) in the second.

34

Moreover, its antiquity is underscored by the laconic listing of the various categories to be prayed for without the elaboration of the second series. These considerations are confirmed by the close relation the latter bears with the corresponding petitions in the Byzantine liturgy of St. Basil on which the Armenian is likely dependent.[80]

An even more informal practice seems to have obtained in Xosrov's time with regard to the structure of the first litany where, apart from great feasts like Easter, considerable variation was tolerated according to the conscientiousness of the priest. The abbreviated formula he enjoins for regular liturgical worship forms the kernel of the expanded version evinced by Nersēs, which in turn was subject to further growth until the time of Catholicos Simēon Erewanc'i (1710-1780). A significant factor in the process was the desire to express more of the church's autocephalous and ethnic character. Hence, whereas the only Armenian element in Xosrov's commemorations is St. Gregory (who is also recognized as a saint of the universal Church)[81] by the twelfth century all his descendants on the catholicosal throne were recorded along with St. Thaddeus, guarantor of the church's apostolicity.[82] Subsequently, the compass was enlarged to include various medieval theologians and spiritual guides up to the reforming catholicos Movsēs Tat'ewac'i (†1632).[83]

Likewise, the second litany was greatly extended by the insertion of additional petitions and a further litany introduced before the Our Father. Presumably in Xosrov's time the priest's preparatory prayer was audible in its entirety, not just the final exclamation. Thereafter, it became the norm to say it in secret and the litany then became a focus for the people's devotions. Its secondary nature is substantiated by comparison with the Byzantine equivalent which it follows in commemorating the saints and the oblation of the sacrifice, thereby imploring the gifts of the Holy Spirit.[84] Where the latter asks for rescue from various kinds of danger, the Armenian transfers allegiance to the formula of the first three litanies of the Byzantine *enarxis* seeking more general protection, again commemorating the Mother of God and the saints and committing one another to God.[85] At the same time, the non-representation in Armenian of a second litany adduced at this point by the liturgies of St. Basil and St. John Chrysostom[86] has been taken to confirm its late addition from the divine office.[87]

Inclination and Elevation
Prayer of Inclination §§148-154
Hymn of the Elevation (N:551)
Prayer of Elevation (N:551)

Doxology
Blessing of the Holy Trinity (N:551)
Hymn of the Doxology

Intinction and Fraction
Prayer of Intinction §§155-158
Exhortation to Communion §§159-161
Bidding for Psalmody §162
Fulfilment (N:552)

As the transference of the gifts was later embellished by prayers and hymnography before the commencement of the anaphora, so its conclusion has been elaborated with more solemn communion rites developed largely between Xosrov and Nersēs. Thus the hymn and prayer of the elevation as well as the final element of the prayer of the fraction "The fulfilment of the Holy Spirit" derive from the Byzantine liturgy.[88] This is also the source of the second part of the same prayer ("I confess and believe") which seems to have entered the Armenian rite only subsequently.[89] In contrast, the doxology evolved in Armenia. The hymn sung by the clerks simply echoes the preceding priestly blessing which is witnessed by Nersēs. The trinitarian affirmation it embodies is characteristic and parallels that of the later Armenian hymns of the anaphora.

Prayers before Communion
Hymn of Praise (N:552)
Prayers before Communion (post 13th cent.)

The Partaking
Prayer of the Tasting (N:552)
Bidding to Communicants (N:554)
Hymn of Communion

The Thanksgiving
Hymn of Glory (N:554)
Bidding for Thanksgiving §163
Hymn of Thanksgiving §164
Prayers of Thanksgiving §165-175

The communion rite with which Xosrov was familiar is both simple and smooth, but became increasingly complicated in the course of the next few centuries. The diaconal bidding (§162) probably introduced the chanting of responsorial psalmody, according to widespread early practice.[90] We observe the remains of this in the current form of the hymn of praise which was redacted by Catholicos Nersēs Šnorhali (†1173). There we find a stichic arrangement of the first two phrases of Ps. 148 punctuated by the response "Alleluia".[91] Originally, the whole psalm would have been sung in this way during the communion of the clergy. After the people had communicated, a further bidding evoked the response "We give you thanks, Lord" which formed the kernel of the later hymns of thanksgiving. The two following prayers (another was prefixed to these in the thirteenth century) then led into the final blessing and dismissal.

The format Nersēs adduces about two hundred years later, as far as this can be reconstructed, is already more encumbered. The hymn of praise in its redacted form accompanied the second and third elements of the current prayer of fraction, as noted above. This was followed by a few unspecified petitions and a brief prayer of tasting ("May Your precious body be to me for life and Your holy blood for the atonement and remission of sins") the embryo from which the current form evolved. The bidding to communion ("With fear and faith draw near . . .") has been drawn from the liturgy of St. John Chrysostom.[92] Thereafter the people's communion ensues, still apparently without accompanying chant, but followed by the hymn of glory. Whereas the first of Xosrov's prayers of thanksgiving was rather short and directed purely to Christ, Nersēs evinces it in a developed form complete with trinitarian doxology, easing the transition to the second ("To the inscrutable, incomprehensible, triune essence . . ." §174).

Later, we note the further growth of both prayers and hymnody. Three pre-communion prayers were added to the accompaniment of the hymn of praise augmented by an ode (taṭ) proper to the day.[93] After an expanded prayer of tasting, a hymn was inserted during communion. The hymn of glory was then associated with a new trinitarian prayer of thanksgiving while an enlarged hymn of thanksgiving paralleled the traditional opening prayer. Finally, other odes were sung while the priest said the third portion of the thanksgiving prayer in secret. By intensifying the eucharist's awesome climax of receiving Christ's body and blood, this unit underwent the fullest exploitation of its hymnographic potential.

We must assume that the Armenian liturgy of St. Athanasius had been evolving constantly since its appearance in the fifth century through the adoption of such elements as the· *trisagion*, creed etc. in harmony with other rites. By the mid eighth century doctrinal disagreements and political setbacks[94] reduced the volume of contact with the Empire and retarded the advance of theological reflection and exposition. Consequently, Xosrov's commentary offers an incomparable opportunity to explore the structure and cohesiveness of this early phase of the rite.

His very act of commenting in an original way on an authoritative text is an indication of the contemporary renewal in intellectual life we have already broached. Tenth century Byzantine expansion led to the cession of several Armenian kingdoms in the next (Vaspurakan 1021, Ani 1045, Kars 1064) and the settlement of the courts in Cappadocia where unwonted proximity between the communities could issue in friction. Nevertheless, among the clergy and nobility emerged some noted Byzantinophiles such as the catholicos Petros Getadarj (†1058), part of whose studies were spent in Trebizond, and his sententious correspondent Grigor Magistros.

Since, as we have seen, some of the material from the liturgy of St. John Chrysostom borrowed by the time of Nersēs Lambronac'i is only extant from Greek sources of the eleventh century, it is quite plausible that the initiative for the undertaking is to be ascribed to Grigor's enterprising son, Catholicos Grigor Vkayasēr (†1105). Concerned not only with the accomodation of traditional usage to ensure effective local government of his by now far-flung flock, he acquired the characteristic epithet (Lit. 'martyr-lover') from his major task of enriching the Armenian

39

sanctoral, expanding the menologion (*tōnamak*) by the inclusion of countless *vitae* translated from Greek and Syriac. Consistently, he revised the lectionary (*čašoc'*) and initiated other liturgical improvements. Moreover, travelling widely around the mediterranean, the hierarch would have had ample opportunity for exposure to the Byzantine liturgy, especially during his three to four year stay in the capital commencing in 1074. His younger contemporary Pōłos Tarōnac'i (†1128) is a good spokesman for the outlook of the age:

> We [i.e. the Armenians] translate the books of the holy fathers and homilies of the holy martyrs from the Syrians, Egyptians, Romans and Greeks, as well as many [books] of the schismatics which are consonant with the orthodox. As St. Athanasius says, "In many points schismatics share our confession, which one should accept."[95]

Subsequently, as we have seen, the liturgy continued to develop though in a more desultory fashion, by comparison with the Roman rite as well as indigenous moves designed, at least in part, to invest it with a more overtly trinitarian focus. The examination of later commentaries should serve to elucidate the steps by which this occurred over the second half of its millennium evolution, as Xosrov does broadly for the first five hundred years.

Notes

1)   P. Ananian, "La data e le circonstanze della consecrazione di S. Gregorio Illuminatore", *Mus* 84 (1961), pp. 43-73, 319-360.
2)   See N. G. Garsoïan, "Nersēs le Grand, Basile de Césarée et Eustathe de Sébasté", *REA* N.S. XVII (1983), pp. 143-169.

3) See R. W. Thomson, *The History of Łazar P'arpec'i*, Atlanta, GA, Scholars Press: 1991, p. 47.

4) Earlier it appears that at least the scriptural readings were orally rendered into the vernacular. See S. P. Cowe, "The Two Armenian Versions of the Chronicles, Their Origin and Translation Technique", *REA* 22 (1990-1991) (forthcoming).

5) See Engberding, *Hochgebet*, p. LXXXV.

6) Ibid., pp. LXXff.

7) Ibid., p. LXXXIII. For a discussion of the issue and French translation of the complete text see A. Renoux, "L'anaphore arménienne de saint Grégoire l'Illuminateur", *Eucharistes d'Orient et d'Occident* II (*Lex Orandi* 47), Paris, 1970, pp. 83-116. A unique edition of the Armenian text was produced by Gat'rčean/Tašean, *Pataragamatoyc'k'*, pp. 120-159. As Renoux notes, it is not completely reliable. For an English translation of the passage in P'awstos (Bk v, 28) see N. G. Garsoïan, *The Epic Histories Attributed to P'awstos Buzand* Cambridge, MA, Harvard University Press: 1989, pp. 207-209.

8) For the text see Gat'rčean/Tašean, *Pataragamatoyc'k'*, pp. 220-242 and for a Latin translation P. Ferhat, "Denkmäler altarmenischer Messliturgie II. Die angebliche Liturgie des hl. Katholikos Sahaks", *Or Chr* N.S. 3 (1913), pp. 16-31.

9) For the text see Gat'rčean/Tašean, *Pataragamatoyc'k'*, pp. 256-267 and for a Latin translation A. Rücker, "Denkmäler altarmenischer Messliturgie IV. Die Anaphora des Patriarchen Kyrillos von Alexandreia", *Or Chr* 3 ser. 1 (1927), pp. 143-157.

10) For the text see Gat'rčean/Tašean, *Pataragamatoyc'k'*, pp. 244-254 and for a Latin translation P. Ferhat, "Denkmäler altarmenischer Messliturgie I. Eine dem hl. Gregor von Nazianz zugeschriebene Liturgie", *Or Chr* N.S. 1 (1911), pp. 201-214.

11) For precise details on the manuscript data see I. M. Hanssens,

Institutiones liturgicae de ritibus orientalibus vol. III, Rome, 1932, p. 587.

12) One might compare the process by which at Byzantium the liturgy of St. Chrysostom replaced that of St. Basil in normal usage from the eleventh century. See G. Winkler, "Zur Geschichte des armenischen Gottesdienstes im Hinblick auf den in mehreren Wellen erflogten griechischen Einfluss", *Or Chr* 58 (1974), p. 164.

13) Thus in §35 he states explicitly, "In all anaphorae the first prayer pertains to the offerant's being made worthy and has the same signification." Independent confirmation of the liturgy's widespread usage at this period comes from the following passage which probably refers to c. 980: "We intoned the missal of the Lord of hosts attributed to Athanasius" (Uxtanēs episkopos, *Patmut'iwn hayoc'*, Catholicate Press: Vałaršapat, 1871, p. 12). In addition to the anaphorae already mentioned, there is a reference to an otherwise unknown anaphora of St. Epiphanius in an Armenian Chalcedonian work. See G. Garitte, "Un opuscule grec traduit de l'arménien sur l'addition d'eau au vin eucharistique", *Mus* 73 (1960), pp. 306-308 and B. Botte, "Fragments d'une anaphore inconnue attribuée à s. Epiphane", ibid., pp. 311-315.

14) For the text see Gat'rčean/Tašean, *Pataragamatoyc'k'*, pp. 435-450 and for a Latin translation Baumstark, "Denkmäler".

15) Baumstark, "Denkmäler", p. 8.

16) For a brief discussion of this community see Hage *Syrisch-jakobitische Kirche*, p. 80.

17) Nersoyan, *Divine Liturgy*, p. 298.

18) For the text see Gat'rčean/Tašean, *Pataragamatoyc'k'*, pp. 180-216.

19) Tašean ibid. dates the version to the ninth-tenth centuries whereas N. Akinean (*Simēon Płnjahanec'i ew ir t'arg-*

42

manut'iwnnerĕ vrac'erenē [Sim ēon Płnjahanec'i and His
Translations from Georgian] Vienna, Mxit'arist Press: 1951, pp.
228-229) argues on linguistic grounds that, at least in its present
form, a thirteenth century dating is warranted.

20) See Engberding (*Hochgebet*, pp. LXVI-LXVIII and
LXXXVI).

21) For the text see Gat'rčean/Tašean, *Pataragamatoyc'k'*, pp.
414-450.

22) For the text see ibid., pp. 353-384. Tašean postulates that
the same hand was responsible for the version of both the liturgies
of St. Basil and St. Chrysostom.

23) For the text see Gat'rčean/Tašean, *Pataragamatoyc'k'*, pp.
455-466.

24) Nersoyan, *Divine Liturgy*, p. 297.

25) For the text see Gat'rčean/Tašean, *Pataragamatoyc'k'*, pp.
389-411 and for a Latin translation A. Rücker, "Denkmäler altarmenischer Messliturgie. 5. Die Anaphora des heiligen Ignatius
von Antiochien" *Or Chr* ser. 3, 5 (1930), pp. 56-79.

26) One might compare the creation of the one-volume Bible in
the previous century uniting all of scripture into one codex which
is attributed to Nersēs Lambronac'i. See S. P. Cowe, *The
Armenian Version of Daniel*, UPATS Scholar's Press, Atlanta,
GA (forthcoming).

27) For a description of MS 17 of the city library of Lyon see
Molinier and Desvernay, *Catalogue général des manuscrits des
bibliothèques de France*, Départements, vol. xxx, part 1, Paris,
1900, pp. 5-6.

28) The first printed missal was probably the second book off the
Armenian press, appearing in Venice in 1513. Subsequently edi-
tions were produced in the capitals of the Ottoman (1568) and
Safavid (1641) empires, as well as in Rome at the press of the

Congregatio de Propaganda Fide (1642). For details see Oskanyan, *Hay girk'ĕ*, pp. 10, 22-24, 25.

29) The initial M indicates the manuscript belongs to the Matenadaran collection in Erevan.

30) For a brief description of those manuscripts see L. Xač'ikyan and A. Mnac'akanyan (eds.), *C'uc'ak jeragrac' Maštoc'i anvan Matenadarani* [Catalogue of the Manuscripts of the Ma,toc' Matenadaran] vol. 2 Erevan, Armenian Academy of Sciences: 1970, coll. 904, 326.

31) See Xosrov, *Meknut'iwn*. The work was edited by the celebrated savant and poet Ł. Ališan for the fiftieth anniversary of Gēorg Hiwrmiwz's ordination to the priesthood.

32) These scholia have been translated in the notes to the present translation and are to be found in §§15, 17, 102, 105, 113, 147, 154. For the similar phenomenon of later accretions to a liturgical commentary in Byzantium see Meyendorff, *St. Germanos*, p. 12.

33) This applies to §§102, 154.

34) In this connection it is worth recalling the variation in liturgical usage which obtains at present within the traditional jurisdictions. See Taft, *Great Entrance*, pp. 103-104.

35) The work has twice been edited: 1) *Xorhrdacut'iwn srbazan pataragi bac'atrut'eamb Nersesi Lambronac'woy* [Meditation on the Holy Liturgy with explanation by Nersēs Lambronac'i] Jerusalem, St. James Press: 1842;

2) *Xorhrdacut'iwnk' i kargs ekelec'woy ew meknut'iwn xorhrdoy pataragin* [Meditations on Church Order and Commentary on the Mystery of the Liturgy] Venice, St. Lazar's Press: 1847. For a reconstruction of the formular with which Nersēs was familiar see Gat'rčean/Tašean, *Pataragamatoyc'k'*, pp. 508-556. The currency of this form is indicated by the second liturgy preserved in

manuscript VI of the Armenian collection at the Bayerische Staatsbibliothek in Munich which derives from an exemplar of 1288. For a description see G. Kalemkiar, *Catalog der armenischen Handschriften in der k. Hof- und Stadtsbibliothek zu München*, Vienna, 1892, pp. 14-22.

36) According to Nersoyan's categories (*Divine Liturgy*, pp. 231-233). See also G. Shrikian, *An Interpretation of the Holy Liturgy or Soorp Badarak of the Armenian Apostolic Church*, New York, 1984. The book's photographic documentation offers a vivid evocation of the liturgical celebration.

37) Gat'rčean/Tašean, *Pataragamatoyc'k'*, p. 299 cf. the second Armenian translation of the liturgy of St. Basil (ibid., p. 157). By Nersēs' time this was preceded by the Prayer behind the Ambo adopted from the liturgy of St. John Chrysostom and Ps 112:2 ("Blessed be the name of the Lord . . ."). It is noteworthy that Justin Martyr also omits mention of the dismissal in his account of the eucharist (*PG* 6, p. 429). The last Gospel of the *textus receptus* was added under Latin influence at the end of the 17th century.

38) Taft, *Beyond East and West*, p. 171.

39) This is at least implied in the statement that the prothesis developed "during the period between the tenth and twelfth centuries" (i.e. between the commentaries of Xosrov and Nersēs) in Nersoyan, *Divine Liturgy*, p. 298.

40) This work has been published twice, though not in its original form but as part of a redaction by Movsēs Erznkac'i (†c. 1323): 1) *Meknut'iwn ałōt'ic' arareal eranelwoyn Xosrovu Anjewac'eac' episkoposi* [Commentary on Prayers by Xosrov, Bishop of Anjewac'ik'] Constantinople, 1730-1737; 2) *Meknut'iwn žamakargut'ean arareal . . .* [Commentary on the Breviary] Constantinople, 1840.

41) Ōjnec'i, *Matenagrut'iwnk'*.

42) S. Amatuni (ed.), "Žamakargut'ean meknut'iwn Step'annosi imastasiri Siwneac' episkoposi" [Commentary on the Breviary by Step'annos the Philosopher, bishop of Siwnik'] *Ararat* (1915), pp. 225-239, 361-364, 495-496, 634-639; (1916) 129-141, 406-412, 694-703.

43) For an edition see F. E. Brightman, *Liturgies Eastern and Western*, Oxford, Clarendon Press: 1896, pp. 311-314.

44) See Nersoyan, *Divine Liturgy*, pp. 52-53.

45) The Byzantine equivalent had been displaced by the eight century (Taft, *Beyond East and West*, p. 178).

46) Nersoyan, *Divine Liturgy*, pp. 118-125. The readings and variable elements associated with it are contained in a related manual called *čašoc'*.

47) Nersoyan, *Divine Liturgy*, p. 37.

48) Ibid., p. 41. For the original form and function of this chant see Taft, *Beyond East and West*, pp. 157-159 and 176-177.

49) Nersoyan, *Divine Liturgy*, p. 45.

50) Ibid., p. 47.

51) Ōjnec'i, *Matenagrut'iwnk'*, pp. 124-125. For a Latin translation see J. B. Aucher, *Domini Johannis Ozniensis philosophi Armenorum Catholici opera*, Venice, St. Lazar's Press: 1834, pp. 500-501. See also the very similar description in an anonymous text, attributed to Ōjnec'i by the Mxit'arist editor, which contains verbatim parallels (ibid., p. 165).

52) The *enarxis* of the *textus receptus* has borrowed various elements from the liturgy of St. John Chrysostom: 1) the initial blessing (of which the oldest extant sources date to the eleventh century) 2) the *monogenēs* (introduced in the sixth century) 3) prayers of the three antiphons (introduced between 630-730).

53) The form is derived from $\mu\epsilon\sigma(\sigma)\acute{\iota}\delta\iotaо\varsigma$, an intermedium.

54) See pp. 223-229.

55) See pp. 67-68 and 229.

56) With the establishment of a major Armenian diaspora in Cilicia and later in various parts of the Middle East and Eastern Europe an increasing amount of digests of paraenetic and canonical materials were prepared for wide circulation in a simple style and format (e.g. Yovhannēs Erznkac'i's *Xrat hasarakac' k'ristōnēic'* [Advice to Common Christians] of 1289).

57) For an illustration of the process of an assistant reading *lemmas* from a textbook while the master gives his interpretation to the assembled students see S. Der Nersessian, "Les portraits d'Esayi Nč'ec'i, supérieur de Glajor", *ASIMHB*, pp. 229-241.

58) See Conybeare, *Rituale*, p. 535 under *qaroẓem*.

59) In fact they are only explicitly mentioned in §47 and §162.

60) Nersoyan, *Divine Liturgy*, p. 310.

61) The following numeral pertains to the page in Gat'rčean/Tašean's reconstruction of the liturgy as Nersēs describes it (*Pataragamatoyc'k'*, pp. 519-556.

62) Unless otherwise specified, information concerning post-Nersesian features are drawn from Nersoyan, *Divine Liturgy*, pp. 301-311.

63) Taft, *Great Entrance*, pp. 338-339.

64) Prayers invoking the cross are particularly plentiful e.g. at the dismissal of the *textus receptus* (*pahpanea ẓmeẓ, K'ŕistos Astuac mer*—Preserve us, Christ God, under the protection of Your holy and precious cross . . .), Nersoyan, *Divine Liturgy*, p. 103.

65) See Chapt. 1, p. 7.

66) Taft, *Great Entrance*, p. 359, n. 45.

67) F. X. Funk (ed.), *Didascalia et Constitutiones Apostolorum* vol. 1, Paderborn, Schoeningh: 1905, pp. 480-488. Ps.

Dionysius at the end of the fifth century mentions the categories of catechumens, energumenoi and penitents (J. Parker (trans.), *The Celestial and Ecclesiastical Hierarchy of Dionysius the Areopagite*, London, Skeffington: 1894, p. 61).

68) Taft, *Great Entrance*, PP. 35-38.

69) V. Hakobyan, *Kanonagirk' Hayoc'* [Armenian Book of Canons] vol. 1 Erevan, Armenian Academy of Sciences: 1964, p. 519.

70) The prelude to the collection contains too many historical and theological inaccuracies to be accepted, however the canons reflect Armenian practice. Ibid., vol. 2, 1971, p. 257.

71) This arrangement with a prothesis niche is already evidenced in side chapels from a variety of Byzantine provenances including Sinai and Cappadocia from the sixth century onwards. See T. F. Mathews, "'Private' Liturgy in Byzantine Architecture: Towards a Re-appraisal", CA 30 (1982), pp. 125-138. As yet no research has been conducted on the Armenian architectural evidence to ascertain when this innovation was introduced into the Athanasian rite.

72) On the origin and significance of these units see Taft, *Great Entrance*, pp. 53-148. N.B. the author's elucidation of the last line of the Armenian Cherubicon in terms of a mistranslation of the Greek on p. 62.

73) Ibid., p. 90.

74) Ibid., p. 115.

75) Outside Xosrov's purview as not featuring in the text proper, the Armenian rite maintains the priestly washing of the hands before receiving the gifts at the altar.

76) The diaconal reference at this point to the catechumens and other groups is an indication of the extremely short expanse of time which has elapsed since their departure. They were admon-

ished to leave at §17 after their blessing and may just have taken their position outside the doors and consequently were well within earshot.

77) See *Tałasac'ut'iwnk' Grigori Magistrosi Pahlawunwoy* [The Poems of Grigor Magistros Pahlawuni] Venice, St. Lazar's Press: 1868.

78) That dedicated to the Holy Spirit follows in the next section. For a recent consideration of the *Sanctus* of the Armenian ordo in comparison with other Armenian anaphorae see B. D. Spinks, *The sanctus in the eucharistic prayer*, Cambridge, University Press: 1991, pp. 134-138.

79) Nersoyan's employment of the distinction between the general and individual in connection with these prayers and litanies is more appropriate to the later form where individualized elements increased in the second set. However, this is foreign to Xosrov's time, as is clear from his comment isolating §118 somewhat from its surrounding context—"among our general petitions we pray especially for our own *bishop*.".

80) See H. Engberding, "Das anaphorische Fürbittgebet der armenischen Athanasiusliturgie", REA N.S. 4 (1967), pp. 49-55.

81) For an overview of the subject see G. Winkler, "Our Present Knowledge of the History of Agat'angełos and its Oriental Versions REA N.S. 14 (1980), pp. 125-141.

82) Gat'rčean/Tašean, *Pataragamatoyc'k'*, p. 547.

83) Nersoyan, *Divine Liturgy*, p. 77.

84) Trempelas, *Three Liturgies*, p. 125.

85) Ibid., pp. 26, 32, 35.

86) Ibid., pp. 127, 190.

87) Taft, "Liturgies", p. 183.

88) Trempelas, *Three Liturgies*, pp. 129, 131, 135. For the secondary character of the prayer of elevation see Taft, "Liturgies",

p. 184.

89) Trempelas, *Three Liturgies*, p. 140.

90) For details see Taft, "Liturgies", p. 187.

91) Nersoyan, *Divine Liturgy*, p. 91. The first verse of the same psalm is a similar remnant in the *textus receptus* of the liturgy of St. John Chrysostom.

92) Trempelas, *Three Liturgies*, p. 148.

93) Nersoyan, *Divine Liturgy*, p. 91.

94) Significant among these was the tightening of control over Armenia by the Abbasid Caliphate. In the course of time the Muslim threat came to be perceived as the contemporary embodiment of the barbarian peril which featured in the litanies (see §108).

95) The citation derives from his *T'uł' ěnddēm T'eopistē hoŕom p'ilisop'ayi* [Epistle against the Byzantine Philosopher Theopistēs] in its original form of 1101 quoted from MS J1272, ff. 285-286 in Bogharian, *Hay groŕner*, pp. 208-209.

96) The precise motivation for these additions has not been investigated but may be connected with disputes over the recipient of the eucharistic sacrifice. In the west under Anselmian influence the view prevailed that the Son offered it to the Father. The issue was debated in Constantinople in 1155-6 as a result of Soterichos Panteugenes' arguments that the Son, as both giver and gift, could not also participate in receiving the sacrifice. A synod of the twenty-sixth of February, 1156 approved rather the contrary position that all three persons of the trinity received it jointly, since they are one in external relations. See Beck, *Kirche*, p. 623. This latter is also Xosrov's understanding (§43 A victim made alive by His divinity, He is *offered as sacrifice* to the Holy Trinity; cf. §34). Consequently, the later hymns and prayers may have been inserted in defense of that doctrine.

Xosrov's Method and Style

As to the medieval Armenian mind literature (particularly prose works) was essentially utilitarian, most books tended to be commissioned to fulfill a specific purpose. However, as bishop, Xosrov possessed sufficient authority to generate the present study, though he too is careful to justify his action against a possible insinuation of vainglory ("I ventured upon this boldly out of necessity and not to win myself renown").[1] From what we have gathered of the circumstances behind its composition, it is clear that he was concerned about rampant clerical disorder in his diocese. Presumably, he had attempted on various occasions to ameliorate the situation by instruction and example on a one-to-one basis before coming to the realization that he could combat the problem most effectively in writing.

Nevertheless, a certain oral element was incorporated into its written form in that, from the information conveyed by his son Grigor, we may deduce that his brother Sahak transcribed the text at Xosrov's dictation.[2] As writing tended to be a solitary occupation, few such instances are recorded, one of these being Aṙak'el

Batišec'i's lament on the fall of Constantinople.[3] In the colophon to the poem we encounter the following strophe:[4]

> [Say, "Lord, have mercy"]
> Also for the monk Yakob,
> the secretary, painter and gilder.
> As I composed the lines of verse,
> he transcribed[5] them on paper.

Moreover, the recurrence of certain phrases and metrical blocks within the composition lend their testimony to the mode by which it came into being. Similarly, the approach Xosrov adopts in the study reveals the process of oral commentary on texts as practised in the monastic academies of his time.

Although our writer had few direct models to follow in the liturgical field, Armenia possessed a long tradition of Bible study and his prodigious knowledge of scripture suggests this had played a major part in his formation. Indeed, even at institutions engaged in philosophical disquisition and rudimentary scientific enquiries, biblical commentary remained throughout the primary focus of their attention. Hardly any major scholar emerged from those schools who did not establish his competence by producing a biblical commentary[6] or translating one, particularly by Fathers of the fourth or fifth century. The latter undertaking had its inception already in the fifth century with the rendering of works by St. Efrem and St. John Chrysostom along with lesser exponents of the School of Antioch. Consequently, although Christologically the Armenian church developed a closer affinity with Alexandria, its exegetical perspective was indelibly molded by Antiochene principles.[7] Accordingly, this impacted not only on minor procedural matters, but also the most fundamental issues of Xosrov's textual interpretation.

It is true that the Alexandrian anagogical approach to the liturgy viewing it as a manifestation of the soul's ascent from the material to the spiritual realm was already familiar in Armenia. The late fifth century Ps. Dionysiac corpus is cited in florilegia of the early seventh century[8] and translated in full a century later.[9] The magnitude of its influence can be gauged by the fact that it merited a commentary on the Heavenly Hierarchy in the late ninth century by the elusive Albanian writer Hamam Arewelc'i.[10] Moreover, Xosrov's acquaintance with its theses surfaces in his dispute with Catholicos Anania over church government.[11] Despite the deep dependence his successor Nersēs owes that source, our author reveals little empathy with its outlook and equally little attraction to its more systematic structure.

Instead of emulating the Dionysiac formula of introducing the subject by a general definition of what constitutes a sacrament, outlining (rather succinctly) the peculiarities of the rite and then expatiating on its mystical dimensions, Xosrov opts for an unabashedly textual orientation, unhurriedly explicating the ramifications of each phrase in turn. This, then, was the Armenian classroom approach to biblical commentary and indeed the tone of the present work maintains an immediacy and liveliness indicating the writer's tangible awareness of his audience's presence and his task of engaging and sustaining their interest in a text inherently dense, whose communicability they were partly inured against by so frequent contact. The demise of rhetorical potential in the political sphere had been accompanied by the expansion of new possibilities in the pulpit and hence its study had found a place in ecclesiastical education. However, there can be no suggestion that the rhetorical questions and instances of direct address interspersed throughout the work represent the laborious application of textbook rules. These have rather been appropriated by the author and function naturally as channels for his energy and conviction. This may be seen to best advantage in the 'sermon' he inserts at the end of the *synaxis* §16) where he adopts a pronouncedly confrontational stance against a certain group in the community which has tried to excuse their disinclination to attend church by specious logic.

Consequently, although Xosrov's delivery is extempore, we are not to assume it lacks form or consistency. Flexible in its application, he nevertheless follows a fairly clear, stable method. Dividing the passage into clauses, he sets about interpreting their component parts phrase by phrase and, if need be, word by word, perhaps on the basis of marginal annotations in the manuscript before him. Imitating the early compilers of wordlists (*baṙgirk'*) he glosses each term in turn, even where this might be considered strictly superfluous (e.g. §33 *non-existence* is non-being. *All things* is everything. *Into visible reality* is into sight and view). Hence the first semantic level is that of paraphrase which he displays in its most extreme form in his synopsis of the creed (§26). Thereafter he often questions the appositeness of a statement or idea and in responding establishes its validity by the time-honored principle of interpreting scripture by scripture. Where an aspect of the relation between the human and divine is at issue, he further clarifies it by analogy with interaction between different social classes, especially the king and his servants, as has been noted. At the same time, he is not slow to point out the incommensurability of the two situations (e.g. §3 if there is often rejoicing when we receive some request from those puny lords who exercise rule over man, when we come before the measureless might of the Lord who is fearful to the angels and are granted our petition from Him, what exultation it should bring us . . .). Particularly where moral paraenesis is involved he may substantiate the injunction by condemning a contrary course of action. The positive teaching is often reaffirmed by a final appeal to scripture.

Although operating on such a small scale, his exegesis is not allowed to become atomistic. Rather, Xosrov is constantly at pains to underline the continuity of thought from phrase to phrase and from one unit (prayer or litany) to the next (e.g. §146 . . . keep *us from evil, since* You are capable of all things and Your lordship rules over all. Consequently, it continues §147 *Yours is the power and the kingdom* . . .). A given section's internal cohesion may be enhanced by appeal to a technique which again presupposes sermonic or pedagogical background viz. the repetition with variation of its central themes (e.g. §1 to entreat Him in hope . . . and place all our hope on Him . . . how much greater hope ought we to put in the all-compassionate One).[12]

Since, apart from the sermon, Xosrov elected to pursue a rigidly textual mode of interpretation, one might imagine this restricted his scope for free expression. Nevertheless, precisely the concentrated formulations encountered in the text afford him an occasion for personal elaboration. From the oxymoron with which they begin (§7 *sakawun bazums* . . . It attempts in a small compass to suggest a lot cf. §33) we are exposed to a vivid display of verbal scene-painting. One of his favorite subjects for depiction is the varied phenomena of the physical universe in the tradition of Hexaemeral literature.[13] Thus in §7 our author seeks to define in detail the identity of the crucified One:

> *You* are God and Son of God, consubstantial with the Father, creator of all whom countless heavenly hosts worship in great fear. At Your command the sea was set in bounds and the dry land fixed, at Your word the luminaries in the firmament of

heaven proceed, rank upon rank, by Your hand every kind of living thing is fed. You rule over all
and fill all and cannot be contained by anything,
unapproachable, ineffable and incomprehensible.

The mystery of *creatio ex nihilo* is embellished with even greater
poetic verve and forcefulness in §33:

The heavens were not, nor the heaven of heavens,
not innumerable, diverse multitudes of celestial
beings. No sun, no moon, no stars, no air, no
clouds, no rains, no earth, no fire, no springs,
rivers and seas. None of the various kinds of
plants, trees and seeds, each with their own fragrance, blossom, fruit and flavor. No variety of
species of animals, beasts, reptiles, birds and the
like. These and all other existing things came into
being from nothing at God's will and assumed activity and visible form.

Moreover, God's providential ordering of creation is the theme
with which he chooses to mark the work's final cadence in §170:

He is *founder* because He founded creation, bringing creatures to existence from non-existence and
keeps them firmly in each one's genus. He is *receiver* because He receives and cares for everything
which came into being through Him and cares for
the needs of each, not only angels and men, but
also other animals and gives Himself as an embellishment and support to all that exists. He sustains the sky from falling and keeps it illumined by
the orbit of the luminaries. He maintains the earth

unshaken and beautifies it with various plants,
shrubs and seeds which He irrigates to satiety with
rain-bearing clouds. He also confines the sea
within its limit, so as not to sink beneath its depths
or extend its shores beyond measure.

Parallel with Christ's activity in creation is the renewal
brought by His direct involvement in the economy through incarnation, death and resurrection. This is another of the commentator's central themes which he similarly elaborates at various
points. The passing allusion to the passion in the *lemma* to §7
stirs Xosrov to heighten the pathos of Christ's self-immolation by
a climactic enumeration of the process:

bound, brought to trial, insulted, spat upon, beaten,
struck, mocked, ridiculed with a crown of thorns
and burlesque clothes, smitten by a cane of reeds,
now by Pilate's lash and now by the soldiers' cane.
All this and the like is meant by *You endured suffering.*

When the theme recurs in the *anamnesis* the tone is even more
elevated through emphasis on the paradox of divine condescension
(familiar especially from Holy Week services) and its salvific efficacy for mankind in §91:

Let us ponder that the Son of God was bound in
order to free us from the bonds of sin. He was
condemned by reprobates to cancel our condemnation when He judges the earth. He endured spittle
on His divine face, a blow to His cheeks to renew
His image in us which we had defaced.
Blindfolded, He tolerated buffets on His stainless
head to withdraw the mantle of darkness from our

57

souls and similarly underwent the various other vicious torments. He was made a laughingstock by the soldiers who dressed Him in purple, with a crown of thorns and a cane, making mockery of veneration to make us truly kings and divine, granting us a glorious robe, royal crown and scepter of office. He was dishonored by Herod and scourged by Pilate to endow us with honor and prepare a path for us to life eternal.

The incarnation also evokes some of Xosrov's most arresting imagery. Throughout Christ's conception and birth is likened to the sanctification of the gifts on the altar and in §43 it is closely linked with the representation of His death in the eucharistic sacrifice, portrayed in graphic, physical terms:

He is the One who took flesh from Mary's virgin womb and united to this His entire Godhead and now unites with this bread and cup in similar fashion. He who breathed His last upon the cross exhibits the same breath-less mortality according to the flesh upon this altar.

Later, this realist tendency is manifest in the explication of the economy in terms of a *Logos* Christology. Already well established in the second century, Xosrov nonetheless develops the metaphor beyond the communication of thought by the spoken word to consider the latter's embodiment on the written page (§57):

Word refers to the Son, for He is begotten purely by the Father as speech by the mind, and He makes known the Father's will as speech makes known the speaker's intention. As speech with one sound

penetrates many things whole and not in part, so
He who was bodiless took flesh and was seen and
touched like speech which becomes embodied and
thus visible and tangible on paper.

The writer's verbal expression matches the artistic diversity of
his images. At times it is staccato and elliptic, at other times
fuller and smoother, utilizing features characteristic of elevated
discourse, some of which can be traced to Greek models that had
become indigenized.[14] Significant too is his harmonic linguistic
sense which exults in the assonance, alliteration and various types
of wordplay which his son Grigor developed to an unprecedented
degree in his poetry.[15]

Despite what has been said about his knowledge of and sympathy with certain facets of Byzantine faith and order, it is noteworthy how far his overall perspective differs from that of Greek
commentaries. We have observed the greater impact of the school
of Antioch on the Armenian tradition. However, exponents such
as Theodore of Mopsuestia, no less than their Alexandrian coun-
terparts, viewed the liturgy fundamentally in symbolic terms, di-
verging rather on the focus of their speculation. In contrast,
Xosrov's textual orientation eschews constructing such an inter-
pretive superstructure.

A number of factors would seem to bear on this situation. Not
unimportant is the fact that many of the Byzantine treatises were
addressed to lay monks, while the readership targeted by this work
was priestly (and not necessarily monastic). The Byzantine specu-
lative tendency was also facilitated by the silent recitation of the
anaphora prayers.[16] Consequently, it was natural from the view-
point of worshippers in the nave to concentrate more on the
movements and entrances and assign them spiritual significance

59

within the mystery of salvation, whether historical or mystical. Since Xosrov's task relates primarily to an elucidation of the theological and moral implications of the prayers spoken at the altar, there was less occasion to pursue such trends.

These had already been explored by previous Armenian authors in writings devoted to the church, its orders and structures. One of the earliest of these is attributed to the highly controversial seventh century figure, Yovhan Mayragomec'i who was finally condemned for his Apollinarian Christology.[17] Similar treatments have been ascribed to the combattant of Mayragomec'i's later followers, the eighth century catholicos Yovhannēs Ojnec'i. An interpretation of the rite of consecrating a church consistently refers each item in the service to the old covenant and its fulfilment in the new with its Christological corollary discussed above in terms of creation and incarnation.[18]

The other work is a homily on the church pronounced at the feast of encaenia[19] which enlarges on the theme of the two covenants as well as the interpenetration of the earthly and heavenly realms. Thus the church is regarded as the spiritualization of Old Testament types. The tripartite division of Noah's ark is reflected in the church plan consisting of *gawit'* (narthex), nave and sanctuary. Its unitive function in drawing the nations into one is contrasted in Pentecostal imagery with the divisive nature of the Tower of Babel. Similarly, the physicality of the description of Abraham's hospitality, Moses' vision on Sinai and the sacrificial victims and cultic paraphernalia associated with the temple prefigure the present spiritual reality which in turn is a foretaste of the awaited consummation. The church betrays in manifold ways its origin in Eden as well as intimations of its heavenly recapitulation.

This last point emerges with particular clarity in his brief handling of the eucharist where, after following the pattern of the *synaxis* indisputably ascribed to ојnec'i,[20] the writer goes on to discuss communion:

> After the prayers, above all the enjoyment and savor of the immortal cup and bread of life signifies the joy of those there who have been crowned in light when He will drink it new with us in His Father's kingdom, openly teaching his disciples the ineffable mystery contained in the verse, "You will eat and drink with me at my table in my kingdom" (Lk 22:30). (These are indications of future good things in the church).[21]

Only at the great entrance (§17) does Xosrov apply this sort of symbolism directly to an action without explicit textual warrant, envisioning a corresponding descent of the heavenly host to surround the altar at the elevation of the gifts. This is then proposed as the grounds for the deacon's proclamation for the departure of the 'impure'. Although the agreements are not quite verbatim, in all likelihood this passage depends on a homily attributed to the late fifth century catholicos Yovhannēs Mandakuni whose liturgical initiatives we have already encountered. In a detailed consideration of how one should worthily approach the sacrament the hierarch acknowledges that the Christian should be holy as Christ is holy. Distinguishing this attitude from the opposite, he remarks that communion is a light to such recipients, but a destroying fire to those unprepared.[22] Accentuating the awesome presence of the sacrament, he states:

> When the sacred mystery ascends to the holy table,
> the heavens open from above and Christ descends

there.   The hosts of angels swell from heaven to
earth and surround the altar where the dread mystery of the Lord is.[23]

In general Xosrov cleaves fairly carefully to the text to be commented upon and is cautious of interpolating material even when
this is broadly germane to the point under review. Thus, in treating the final bidding for thanksgiving (§163), he draws out the
significance of participating in the immortal, incorrupt and divine
mystery through the doctrine of divinization[24] whereby "others do
not possess immortality and incorruption by nature, but receive it
from Him."   Nevertheless, in the preface to the *eucharistia* (§61)
where a similar theme is announced, he is at pains to distinguish
the precise nuance of the moment:

> He descended to our poverty and granted us His di-
> vinity, though that is not the point made here, but
> rather that He made us equal to the *angels*.

Although he shares the Antiochene emphasis on salvation history,
Christ's earthly ministry and the anticipation of the heavenly
banquet, Xosrov expresses this through the mode of exegesis
rather than speculation on the rite itself.[25]

Notes

1) See *Afterword* p. 229.
2) See the colophon on p. 231.
3) For a full English translation of the poem see A. K. Sanjian,
"Two Contemporary Armenian Elegies on the Fall of
Constantinople 1453", *Viator* 1 (1970), pp. 223-261.
4) A. Łazinyan, *Aṙak'el Baťišec'i* Erevan, Armenian Academy of
Sciences: 1971, p. 236.

5) Both this colophon and that of Grigor employ the same technical term *gcagrel*.

6) The latter trend is already adumbrated by Xosrov's son Grigor who commented on Song of Songs. For an analysis see R. W. Thomson, "Gregory of Narek's *Commentary on the Song of Songs*", *JTS* 34 (1983), pp. 453-496. For the situation at Glajor and Tat'ew see Mathews/Sanjian, *Armenian Gospel*, pp. 22-26.

7) For facets of the Antiochene impact on Armenian exegesis see Cowe, *Daniel*,(forthcoming).

8) For a survey of Armenian authors' acquaintance with the corpus see R. W. Thomson, "The Armenian Version of Ps. Dionysius Areopagita", *AJ* 56, 1982, pp. 115-123.

9) Id. (ed.), *The Armenian Version of the works attributed to Dionysius the Areopagite*, CSCO script. arm. 17 (Armenian text), 18 (English translation) Louvain, Peeters: 1987. Ps. Dionysius is also referred to in a homily on the rite of consecration of a church attributed to Catholicos Yovhannēs ōjnec'i (ōjnec'i, *Matenagrut'iwnk'*, p. 149).

10) For the problem of his identification see *AnjB*, vol. 3, 1972, pp. 23-25.

11) See Anania Mokac'i, "Letters", pp. 280-288.

12) Naturally, Xosrov's stylistic finesse in varying the morphology and syntax of these phrases is best exemplified by reference to the Armenian text . . . *yusov* . . . *yusasc'uk'* . . . *mecayoys* (p. 2).

13) One of the most influential texts of this genre composed by St. Basil already existed in Armenian in the first half of the fifth century. Significantly, this loose translation was effected from the already expansive Syriac version. Another verse treatment by the Byzantine writer George Pisides was translated in the first decades of the eighth century.

14) These features are already observed in Armenian writers of

the fifth century and include left branching, placing a noun in the genitive case in front of the related substantive (e.g. *caṙayut'ean anun*, p. 3). Another facet is the enclosing of verbal forms within nominal phrases (e.g. *zanbaw nora yaytnelov zoḫormut'iwn*, p. 4). A third significant element is the absolute use of verbs in association with prepositions which function like Greek preverbs and hence do not govern dependent nouns (e.g. *zoḫormut'ean šnorhn iwr i veray aṙnē* in contrast to the *lemma zoḫormut'ean zšnorhs iwr arasc'ē i veray mer*, p. 4).

15) One might cite the *figura etymologica* of §33: "in order that . . . we might stand before Him in deep reverence, offering (*matusc'uk'*) our prayers and approach (*matic'uk'*) the holy mystery with all holiness." So also at §71 "in placing the sacrifice on the altar we begin (*zskizbn aṙnemk'*) to render thanks from the elements (*yiskzbanc'n*). He also makes frequent use of *chiasmus* as in §89 in the consideration of mercy and justice. Similarly, he epigrammatically contrasts the punishment (*patžēr*) of the transgressor with the honor (*patuēr*) bestowed upon the righteous in §72. Another example of wordplay is the contrast between those of clay (*hoḫeḫēn*) and the spiritual (*hogeḫēn*) in §61.

16) In Constantinople the practice was current since at least the sixth century (Meyendorff, *St. Germanos*, p. 22).

17) Archbishop N. Bogharian, "*Verlucut'iwn kat'oḫikē ekelec'woy ew or i nma yōrineal kargac'*" [Analysis of the Catholic Church and Its Orders] *Sion* (1967), pp. 70-75.

18) Ōjnec'i, *Matenagrut'iwnk'*, pp. 139-150.

19) Ibid., pp. 151-167.

20) See pp. 26-28 and cf. Meyendorff, *St. Germanos*, p. 25.

21) Ōjnec'i, *Matenagrut'iwnk'*, p. 165.

22) With this one may compare Xosrov's comments in §159.

23) Mandakuni, *Čark'*, pp. 167-168. A writing traditionally ascribed to the founder of Armenian Christianity also deals with repentance. See *Srboy hōrn meroy Grigori Lusaworč'i yačaxapatum čaŕk' ew aŕōtk'* [The Homilies and Prayers of our Holy Father Gregory the Illuminator] Venice, St. Lazar's Press: 1954, pp. 199-209. Mandakuni's formula of dismissal varies slightly from Xosrov's in representing the third term as the hopeless (*mi ok' yanyusic'*) instead of the impenitent (*mi ok' yanapašxaric'*) in §17. As in many instances of patristic citation, the discrepancy may result from quotation from memory.

24) For a treatment of the doctrine of divinization see V. Lossky, *The Mystical Theology of the Eastern Church*, Crestwood, NY, St. Vladimir's Seminary Press: 1976, pp. 196-216.

25) As Theodore of Mopsuestia interprets the great entrance as Christ's passion and the deposition of the gifts on the altar as His entombment, so by his comments at the end of the *epiclesis* Xosrov indicates his broad agreement with this schema:

> We acknowledge the Son of God on the holy altar, making visible to us His mortality for our sake, so that hereafter it may become the body which hung on the cross and lay in the tomb." (§105).

An Overview of Xosrov's Theology

Although the format of the present work does not afford the opportunity for a systematic doctrinal exposition, it may be useful to outline the main features of the author's thought, bearing in mind that many Armenian scholars adopted the commentary genre as a vehicle for their views on a given discipline.[1] Apart from the factor of medium, we have already noted how readership too impinges on the sort of material to be included and the perspective assumed. The stern admonition of priests on the gravity of their responsibility is a *topos* which emerges early in Armenian paraenetic literature[2] and can, of course, be paralleled in most Christian traditions. However, Xosrov and his successors faced a particular set of abuses which had been compounded by the church's geographical and social situation.

Arab suzerainty of the Caucasus under the Umayyads since the 640's had been relatively moderate, but became more oppressive under the Abbasid dynasty. Politically Armenia had regained independence with the recognition of Ašot I as king in 884. Still, the effects of the previous regime in impeding the church's educative role were only gradually being remedied by the efforts of bishops like Xosrov and a revival of monastic life under aristocratic patronage. More endemic was the institution's conformity to the hereditary principle fundamental to Iranian culture on the proclamation of Christianity as state religion. Not only did it fall heir to the Zoroastrian temple lands, but also to the social status of its priesthood.

Hence tenure of office on the local level corresponded to that of the house of St. Gregory in occupying the primacy during the early period.[3] Some of the problems which ensued from this procedure are eloquently summarized by Movsēs Erznkac'i at the turn of the fourteenth century. The following excerpt from one of his letters helps clarify the background to Xosrov's pervasive ethical concern:

> When someone falls from the priesthood, he should leave the church even though he or his forebears had built it; for sanctity befits the saints. Similarly, if anyone falls into schism, he is unworthy to retain the church, since if someone polluted by his actions is unworthy of the holy things, how much more someone found wanting in faith. It is written, "The priest shall erase the people's sin", yet a culpable priest cannot erase a sinner's sins. When he himself is in need of an intercessor, how can he intercede for others? As water does not burn grass but nourishes it and makes it grow, the culpable priest not only does not atone for his people's sin, but can actually be a cause of sin and encourage his people to sin. The blind cannot lead the blind: both will definitely fall into the pit, as the verse says. Therefore it is first necessary for

the priest to cleanse himself and then to erase other people's sins and extinguish them with divine fire. For the priest may be interpreted as the purifier, purifying his people's sin through his upright life and pure prayer. From another perspective the priest may be called father, showing a father's care for those who have become his children, counting their lack his own and attending to them as to himself, as having to give an account for them all before God. Hence God's church is not one's private inheritance, but belongs to true priests who serve properly . . . And where are we to put those infected with simony, blind in mind and foolish of heart, who charge to remit sin or sell the faith?[4]

It has also been argued that the political and ecclesiastical vicissitudes of the tenth century had a certain bearing on Xosrov's theological opinions, particularly regarding Christology. The issue of his possible Chalcedonian leanings was adumbrated earlier and merits more detailed discussion here. At the outset it must be admitted that much of the argumentation has relied on indirect evidence such as the bishop's acceptance of aspects of Byzantine ecclesiastical theory and practice as well as the reputed openness to such doctrines in the surrounding region of Vaspurakan.[5] Other theories attempt to achieve the same goal through association with his wife's cousin Anania[6] or his own son Grigor.[7]

Anania's implication is somewhat problematic in light of the refutation of Chalcedon which has been attributed to him,[8] although some manuscripts assign the work to his namesake from the monastery of Sanahin who flourished in the next century. The matter is complicated by the fact that the text exists in three different recensions.[9] Regardless of whether this extant composition belongs to him, the independent witness of his spiritual son Uxtanēs, bishop of Sebastia[10] explicitly confirms that he presented an anti-dyophysite treatise to Catholicos Xač'ik in c. 980.[11] Moreover, he sponsored the latter's history of the severance of the Georgian and Armenian churches which interprets events from a similar dogmatic standpoint.[12] Indeed the third part of that history (which unfortunately does not survive) treated of the Armenian mission in Cappadocia and other places to regain converts to the Byzantine fold, an activity in which the writer was personally involved.[13] In this connection Anania insisted on the rebaptism of such converts and their families on their return to the mother church.[14]

With regard to Xosrov's confession, two passages of the commentary require investigation. Reviewing the qualities the worthy communicant should exhibit, the author pauses over the stipulation of "perfect faith" (§26) to offer a synopsis of the creed. The clause delineating the incarnation is as follows:

> He [Christ] is true God and perfect man, as God
> displaying the power of divinity and bearing the
> human condition as man, yet without sin, united in
> nature (*miawor bnut'eamb*).[15]

The attempt has been made to interpret this last term as the equivalent of 'person' in the Chalcedonian definition, denoting the Word's concrete existence,[16] yet that would be highly unidiomatic usage. On the contrary, the phrase is more reminiscent of a portion of Catholicos Komitas' confession of the early seventh century which similarly speaks of the Cyrilline union of natures:

> He [Christ] appeared on the earth [and] moved
> about among men. By the union of the economy

> (*miaworut'eamb tnōrēnut'eann*) He hungered and
> thirsted, not merely through His human nature
> (*mardkayin bnut'eamb*), but by the union of the
> economy.[17]

This emphatic statement is a cautionary corrective to the
Nestorian understanding of the union which was perceived as an
unduly loose association. This misgiving applied equally to Pope
Leo's account of Christ's human and divine activities in his famous tome.[18]

The second relevant passage derives from the *anamnesis*,
affirming the lack of confusion in effecting the union
(§79):

> It says He united with the flesh *without confusion*
> for He effected no change or diminution to either
> the divine or human nature. Rather He united the
> natures to be both God and man, so that God the
> Word might be flesh and that which was incarnate
> of the Virgin might be God and He himself both
> God and man.

Scholars have regarded this declaration as even more indicative of
Chalcedonian influence with its reference to the union of natures.[19] Yet without the characteristic prepositional phrase "in
two natures" the affinity is more illusory than real, since the
Armenian church maintained the older eastern formula of union
"out of two natures". The latter is well illustrated by a pic-
turesque metaphor utilized by the eighth century catholicos,
Yovhannēs Ōjnec'i:

> The incorporeal nature of the divine Word assumed
> the corporeal nature from the Virgin and united it
> to Himself. Hence, according to nature He is from

70

two, divine and human, yet one according to the union (*miaworut'eann*). If you are not founded on those two most beautiful feet of faith in rising toward the truth, whichever one of these you rest on, you will be found lame in your confession of the truth.[20]

The implication is thus that, though not averse to certain Byzantine ecclesiastical borrowing, Xosrov did not actually adopt their Christological formulation. This is indeed the status which seems presupposed by his outburst in the commentary on the office that if someone feels other nations are right on some issue out of love for the truth, he is regarded as a Chalcedonian and deficient in faith.[21] If the bishop were really a dyophysite, his indignation would be excessive. Moreover, it is hard to imagine if he were in fact a Chalcedonian sympathizer that he would have phrased his comment on catholicity in the general intercessions (§116) in the way he did. In that case his remark that "those who have diverged from the confession of the apostles are no longer called *apostolic*" would presumably be addressed to his very readers.

Similarly, Xosrov has emerged as a man of such independence of judgment that he would hardly have imbibed such views by osmosis from his surroundings. More importantly, if Catholicos Anania had any suspicion of the bishop's wayward Christology, it is completely inexplicable why this major error is ignored in his formal condemnation while space was found for the minutiae of Greek pronunciation. Finally, his son's admiration for Basil II need not be viewed as a further Chalcedonian impetus in Xosrov's immediate vicinity[22] since it is well known that the emperor made a policy of religious lenience towards the Armenians in order to win them over to his political advantage.[23]

71

The situation is rather different with regard to T'ondrakitism. Certainly the very act of composing a commentary on the liturgy already suffices to demonstrate Xosrov's orthodoxy in this respect, since the sectarians rejected the church's sacraments along with its orders and structures. On the contrary, it may be that certain facets of his approach were intended to refute such aberrations. Foremost among these is the insistence on the transformation of the gifts, so that they should not be looked upon as "mere bread and wine" (§42, cf. §22) but reverenced with awe. So basic is this teaching considered that Xosrov appended it to his mini creed (§26). In elucidating the process it has been noted how frequently he employs the analogy of the incarnation, Christ's assumption of the elements corresponding to the union with His human nature[24] e.g.

> (§42) He is the One who took flesh from Mary's virgin womb and united to this His entire Godhead and now unites with this bread and cup in similar fashion.
>
> (§82) [The Holy Spirit] was sent to Mary, effected the ineffable economy in her and united to God the Word the flesh from the Virgin, so that in the same way He might miraculously bring the *bread* into unity with the Son of God.[25]

This association of the two doctrines is one of comparative antiquity in Armenia, indications of which are found from at least the sixth century.[26] Whereas it often appears in the context of liturgical discussions with Byzantium, its utility in the debate with the Paulicians and the rejected T'ondrakite movement is evident since it appears that they rejected Christ's divinity.[27] In his refutation of the sect Ojnec'i employs a similar argument, parrying the sectarians' allegations of idolatry in venerating images and the cross. Summarizing the significant impact of the ark on salvation history, he retorts, "Was it a tablet carved of inanimate stones which did these or was it not God Himself who was united (*miaworeal ēr*) to these?"[28]

The same writer develops the theme further to affirm that images are means of grace for the believer, stating:

> We represent Christ alive and making [others] alive on all materials in human resemblance. For this reason also our hope is sure; for He said, "Whoever believes in Me will not see death, but even if he dies, he is alive" (Jhn 8:51, 11:25).[29]

Xosrov likewise argues that partaking of the sacrament is a vital element in divinization (§127):

> The same vivification of divinity united to the bread and cup is *immortal* and gives immortality to those who approach.[30]

Furthermore, in contrast to the T'ondrakite common meal, he underlines the fundamental sacrificial nature of the rite. For this Christ has appointed a human order of priesthood not vouchsafed to the angels (§34). It is the fulfilment of the sacrifices of the old covenant (§73), yet although the sacrifice is performed on earth, the reality is in heaven (§48). The priest is a minister, but Christ is celebrant (§101); in fact He is both sacrificer and sacrificed (§76) and the sacrifice He offers is that of the cross (§86).

Commemorating the gathering in the upper room (§164), the eucharist provides present assurance of blessings to come (§16) anticipating the eschatological banquet by uniting us to the Father in love through participation in the Spirit and our entering the bridal-chamber to be with the immortal bridegroom (§46).[31] Sustaining the imagery from the Matthean parables of the kingdom, those unworthy of this (catechumens, penitents etc.) are led away from the holy nuptials to mourn their exclusion at the doors (§40). With this in mind, the faithful are to purify themselves through confession (§19) and devote themselves to fasting (§155) and almsgiving with tears of entreaty for forgiveness (§16).

Acknowledging that the liturgy is ultimately a mystery, the fullness of which no one has experienced (§34), Xosrov further reveals his basically apophatic or negative orientation characteristic of the eastern theological tradition by his frequent testimony to the incomprehensibility of the divine essence (§174), inscrutable alike to men and angels (§56). Indeed the latter cower before the radiance of the divine effulgence (§61). Distinct in hypostasis (§26), the persons of the trinity are one in essence (§104) and lordship (§64) and the universe is their common creation (§57).

God is creator by nature (§133), calling the world into being from non-being by His will (§32), but became father by showing compassion. His fervent love for man was not content with having one son by nature (§156): He adopted others by grace (§46) which is manifested in the baptism of regeneration (§1). Thereby God overlooks our sins as if He had not noticed them (§99): postbaptismal sin is purged by the eucharist (§160).

As we have already noticed, a cataphatic or positive analogical approach is sometimes adopted to clarify divine-human interrelations. In this sphere it is notable that where the issue at stake turns on the obligations incumbent upon the lesser party in the relationship, the comparison is made directly e.g. (§1) "Similarly, it is normal first to serve human lords and then bring petitions."

> (§74) *Reckoning* is what kings draw up against
> criminals and keep sealed until they repay them as
> their crime requires. Similarly, human nature
> from the first man until Christ was held in custody
> by a writ sealed till the day of retribution.[32]
>
> (§122) As a coachman steers the horses and does
> not allow them to veer from the highway, so may
> You *steer our prayers* so as not to diverge from
> Your will.

Instances illustrating benefits accruing from earthly patrons or
benefactors are always introduced in terms of contrast with the
divine. Perhaps the most striking case is the relativizing of human parental affection by reference to the animal world:

> (§71) *Lovingkindness* is more forceful than ten-
> derness which parents exhibit towards their off-
> spring with warm affection and great fondness
> which can be observed not only among men, but
> also on many occasions among other animals such
> as hens.[33]

The effect of gaining a lord's favor also palls before that of receiving God's bounty (§2). Moreover, since He is father as well
as physician, His caring concern is far more dependable than the
attention of ordinary doctors (§16). In this way the commentator
marks the limitations of the symbol by an apophatic corrective.

In discussing Xosrov's Christology we have considered the theory of Chalcedonian affinities and possible anti-T'ondrakite measures. Another important facet of his teaching central to the interpretation of the eucharist is the reality and efficacy of Christ's
passion. If the T'ondrakites held that a "mere man" had suffered

on the cross, another sect prevalent in parts of Armenia preached a view diametrically opposed to this that docetically limited the degree to which the Word shared the human condition. Founded by the controversial seventh century figure, Yovhan Mayragomec'i, the group claimed features such as Christ's ignorance were a semblance and that it was impossible that He could have feared death in the agony of Gethsemane as He assumed Adam's prelapsarian flesh.[34]

Whereas Mayragomec'i drew a sharp distinction between Christ's being "in the likeness of sinful flesh" (Rom 8:3) and regular human existence, Xosrov is at pains to reaffirm His consubstantiality with us (e.g. §9 *"To dwell among us* means being as we are") which is further defined as meaning "without appearance" (§78). As Mayragomec'i's "unitarian" understanding of the relation of Godhead and manhood in Christ suggested some sort of Eutychian mixture, so our author emphasizes the lack of confusion in the union of natures (§§79, 127).

In contrast to Mayragomec'i's docetic presentation of Christ's humanity, Xosrov elaborates all the natural passions of the flesh and rational soul which He shared (§80):

> He was born, nourished, hungered, thirsted, grew tired, ate, drank, felt, became anxious, sorrowed, wept and took upon Himself all else entailed by the flesh. And remaining free from *sin*, He became victorious over fleshly shortcomings.

Moreover, he underlines the soteriological importance of Christ's consubstantiality with us in transfiguring human nature (§171):

> By Your sufferings by which we have received incorruption You made us worthy to be under Your rule.

76

This was possible because He was raised in the same body of flesh, now glorified (§127) and by His ascension "He exalted our earthly nature to the divine throne" (§95). As we have already seen, the eucharist is a vital means of realizing the union of the faithful with their resurrected Lord in Xosrov's theology.

His ethical preoccupation also perceives in Christ's condescension a valuable object lesson in Christian living. The circumstances of His life incorporate an implicit critique of the extravagance to be witnessed at the independent princely courts and in the merchant communities of cities like Arcn and Ani as a result of reinvigorated trade between the Empire and Caliphate.[36] Its destruction in the middle of the following century is seen in part as retribution for its citizens' luxury and exploitation by the historian Aristakēs Lastivertc'i.[37] Hence for Xosrov, Christ's lowly birth teaches us not to despise poverty, His dress, table habits and behavior at wedding celebrations encourage moderation and temperance and His riding on a donkey and washing of His disciples' feet advocate humility for those who would pursue the *imitatio Christi* (§85).

If much of the commentator's focus on Christ is occupied with the understanding of His person, his pneumatology concentrates rather on the Spirit's activities.[38] As affirmed in the Nicene creed, He was poured out upon the prophets, but was present in even greater abundance in the apostolic gathering at Pentecost (§8). The Spirit is life-creating in the sacraments through the regeneration of baptism (§38) and in the purification from sin of the eucharist (§11) in which He unites Christ with the elements as He united the Logos to His human nature in the incarnation (§103). He bestows charisms on those who ask to confirm them in faith and works of righteousness and is a comfort in tribulation (§4).

77

With regard to Xosrov's ecclesiology, it is surely significant that he omits any mention of the one catholic and apostolic Church from his synopsis of the creed (§26) and has to be prompted to handle the subject in treating the special intercessions (§116). There too the commentator is more at home with the plural number, implying the individual structures "erected in the entire world according to the preaching of the apostles" as well as the various autocephalous jurisdictions claiming apostolic origin.[39] It is only in connection with the sacrament of baptism and unity in the faith that Xosrov speaks of the oneness of churches, employing the traditional image of a mother nurturing her offspring.[40] Betraying the seminal importance of Jerusalem for Caucasian Christianity, he would assign it primacy over all others because of the holy places under its oversight.[41] Still he has to concede that even the faith is not fully uniform, recognizing that certain churches have erred from apostolic doctrine.

Nevertheless, in characteristically Armenian fashion, Xosrov takes a quietist approach to issues of dogmatic disagreement, seeking protection from schismatic harassment (§108) but not advocating mounting the ideological offensive against them. Hence generally in the doctrinal consultations and correspondence in which the Armenians were involved with the Byzantine, Syrian and Latin churches the initiative was taken by the other side.[42] It was only when Nestorian proselytizers established a congregation in the capital of Duin during the sixth century and began to spread their propaganda among the local population that Catholicos Nersēs was impelled to convene a synod to take defensive action.[43] Similarly, Armenian measures against the Paulicians, followers of Mayragomec'i and T'ondrakites[44] were undertaken when the welfare of the church itself was deemed to be in jeopardy. Under other circumstances co-operation was counselled despite theological disagreements as, for example, by Vardan Aygekc'i (†1235).[45]

One of the latter's motives was presenting a united front against Muslim attack. Their threat to Christendom for Xosrov was tantamount to that of the barbarians cited in the liturgical text (§108).[46] Yet once again, in view of the swift and persistent Byzantine and Syrian polemic against the new community, the paucity of corresponding Armenian material is striking.[47] At the same time the commentator envisions a day when the Church will encompass the earth, impiety cease and all perform God's will like the angels (§139).

Furthermore, through the communion of saints the present and future coinhere with the past in timeless unity. Accordingly, Xosrov emphasizes that there are those also under the old covenant who fell asleep in Christ (§108) and gives detailed instructions on how the different ranks of saints should be invoked as intercessors at the liturgy (§113). Supplications are also enjoined for the souls of those departed this life in faith and hope (§§114, 131).

In a somewhat invidious position as bishop himself, Xosrov takes time to explain the benefit to believers of praying for their overseers. If the latter are committed to the flock's spiritual welfare, the mutuality of concern renders their petitions for the people of more avail (§118). As the hierarchy's supervisory responsibilities are outlined there and at other points (§117), the laity also have a ministry to contribute to the church's needs in various ways. They sustain the church's liturgical service by gifts of vessels and texts and the officiating clergy by the bounty of their herds and land. In their provision for the eucharist as their participation in it, their attitude is of paramount importance for the commentator (§120).

As previously adumbrated, Xosrov's primary soteriological focus is divinization. That is the process the devil hoped to thwart by beguiling Eve through the snake to accept a counterfeit which resulted in expulsion from paradise (§16). The sin of transgression made man vulnerable to death and the curse it inflicted on him (§57) imposed an impenetrable obstacle in his relation to God. Consequently, all are subject to temptation (§14) and the torment of demons (§13) from whose fear the faithful are to pray Christ's deliverance.

The extent to which the fall influenced human nature has been variously debated and a distinct tension is perceptible in the commentator's handling of Satan's authority over humanity. On the one hand statements like "he prevents your acceptance of divine seeds" (§16) and "the devil does not permit us to hear what is of God" (ibid.) suggest he is all-powerful. However, imperatives such as "do not favor the devil's deceit" and "listen to God" from the same section imply that our volitional freedom is not entirely compromised. Indeed, he remarks that Adam's punishment was also meant to foster caution in others (§72). And yet our proclivity is to "prefer to listen to Satan rather than God" (§16).

The principle is once again expressed with clarity by Catholicos Yovhannēs Ōjnec'i:

> Then [before the fall] only with difficulty could [our nature] be moved to sin, but most easily to good, whereas now that we have fallen into this corruptible life, we are threatened by the opposite condition, turning easily to sin, but with difficulty to virtue.[48]

The greater concern for guarding thoughts and institutionalization of confession, originally a monastic discipline, to lend it direction and support intensified the church's sense of unworthiness (§14) and relativized the earlier practice of categorizing the congregation according to merit. Nevertheless, it is still regarded as possible to "strip off the Spirit with [postbaptismal] sins" (ibid.) and be given over to the demons completely.

Salvation is therefore only possible through Christ's vicarious death which trampled down death and released its captives. The commentator briefly considers alternatives (§57), but concludes only Christ's sinlessness would provide a solution congruent with divine justice (§89). His death being re-presented in the eucharist, the latter becomes a weapon against the devil's assaults (§57) and strengthens worshippers in welldoing (§165). While the Our Father looks towards the consummation of the kingdom in power (§138), through the illumination of the Spirit the liturgy already initiates the faithful into the contemplation of "the glory of God with uncovered face as in a mirror" (§14).

In the above the theologian will find little that is novel or strives to be original: that was not the task the author set himself. Instead, we find him fulfilling his episcopal duty to provide "precise, straightforward and accurate teaching" (§117), steering the monastic students and parish clergy away from any tendencies to "perversion or deviation to right or left" (ibid.). The extent to which he achieved this may be gauged by his impact on the commentators who followed after him.

Notes

1) Perhaps the most characteristic example of this phenomenon is the series of grammarians over about a millenium from the sixth century who advanced the field by commenting on the fundamental treatise of Dionysius Thrax. In theology attention focused particularly on the patrimony of the Cappadocian Fathers along with Evagrius and (uniquely among the eastern churches) Philo.

2) One of the earliest occurs in a fifth century homily on the worthy reception of communion (Mandakuni, *Čaṙk'*, p. 168).

3) One of the most enduring applications of the principle of heredity was maintained by the catholicoi of the see of Aɫt'amar who for much of its duration claimed descent from the Arcrunid royal house. See R. H. Hewsen, "Artsrunid House of Sefedinian: Survival of a Princely Dynasty in Ecclesiastical Guise", *JSAS* 1 (1984), pp. 123-138.

4) E. Petrosyan (ed.), "*Movsēsi hayoc' vardapeti greal patasxanik' t'ɫt'oy Trapizoni aṙ hatuacealn Grigor erēc'*" [The Reply Written by Movses, Vardapet of the Armenians to the Priest Grigor who had settled in Trebizond] *Eǰmiacin* 31 (1975) March, p. 54.

5) E.g. Salaville, "Explication", p. 351, Mécérian, *Livre de prières* p. 18 and Yarnley, "Armenian Philhellenes", pp. 46-47. Earlier when it was thought that the Armenians had already rejected Chalcedon in the fifth century, it was fashionable to view the persecution of Ɫazar P'arpec'i and the philosopher Movsēs (identified with the historian Movsēs Xorenac'i) as a reaction to their putative Chalcedonian sympathies, purely on the basis of speculation.

6) Salaville, "Explication", p. 351 and Yarnley, "Armenian Philhellenes", p. 47.

7) Mécérian, *Livre de prières*, p. 25 and Yarnley, "Armenian Philhellenes", pp. 48-49.

8) E.g. Archbishop N. Bogharian, *Hay groɫner* [Armenian Writers], Jerusalem, St. James Press: 1971, p. 151. This may be partly supported by the early eleventh century historian Asoɫik's account of Anania's having composed writings against other heresies as well as T'ondrakitism. See Ɫ. Ališan, *Hayapatum*, Venice, St. Lazar's Press: 1901, p. 287.

9) For details see H. Anasyan, *Haykakan matenagitut'yun e-ẊẊ darer* [Armenian Bibliography of the Fifth to the Eighteenth Centuries] vol. 1 Erevan, Armenian Academy of Sciences: 1959, coll. 775-782. The issue is currently under investigation by H. Kyoseyan and H. H. Tamrazyan of the Matenadaran Institute of Manuscripts, Erevan. See in particular the latter's monograph, *Anania Narekac'i* Erevan, Armenian Academy of Sciences: 1986.

10) For the resolution of the question of which see he occupied see Kolandjian, "Uxtanēs", pp. 397-413.

11) Uxtanēs episkopos, *Patmut'iwn hayoc'* [History of the Armenians] Vałaršapat, S. Kat'ołikē: 1871, p. 11.

12) Ibid.

13) See Kolandjian, "Uxtanēs", p. 398.

14) K. Šahnazareanc' (ed.), *Tiezerakan Patmut'iwn Step'annos Vardapeti Tarōnec'woy* [The Universal History of the Vardapet Step'annos Tarōnec'i], Paris, 1859, p. 165.

15) Xosrov, *Meknut'iwn*, p. 15.

16) Salaville, "Explication", p. 355. See esp. n. 3 ibid. and cf. Vetter, *Explicatio*, p. x.

17) "*T'ułt' Komitasay hayoc' katułikosi i Parss*" [A Letter of Komitas the Armenian Catholicos to the Persians] *Ararat* 30 (1896), pp. 532-533.

18) See the verdict of Vrt'anēs k'erdoł, *locum tenens* of the catholicate at the turn of the seventh century in the *Girk' t'łt'oc'*, p. 124.

19) Salaville, "Explication", p. 361 and Mécérian, *Livre de prières* p. 22.

20) Ōjnec'i, *Matenagrut'iwnk'*, p. 68.

21) See Constantinople, 1840, p. 199 and cf. Mécérian, *Livre de*

prières, p. 23 and Yarnley, "Armenian Philhellenes", pp. 47-48.

22) Yarnley, "Armenian Philhellenes", p. 48.

23) H. M. Bart'ikian, "The Religious Diplomacy of Byzantium in Armenia During the Tenth and Eleventh Centuries", *ASIMHB*, pp. 59-60.

24) Vetter, *Explicatio*, pp. x-xi, Salaville, "Expliation", pp. 380-381.

25) See also the similar formulation at §104.

26) For details see Cowe, "Job Fragment".

27) See Nersessian, *Tondrakian Movement*, p. 57.

28) Ojnec'i, *Matenagrut'iwnk'*, p. 57.

29) Ibid., pp. 52-53.

30) See also the similar language employed by Xosrov's son Grigor in relation to Anania's refutation of the T'ondrakites in Nersessian, *Tondrakian Movement*, p. 57.

31) Equally the eucharist is related to the paradise of Eden: as St. Paul depicts Christ as the new Adam and the fathers extend the analogy to the Mother of God as second Eve, so it is by tasting the eucharistic food that the effects of the first transgression are overcome (§37).

32) See also the consideration of the same topic in §16.

33) See also the parallel in §1.

34) Karapet episkopos, *Knik' hawatoy* [Seal of Faith] Ejmiacin, Mayr At'oł, 1914, pp. 363-364.

35) Ibid., p. 254.

36) For an overview of the process see H. Manandian, *Trade and Cities of Armenia in connexion with the Ancient World*, Bibl. C. Gulbenkian, Lisbon: 1965.

37) See K. N. Yuzbašyan (ed.), *Patmut'iwn Aristakisi Lastivertc'woy* [The History of Aristakēs Lastivertc'i], Erevan, Armenian Academy of Sciences: 1964, p. 136 and for an English

translation R. Bedrosian, *Aristakēs Lastivertc'i's History*, New York, 1985, p. 165.

38) The internal relations of the Spirit with the other persons of the trinity are dealt with briefly in §§26, 104.

39) On the early significance of St. Thaddeus for Greater Armenia and its subsequent adoption of traditions relating to St. Bartholomew see the discussion and literature cited in Cowe, "Job Fragment".

40) In keeping with this, his son portrays the Church in striking fashion as the bride of Christ. See A. K'yoškeryan (ed.), *Grigor Narekac'i taɬer ew ganjer* [Grigor Narekac'i Taɬ and Ganj Poems] Erevan, Matenadaran: 1981, pp. 120-125.

41) For the impact of the Jerusalem pilgrimage on Caucasian Christianity see S. P. Cowe, "Pilgrimage to Jerusalem by the Eastern Churches", L. Kriss-Rettenbeck and G. Möhler (edd.), *Wahlfahrt kennt keine Grenzen*, Munich, 1984, pp. 316-330.

42) The case of the dialogue between the Armenian and Georgian churches at the turn of the seventh century which led to the rupture of communion between them is exceptional. The Armenian reaction there is to be explained by the close association which had existed between them in times past which had been cemented by their joint presence at the Synod of Duin of 505/6.

43) *Girk' t'ɬt'oc'*, pp. 72-75.

44) The movement was largely crushed by the campaigns of an Armenian prince in the mid eleventh century. For his account of the events see K. Kostaneanc' (ed.), *Grigor Magistrosi t'ɬt'erǝ* [Grigor Magistros' Letters] Alexandropol, 1910 and for an English translation F. C. Conybeare, *The Key of Truth*, Oxford, Clarendon Press, pp. 143-149.

45) See Y. A. Anasean, *Manr Erker* [Short Monographs] American Armenian International College, La Verne, CA: 1988,

85

pp. 217-220. Similarly, the vardapet Samuēl Kamrǰajorec'i, replying to a doctrinal tract by the Metropolitan of Melitene c. 986, emphasizes Armenian willingness to serve both emperor and patriarch. At the same time he appreciates the irremediability of the longstanding schism and leaves the issue to God's inscrutable judgment. *Girk' t'łt'oc'*, p. 322.

46) This must also be the allusion in a coronation anthem which speaks of the king "obtaining revenge upon Hagar and the Canaanite". See A. Siwrmēean, *Mayr c'uc'ak hayerēn jeṙagrac' Halēpi ew Ant'iliasi ew masnaworac'* [Grand Catalogue of the Armenian Manuscripts of Aleppo, Antelias and in Private Collections] vol. 2. Aleppo: 1936, p. 29.

47) For a survey see R. W. Thomson, "Muhammad and the Origin of Islam in Armenian Literary Tradition", *ASIMHB*, pp. 829-858.

48) Ojnec'i, *Matenagrut'iwnk'*, p. 85.

Xosrov and His Successors

The prestige our commentator enjoyed can partly be gauged by the range of extant manuscripts of his writing, as well as scattered scribal testimonials to his authority.[1] More important, however, is the seminal influence he exerted over subsequent cultivators of the genre he had initiated. The main exception to the trend is formed by Nersēs Lambronac'i whose study of 1177 was produced when the writer was only twenty-four years of age and had but recently been consecrated bishop of Tarson. Despite this, it reveals maturity and wide erudition in the examination of exemplars of the missal, though nowhere is there mention of or citation from his predecessor's work.

Like most texts of this kind, it was commissioned by priests and complains of clerical ignorance and indifference. More comprehensive in scope than Xosrov's, before embarking on the rite itself it treats such general questions as the symbolism of ecclesiastical architecture and vestments and the parallelism between the earthly and heavenly aspects of the rite under the influence of Ps. Dionysius, as frequently in the body of the commentary.

Reflecting, as we have observed, the more detailed rubrics of his time, Nersēs indicates variations in the common rite when the celebrant is a bishop and during ordinations, as well as contrasting Byzantine and Roman practice. In this connection he also enters into the debate concerning the transformation of the elements,[2] azymes and the unmixed cup, breaking with Armenian tradition in regarding the latter as purely issues of usage unaffecting the efficacy of the sacrament.[3]

The next commentary we encounter was completed by Movsēs Erznkac'i (†1323) in 1293 at the behest of the renowned scholar Yovhannēs Erznkac'i (also credited with having commented on the liturgy)[4] who died that same year.[5] Like Xosrov's it was conceived as the sequel to an investigation of the divine office.[6] However, it betrays a familiar trend toward compilation, abbreviation and simplification which had already infiltrated the biblical sphere with Anania Sanahnec'i's commentary on the Pauline Epistles of 1055. Obviously curriculum expansion at the monastic academies and the reconciliation of authorities was a matter of growing concern as in the west. The result is a handy digest and hence, although intermittently venturing his own opinions, most of his effort was devoted to collating Xosrov and Nersēs. Indeed, the former appears almost word for word, while treatment of the latter is more selective.[7] The compiler followed Xosrov's advice about consulting St. Gregory of Nyssa on the Lord's Prayer (§136) and occasionally cites Ps. Dionysius. He seems to have been particularly exercised about the implications of the reference to Christ's descent into Hell in the great anaphoral prayer, on which he offers an unprecedentedly broad spectrum of sources.[8] The text remains unpublished: the earliest manuscript is M9292, copied only four years after the composition itself in 1297.

This was followed by a rather similar undertaking of

Yovhannēs Arčišec'i (†c. 1330) whose mandate from the priests who commissioned the work was to render even more accessible to ordinary clergy the by now standard treatments of Xosrov and Nersēs. With the latter particularly in mind, the epitomator rehearses popular complaints of their prolixity and over-subtlety of thought.[9] Meanwhile, some local clergy recite even the liturgical prayers without comprehending them and hence incline towards a perfunctory performance of their duties.[10] In fact, he alludes not only to laymen but even celibate priests who would not communicate until near death and then not out of hope but to avoid scandal.[11] Apart from such vignettes of contemporary religious mores, the author largely restricts himself to following his prototypes. In view of the book's aims and format it is hardly surprising that it went through four editions by the end of last century.[12] The earliest extant textual witness is J1698 penned probably still within the writer's lifetime in 1326.[13]

Other anonymous commentaries on the full liturgy survive in later codices such as M3050 of 1592 and M8689 of the seventeenth century which await identification and research. In addition, certain more technical studies exist as, for example, a disquisition entitled *Vasn xorhrdoy pataragi* [On the Sacrament of the Eucharist]. The piece is attributed to the eminent scholar Vardan Arewelc'i (†1271) who is known to have dealt with related subjects in other works.[14] Naturally, the same topic is represented (albeit briefly) in Grigor Tat'ewac'i's theological *summa* about a century later. The savant displays his customary eclecticism in defending the traditional Armenian unmixed chalice[15] while subscribing to the Thomist view of transsubstantiation.[16]

Even this spare synopsis which makes no pretense of being exhaustive should suffice to indicate something of the range and variety of medieval Armenian commentary and doctrinal literature pertaining to the eucharist's form and meaning. It has been stated that investigation of the liturgy of St. Athanasius is still in its infancy[17] and this is corroborated by the amount of relevant material as yet unpublished. Moreover, even where a text has appeared in print, the edition is hardly satisfactory, often in the editor's opinion first and foremost. Thus Ališan remarks his three witnesses to Nersēs' composition require correction on the basis of more authentic copies.[18] Likewise, Sargis Dpir laments lacunae in his copy of Yovhannēs Arčišec'i's epitome which had occasioned a long typographical delay.[19]

Nevertheless, one should recognize that some progress has been made. Sargis' dilemma over the absence of St. John Chrysostom's prayer of thanksgiving (prefixed to the original two in the *textus receptus*) is no longer a cause of mystification. Neither does one need to suppose the epitimator overlooked these passages, deeming the sense lucid enough, nor that the manuscript in question was defective in this regard.[20] When we consider the late position they occupy in the rite's evolution, a very different solution imposes itself. The present translation is offered in the hope of fostering a broader appreciation of the value of the genre in general and of Xosrov Anjewc'i's formative role in creating it. Despite changes in the rite, his work may still be a worthy spiritual guide to the liturgy.

Notes

1) See, for example, the marginal note in J1946 of 1310 advising readers not to diverge from the pattern of the litany of intercessions great Xosrov had established (Bogharian, *Mayr c'uc'ak*, vol. 6, 1972, p. 499.
2) See Salaville, "Consecration", p. 29.

3) For further details see Cowe, "Job Fragment".

4) This too seems to have been an epitome of Nersēs' work. See N. Akinean, *Nersēs Lambronac'i*, Vienna, Mxit'arist Press: 1956, p. 176. A work with this ascription is to be found in various manuscripts usually of rather late date (e.g. M2993 of 1679 and M3433 of 1720).

5) For the author's final colophon where this information is presented see A. S. Mat'evosyan (ed.), *Hayeren jeṙagreri hišatakaranner žg dar* [Thirteenth Century Armenian Manuscript Colophons] Erevan, Armenian Academy of Sciences: 1984, pp. 714-715.

6) *Meknut'iwn aṙōt'ic'* . . . *hawak'eal ěst kargi i mium tětpi i Movsisē umemē ašxatasēr vardapetē* [Commentary on the Prayers . . . compiled by the diligent vardapet Movsēs] Constantinople, 1730. For details see Oskanyan, *Hay girk'ě*, pp. 292-294.

7) See E. Petrosyan, "Movsēs Erznkac'u 'Hawak'umn hamaṙōt meknut'ean srboy pataragin zor yaṙajagoyn arareal ē srboc' lusawor harc'n ašxatut'yuně" [Movsēs Erznkac'i's "Brief Collection of Commentaries on the Holy Liturgy Produced by Earlier Holy, Enlightened Fathers] *Ejmiacin* 30 (1973) Nov., pp. 43-45. Significantly Movsēs does not witness the marginal additions to Xosrov's text in later manuscripts.

8) Ibid., p. 47.

9) Yovhannēs Arčišec'i, *Meknut'iwn Pataragi* [Commentary on the Liturgy] Constantinople, 1717, p. 18.

10) Ibid., pp. 15 ff.

11) Ibid., p. 273.

12) For the second edition see Oskanyan, *Hay girk'ě*, pp. 742-743. The third appeared in Calcutta in 1830 and fourth at Ejmiacin in 1860.

13) Bogharian, *Mayr c'uc'ak*, vol. 5, 1971, pp. 572-573.

14) He handled the sacraments in an anti-dyophysite treatise preserved in J888 (ibid., vol. 3, 1968, p. 391). Additionally, an article on unleavened bread is found in his compendious encyclopaedia. See P'. Ant'abyan, "Vardan Arewelc'u 'Žłank'ĕ'" [Vardan Arewelc'i's "Conversations"] BMat 8 (1967), p. 165 (item 24 in the table).

15) Grigor Tat'ewac'i, *Girk' harc'manc'* [Book of Questions] Constantinople, 1729, p. 594.

16) Ibid., p. 597. In this he displays his knowledge of Yovhannēs Corcorec'i's Armenian translation of Aquinas' sacramental theology effected in 1321. His eclecticism is paralleled by that of his teacher Esayi Nč'ec'i who in one of his doctrinal letters seems to have adopted the latin doctrine of the trinity while maintaining the traditional Armenian position on the incarnation. See Mathews/Sanjian, *Armenian Gospel*, p. 30.

17) R. Taft, "Psalm 24 at the Transfer of Gifts in the Byzantine Liturgy: A Study in the Origins of a Liturgical Practice" in *The Word in the World*, R. J. Clifford and G. W. MacRae (eds.), Cambridge, MA, Weston College: 1973, p. 162.

18) See the introduction to Nersēs, *Meknut'iwn*.

19) Oskanyan, *Hay girk'ĕ*, p. 223.

20) Ibid.

Commentary Analysis Collated with the Divine Liturgy according to Nersoyan's Diglot Edition:

Synaxis

Prayers after the Lections §§1-5 (Ners. pp. 49-51)
Prayers after the Lections §§6-15 (Ners. pp. 49-53)
Last Blessing of the Synaxis §16 (Ners. p. 53)

HOLY SACRIFICE

1) Offertory
   A) *Great Entrance*
      Dismissal of the Catechumens §17 (Ners. p. 55)
   B) *Laying of the Gifts*
      Litany of the Offertory §§18-31 (Ners. pp. 59-61)
      Prayer of the Offertory §§32-39 (Ners. pp. 59-61)
   C) *Kiss of Peace*
      Bidding for the kiss of peace §§40-41 (Ners. p. 61)

2) Eucharistia
   A) *Prologue*
      Responsory before the eucharist §§42-51 (Ners. pp. 63-65)
      Preface §§52-63 (Ners. 65-67)
   B) *Anamnesis*
      Anamnesis §§64-98 (Ners. pp. 67-69)
      Prayer of Humble Access §§99-101 (Ners. pp. 69-71)
   C) *Epiclesis*
      Prayer of Epiclesis §§102-105 (Ners. pp. 71-73)
   D) *Diptychs*
      Intercessions §106-112 (Ners. pp. 73-81)
      Litany of Intercessions §§113-115, 127-132 (Ners. pp. 73-81)
   E) *Dominical Prayer*
      Prayer of the Paternal Name §§133-136 (Ners. pp. 81-83)
      Lord's Prayer §§137-144 (Ners. p. 83)
      Embolis §§145-147 (Ners. p. 83)
   F) *Inclination and Elevation*
      Prayer of Inclination §§148-154 (Ners. p. 87)

3) Intinction and Fraction
      Prayer of Intinction §§155-158 (Ners. p. 87)
      Exhortation to Communion §§159-161 (Ners. pp. 87-89)
      Bidding for Psalmody §162 (Ners. p. 89)

4) Communion
   Thanksgiving
      Bidding for Thanksgiving §163 (Ners. p. 97)
      Hymn of Thanksgiving §164 (Ners. p. 97)
      Prayer of Thanksgiving §§165-175 (Ners. pp. 97-99)

Commentary on the
Divine Liturgy

Xosrov Anjewac'i

ԽՈՍՐՈՎՈՒ

ԱՆՁԵՒԱՑԵԱՑ ԵՊԻՍԿՈՊՈՍԻ

ՄԵԿՆՈՒԹԻՒՆ

ՍՐԲՈՅ ՊԱՏԱՐԱԳԻ

Զկնի Աւետարանին[1] եւ զՀաւատամքն ասելոյ քարոզէ սարկաւագն.

§1 «Եւ եւս հաւատով աղաչեսցուք եւ խնդրեսցուք յԱստուծոյ՝ 'ի Հօրէ եւ 'ի տեառնէ ամենակալէ, 'ի վերայ ժամու պաշտամանն եւ աղօթից. զի Աստուած արժանի ընդունելութեան արասցէ»:

Ասացաք զեւ եւս թէ ա՛յլ է հաւատով աղաչեսցուք. զի Հաւատքն առանձ լսելի, որպէս ասաց առաքեալն Յակոբոս. եթէ ոք 'ի ձէնջ իցէ նուազեալ յիմաստութենէ, խնդրեսցէ յԱստուծոյ, որ տայ ամենայնի առատապէս եւ ոչ նախատէ, եւ տացէ նմա. բայց խնդրեսցէ Հաւատովք, եւ մի՛ երկմտութեամբ: Զայն եւ 'ի Պօղոսէ խրատիմք, որ ասէ. Կամիմ՛ զի արք կացցեն յաղօթս յամենայն տեղիս, Համբառնայցեն զձեռս ձերս 'ի վեր, առանց բարկութեան եւ երկմտութեան. եւ ինքն իսկ Տէրն մեր զայս Հաստատէ, այսպէս ասելով. Զամենայն ինչ վասն որոյ աղօթս արարեալ խնդրիցէք՝ եւ Հաւատայցէք եթէ առնուցուք, եղիցի ձեզ:

Ընդէ՞ր երկուս դնէ թէ՛ աղաչեսցուք եւ խնդրեսցուք. յուցանէ թէ մեծաւ պաղատանօք զխնդրուածան պարտ է առնել, եւ սրտի մտօք եռանդնալից ջերմութեամբ աղաչել, ըստ խրատու մարգարէին. Ժտեա 'ի տեառնէ, եւ նա տացէ քեզ զամենայն խնդրուածս քո. կոչեաց եւ զԱստուած յերկուց անուանց եւ զեկրորդն եւս յաւել.

«Խնդրեսցուք յԱստուծոյ 'ի Հօրէ եւ 'ի տեառնէ ամենակալէ».

ուսուցանելով դուռ առ Աստուած եւ երկիւղ ունել, եւ 'ի գթութիւն եւ 'ի խնամածութիւն եւ 'ի պաշպանութիւն զնա յուսով կոչել. զի Աստուած է արարիչ, Հարկաւ Հանդիպի, եւ 'ի ստեղծուածս խնամակալութիւն պահանջի. եւ զի հայր է ըստ աւգանին միասնդամ ծննդեանն՝ 'ի դուռ մեզ բորբոքէ սիրով. եւ զի տէր է ամենակալ՝ զպաշպանութիւն եւ զամենայն պիտոյս իբրեւ ծառայից ընորէել յանձն առնու:

Վասն այսորիկ մեք որպէս 'ի Հատիչ եւ 'ի հայր՝ սերտ սի-

96

After the Gospel and recitation of the Creed[1] the deacon proclaims:

§1 *"Let us again entreat and implore God the Father and Almighty Lord in faith to render this hour of worship and prayer worthy of acceptance."*

We said *"again"* because it is something additional *to entreat in faith*, since faith makes our prayers heard. As the Apostle James put it, "If any of you lacks wisdom, he should implore God who gives richly to everyone without reproach and He will give it to him. Only he should implore with faith and not doubt." (Jas 1:5). Paul offers us the same advice: "It is my wish that everywhere men pray they should raise their hands in purity without anger or doubt" (I Tim 2:8). Moreover, our Lord Himself confirms this when He says, "Everything you ask in prayer which you believe you will receive, will be yours" (Matth 21:22, Mk 11:24).

Why is it that two terms are employed *"Let us entreat and implore"*? This indicates that we must make our petitions with great supplication and entreat with conviction and fervent ardour, as the prophet enjoins, "Ask the Lord and He will grant you all your petitions" (Ps 37 [36]:4).

Here God is also invoked by two titles and a third is added: *"Let us implore God the Father and Almighty Lord"*. This instructs us to show affection and reverence towards God and to entreat Him to show affection and mercy on us, care and protect us. Since God is creator[2] it follows of necessity that His creatures need His solicitude. Since He is our *Father* in the baptism of regeneration, He is aflame with love to have compassion on us. And as He is *Almighty Lord* he undertakes to grant protection and everything expedient for us as His servants.

րով ապաւինեսցուք. եւ իբրեւ տեառն երկիւղիւ ծառայեսցուք,
եւ զամենայն հոգս մեր 'ի նա ընկեսցուք, եւ ամենայնիւ 'ի նա
յուսասցուք. զի թէ առ սակաւադուժ մարդկութիւնս[2] վասն
միոյ պատճառի հայրութեան կամ տէրութեան[3] վատահանամք
զամենայն պիտոյից մերոց լլրումն, ապա ո'րքան առաւել
երիւքս այսոքիւք` առ բազմադուժն այն Աստուած եւ հայր եւ
տէր` պարտիմք մեծայոյս լինել։ Միայն զարժանն եւեթ հա-
տուսցուք նմա լաստ ամենայնի. զի արարածն զարաբիէն պատո-
ւէ, եւ 'ի նորա սպաս եւ 'ի պաշտօն հարկի. եւ որդի զճայր
փառաւոր առնէ, եւ ծառայ երկնչի 'ի տեառնէ իւրմէ։ Այս-
պիսիք լեալք` ամենայնիւ 'ի նմանէ բարեգործիցիմք, եւ
զաւետիս կենաց ունիցիմք զաստիս եւ զճանդերձելոցն. իսկ եթէ
ընդ հակառակն յայնցանէ շրջիցիմք, հակառակն եւ մեզ
դիպիցին. եւ զայն լսեմք թէ Չոճացայ, զի արարի զմարդն 'ի
վերայ երկրի, եւ թէ աճա ես ապականեցից զնոսա եւ զերկիր,
եւ զոր մարգարէիւն տրտանջէր` եթէ հայր եմ, ո'ւր են փառք
իմ, եւ եթէ տէր` ո'ւր է երկիւղն իմ:

«Ի վերայ ժամու պաշտաման եւ աղօթից. զի Աստուած
ընդունելութեան արժանի արասցէ»:

Վասն այսր, ասէ, ժամու. զայն ժամանակէ ասէ` յորում ժա-
մու յաղօթս ժողովեալ իցեմք. զոր պաշտօն եւ աղօթս կոչէ,
յայտ առնելով թէ պաշտօնեայք գոլով Աստուծոյ հօրն եւ
ամենակալին տեառն, ճանապազ 'ի նորա պաշտօնն ժամանել
պարտիմք առանց ճեղգութեան. եւ է պաշտուլն ծառայութեան
անուն։ Ոչ վայրապար զպաշտօնն եւ ապա զաղօթսն եդէ` որ է
խնդրուածն. այլ զի ունցիս, թէ ծառայելով պարտ է խնդրել
զպէտս. զի այսպէս եւ առ մարմնաւոր տեարս նախ ծառայէլ,
եւ ապա խնդիրս առնուլ սովոր եմք։ Դարձեալ զի եւ ընդունելի
պաշտօնն եւ աղօթքն լիցին` աղաչել խրատէ. այսինքն թէ զի
որպէս ճաճելին է պաշտեմք զԱստուած, եւ որպէս նայն կամ'ի
աղօթիցեմք, սրբութեամբ եւ սիրով եւ զգաստութեամբ եւ
յստակ մտօք եւ ջերմ ճոգւով. եւ զի խնդրիցեմք զողորմական,
զարքայութիւնն Աստուծոյ եւ զարդարութիւն նորա. զի որպէս

Let us then seek refuge in Him with sincere affection as creator and *Father* and reverently serve him as *Lord*. Let us lay all our cares upon Him and place all our hope on Him. For if we expect other people to satisfy all our needs when they have little capacity for compassion, how much greater hope ought we to put in the all-compassionate One on the grounds that He is both God and *Father* as well as *Lord*. Only our response should be worthy of all He has done. The creature honors the creator and is bound to His service and worship. A son honors his father and a servant respects his master. If we act accordingly, we shall receive His benefits in every way and enjoy the goodness of life both now and hereafter. But if we follow the opposite course, the result we face will be the opposite of that. We recall the verses "I repented of making man on the earth" and "behold, I will destroy both them and the earth (Gen 6:7) and how He complained through the prophet, "If I am a father, where is my honor and if I am a lord, where is my respect?" (Mal 1:6). *"To render this hour of worship and prayer worthy of acceptance."* *This hour* refers to the time we are gathered at prayer. It is called *worship and prayer* to demonstrate that as servants of *God the Father and Almighty Lord*, we must not be lazy but assemble regularly to worship Him. And *worship* is a name for service. Not for nothing does *worship* come before *prayer* (i.e. petitions) but for you to learn that you must be in His service when you bring your needs before Him. Similarly, it is normal first to serve human lords and then to bring petitions. Again we are exhorted to supplicate that our *worship and prayer* be acceptable, i.e. that we worship God as is pleasing to Him and pray according to His will with holiness, love, purity, with a clear mind and fervent spirit. We should also seek what is beneficial, "the kingdom of God and His righteousness" (Matth 6:33). For, as the Apostle John says, "Whatever we request ac-

ասէ առաքեալն Յովհաննէս՝ թէ Զոր ինչ հայցեմք ըստ կամաց
նորա՝ լսէ մեզ. 'ի սոյն միտս եւ քարոզին գան բանք:

§2 «Լուիցէ Տէր ձայնի աղաչանաց մերոց, ընկալցի
զխնդրուածս սրտից մերոց, ողորմեսցի 'ի վերայ մեր»:

Քանզի այսպիսեացն սովոր է լսել՝ որք ըստ կամաց նորա
հայցեն: Դարձեալ ոչ ասաց, թէ ընկալցի զխնդրուածս մեր,
այլ թէ զսիրտից մերոց. զի ոչ եթէ որ 'ի շրթանցն՝ այլ որ 'ի
սրտէն խնդրուածքն ընդունելի է նմա. որ եւ ողորմել մեզ տայ
Աստուծոյ, որպէս եւ պարոնկին եւ քանանացւոյն, եւ որպէս կու-
րացն՝ որ գողորմութիւն խնդրելով ոչ լռէին, թէպէտ եւ բազումք սաստէին, մինչեւ լուսաւորեցան եւ գնացին գետ նորա,
ոչ թողլով զնա՝ թէպէտ եւ հասին պարզելեին: Զոր եւ մեք ա-
րասցուք. մի՛ լուեսցուք 'ի խնդրեին, թէպէտ եւ յոլովիւք խա-
փանողք արգելեաւք լիցուք, եւ մի՛ յառնուլն գխնդրելին՝ 'ի
նմանէ 'ի բաց կացցուք. թէ ոչ եւ նա 'ի բաց⁴ լինի 'ի մէնջ.
եւ այնմ զիպիցիմք, զոր սադմրասանուադն ասէ. Ախաւասիկ որք
հեռի աբարին գանձինս իւրեանց 'ի քէն՝ կորիցեն. այլ ըստ
խրատու առաքելոյն՝ մերձեսցուք առ Աստուած եւ նա մերձեսցի
առ մեզ:

§3 «Աղօթք մեր եւ խնդրուածք յամենայն ժամ մտցեն
առաջի մեծի տերութեան նորա»:

Թէ այնպէս աղօթեսցուք որպէս ասացաւն, եւ զհաճոյս
Աստուծոյ եւ զոգղուտն մեր խնդրեսցուք, ոչ այժմ եւեթ այլ եւ
յամենայն ժամու, աղօթք մեր եւ խնդրուածք մտցեն առաջի
մեծի տերութեան նորա. ապա քանի՛ անչափ խնդութիւն մեզ
գայց. զի եթէ 'ի փոքր տերութենէս որ 'ի մարդիկ' յաձախ
խնդութիւն լինի, զաղաձանս ուրուք ընկալեալ, ապա այնչափ
մեծութեան երկնաւոր տեառնն աձաւորին Հրեշտակաց՝ առաջի
մտեալ մեր եւ գհայցումն 'ի նմանէ ընկալեալ⁵, որպիսի'
զուարձումն մեզ բերիցէ, որ եւ նախ քան զանդ երանութիւնան
ատ պարգեւալից արասցէ, որպէս եւ ասէ:

cording to His will, He hears us" (1John 5:14).

The next phrase in the proclamation reinforces that meaning:

> §2 "*May the Lord hear our cry of supplication, accept our hearts' requests and have mercy on us,*"

since He is accustomed to hear those who make their requests according to His will. Again it does not just say *may He accept our requests* but *those of our hearts,* as not the petitions of the lips but those from the heart are acceptable to Him. This is what moves God to have pity on us as on the prostitute (Matth 26:6-13), the Canaanite (Matth 15:22) and the blind men who would not keep silent until they received sight and followed Him and would not leave Him, even though they had obtained the gift they sought (Matth 20:30-34). We should do likewise and not cease to intercede though beset by every sort of obstacle nor hold back from receiving what we have requested from Him. Otherwise, He may distance Himself from us and we face the situation the Psalmist described: "Behold those who held aloof from You will perish" (Ps 73 [72]: 27). Rather, according to the apostle's advice, let us "draw near to God and He will draw near to us" (Jas 4:8)

> §3 "*May our prayers and petitions at every hour come before His great Lordship.*"

If we pray in the above fashion and seek what is pleasing to God and beneficial to ourselves not only now but *at every hour, our prayers and petitions* will *come before* His *great Lordship.* Then what overwhelming joy should be ours! For if there is often rejoicing when we receive some request from those puny lords who exercise rule over man, when we come before the measureless might of the Lord who is fearful to the angels and are granted our petition from Him, what exaltation it should bring us, whom He will shower with gifts in this life even before the bliss of the

§4 «Եւ նա տացէ մեզ միաբան հաւատով յարդարութիւն
վաստակել. զի գողորմութեան գշնորհս իւր արասցէ 'ի
վերայ մեր տէրն ամենակալ»:

Տեսե՞ր զաղօթիցն չափ, որպիսի՛ եզրյց գմիաբանելն յուղիղ
հաւատս եւ զվաստակելն յարդարութեան. եւ այս լինի յորժամ
Տէրն ամենակալ գողորմութեան շնորհն իւր 'ի վերայ առնէ,
այսինքն գՀոգւոյն սրբոյ շՀորՀս, գոր ողորմի եւ տայ խնդ-
րողացն. այն է որ Հաստատէն 'ի Հաւատս. նոյն եւ որ յարդարութեան վաստական գործացուցանէ. նա է որ գտամանելիան
Հեշտալիս առնէ: Ապա յաղօթս աւարտէ գրանն ասելով,

§5 «Կեցո եւ ողորմեա մեզ, Տէր»:

ԱՂՕԹՔ

§6 «Տէր մեր փրկիչ Յիսուս Քրիստոս, որ մեծդ ես ո-
ղորմութեամբ եւ առատ ես պարգեւօֆ բարերարութեան»:

Երկնից եւ երկրի գլով տէր, ասեմք մեզ յատուկ, յառաւել
գուֆ այնու ձգել. մանաւանդ գիրկիչն կարդալով մեզ, որոյ
մարմնանալովն եւ մաՀուամբն փրկեցաք. բայց զի մեծ ասաց
ողորմութեամբ` գանքաւ նորա յայտնելով գողորմութիւն,
նոյնպէս եւ գառատութիւն նորա պարգեւացն անչափաբար:
Բայց չե՞նչ ասաՆոր կամ 'ի այս նախաշաւիղ աղօֆիցս գող-
քանգի յեւրորդ ժամուն է աղօֆքս, յորում ժամու 'ի խաչ
Հանին գիրկիչն, եւ յորում ժամու Հոգին սուրբ տուաւ առաքելոցն. եւ 'ի խաչի Համբերելն վասն բազում իւրոյ ողոր-
մութեանն էր, զի գմեր մեղացն գպարտան իւրով մարմնովն
Հատուսցէ. նոյնպէս եւ գմեծ պարգեւեսն` գՀոգին սուրբ` շնորՀելն
առատութեամբք, յորդ եւ անՆուն բարերարութեամբք. յաղագս
այսորիկ, ասէ, մեծդ ես ողորմութեամբք 'ի խաչին պատձառս.
եւ առատ ես պարգեւօֆ բարերարութեան, վասն գՀոգին Հեղլոյ.
որպէս յաջորդն իսկ յայտ առնէ.

102

world to come as the proclamation continues:

§4 *"And may He grant us to work for righteousness, united in faith that the Almighty Lord may send down upon us His gift of mercy."*

Did you observe the benefit of prayer mentioned here—unity in right *faith* and *working in righteousness*? And this will come about when the *Almighty Lord* bestows *His gift of mercy* i.e. the gift of the Holy Spirit which in His compassion He gives to those who ask. This is what confirms us in faith and strengthens us for *works of righteousness*. It is what makes tribulations easy to bear. Then the deacon completes the prayer with the phrase,

§5 *"Save us, Lord, and have mercy on us."*

Prayer

§6 *"Our Lord and Savior Jesus Christ who are great in mercy and rich in gifts of kindness."*

Though Lord of heaven and earth, we call Him particularly *our* own to incline Him to be more merciful thereby. We invoke Him especially as *our Savior* (Mk 15:25) since we have been saved by His incarnation and death. But the phrase *"great in mercy"* reveals His boundless mercy and likewise the immeasurable abundance of His gifts. But what is the point of this preliminary prayer being here? It belongs to the third hour in which they crucified the Savior and the Holy Spirit was given to the apostles. His patience on the cross stemmed from His abundant *mercy* in order to pay in His body the debts we incurred by our sins. Similarly, we commemorate the conferring of great gifts i.e. the Holy Spirit in plenitude through His immense, overflowing generosity. It says *"You are great in mercy"* on account of the cross and *"You are rich in gifts of kindness"* because of the outpouring of the Holy Spirit, as the continuation makes clear:

§7 «Որ դու քոյին կամաւ համբերրցեր 'ի ժամուս
յայսմիկ` չարչարանաց, խաչի եւ մահու յաղագս մեղաց
մերոց»:

Ո՛չ 'ի բռնութենէ ասէ ուրուք, այլ 'ի կամաց քոց կրեցեր
զամենայն, ողորմելով մեզ. ոչ զղուն առանց պատճառի զնէ
նախկին, այլ սակաւուն բազումն ընդ միտ ածել պատրաստէ.
Թէ դու Աստուածդ եւ Որդիդ Աստուծոյ Հօր համագոյդ, արա-
րիչդ ամենայնի, զոր անբաւ բազմութիւնք վերնոցն միշաւ երկ-
կիւղիւ պաշտեն, յորոյ Հրամանէ ծով սանձանեալ է եւ ցամաք
հաստատեալ, որոյ բանիւ լուսաւորք 'ի հատատութեան երկինի
գնան ըստ իւրաքանչիւր կարգաց, յորոյ ձեռանէ կերակրին
ամենայն կենդանեաց ազգ, որ ամենայնի տիրես եւ զամենայնն
լնուս, եւ անբովանդակելիդ ես յամենեցունց, անսատ եւ ան-
ծածող եւ անիմանալիդ. համբերցեր չարչարանաց, կապեալ,
յատենի կացեալ, թշնամանեալ, թքալից եղեալ, ապտակեալ,
կոխեալ, ձաղեալ, կատակեալ, փշեայ պսակօք եւ եկերանաց
զգեստուի, եւ եղեգնեայ գաւազանաւ գանեալ, երբեմն 'ի Պի-
ղատոս մօրակաւ եւ երբեմն եղեգամբ 'ի զինուորացն: Զայս
եւ որ սոցին նման ցուցանէ յասէն, թէ համբերցեր չարչարանաց. յուշ առնէ ապա եւ զխաչին կիրսն, միով բանիւ ասէ
զմերկութիւնն, զբեւեռումն, զծարաւն, զլեղոյն ճաշակումն[6],
զբազմաց հայհոյութիւնն եւ զնախատինն եւ զգլուխս շարժելն:
Ապա եւ զմահն 'ի նոյն յարէ` այսպէս ասելով. Քոյին կամաւ
համբերցեր 'ի ժամու յայսմիկ չարչարանաց եւ խաչի եւ
մահու. յորում զխոցումն էառ` մեռելութեամբն եւս թշ-
նամանեալ. եւ թաղմամբն ընդ մեռեալս համարեալ. զայս աս
զամենայն համբերցեր վասն մեղաց մերոց. զի քոյին անպարտ
արեամբդ զգարտաւորս ազատեցես 'ի յախտնական մահ-
լանէն եւ 'ի տանջանացն:

§8 «Եւ պարզեցեր առատապէս զպարգեւս Հոգւոյդ
սրբոյ երանելի առաքելոցն»:

Քանզի առ այնս որբ արբեցութեամբ բամբասէին զառա-
քեալսն 'ի խօսել նոցա զամենայն լեզուս, ասէ Պետրոս. Ո՛չ

104

§7 *"You voluntarily endured suffering, the cross and death at this hour for our sins."*

Not through any necessity, but of Your own will, you bore everything to show mercy on us. Not without reason does it begin with *You.* It attempts in a small compass to suggest a lot i.e. *You* are God and Son of God, consubstantial with the Father, creator of all, whom countless heavenly hosts worship in great fear. At Your command the sea was set in bounds and the dry land fixed, at Your word the luminaries in the firmament of heaven proceed, rank upon rank, by Your hand every kind of living thing is fed. You rule over all and fill all and cannot be contained by anything, unapproachable, ineffable and incomprehensible. *You endured suffering* bound, brought to trial, insulted, spat upon, beaten, struck, mocked, ridiculed with a crown of thorns and burlesque clothes, smitten by a cane of reeds, now by Pilate's lash and now by the soldiers' cane. All this and the like is meant by *You endured suffering.* Then the passion on *the cross* is recalled, recapitulating in a word the nakedness, the nailing, the thirst, tasting gall, the crowd's cursing, taunts and shaking of heads. Then His *Death* is linked with this in the phrase *You voluntarily endured suffering, the cross and death at this hour.* Thereby He submitted to wounds, underwent further indignity in His mortality and in burial was numbered among the dead. This is what is meant by *You endured* everything *for our sins* to free the condemned by Your innocent blood from everlasting death and torment.

§8 *"And You richly bestowed the gifts of the Holy Spirit on the Blessed Apostles."*

Peter said to those who accused the apostles of speaking in every tongue through drunkenness, "They are not drunk, as you think, for it is only the third hour of the day" (Acts 2:15). This phrase from the prayer proclaims that the same third hour when

որպէս դուք կարծէք թէ սոքա արբեալ իցեն, զի դեռ երեք
ժամք են աւուրս. զայն եւ աղօթիցս բան յայտ առնէ, թէ 'ի
սոյն յայս երրորդ ժամուս, յորում 'ի խաչին բեւեռեցաւ, եւ
զՀոգիդ սուրբ Հեղեր յերանելի առաքեալսն: Իսկ առատապէսն՝
զառաւելութիւնն քան 'ի մարգարէսն յայր առնէ, վասն որոյ
երանելիս կոչէ. զի սատիկ յորդութեամբ զէջս Հոգւոյն ընցա
պարգեւաց: Յարէ 'ի նոյն եւ մաղթանս:

§9 «Հաղորդս արա զմեզ, Տէր, աղաչեմք զքեզ աստուածային պարգեւացդ»:

Հաղորդս լինել՝ Հաւասարորդ է լինել. աստուածային պարգեւ ասէ զոր 'ի Քրիստոսի չարչարանացն չնորհեցաւ մեղաց
թողութիւն, եւ 'ի Հոգւոյն սրբոյ գալստեանէն չնորհք. զի եւ ա-
ռաջիկայ բանիւս յայտնագոյնս ցուցանէ զոյն. զի ասացեալ,
Հաղորդս արա զմեզ, Տէր, աղաչեմք զքեզ, աստուածային
պարգեւացդ, յարէ 'ի նոյն.

§10 «Թողութեան մեղաց, ընդունելութեան Հոգւոյդ
սրբոյ»:

Աղաչեմ, ասէ, զի արիւնդ քո պատուական որ մաքրեաց
զոլեզերս՝ եւ զմեզ սրբեսցէ, եւ Հոգիդ սուրբ 'ի վերայ մեր
եկեսցէ. զի եւ մեք այսոցիկ պարգեւացս Հաղորդս լիցուք, եւ
սրբեալ 'ի մեղաց եւ Հոգւով լցեալ՝ քո պարգեւացդ չնոր-
Հակալութիւն արժանապէս Հատուսցուք. այս է գոր ասէն.

§11 «Որպէս զի արժանաւորք եղիցուք զոհութեամբ փառաւորել զՀայր եւ զՈրդի եւ զսուրբ Հոգիդ. այժմ եւ
միշտ եւ յաւիտեանս յաւիտենից. Ամէն»[7]:

§12 Խաղաղութիւն ամենեցուն.

§13 «Խաղաղութեամբ քով, Քրիստոս փրկիչ մեր, որ 'ի
վեր է քան զամենայն միտս եւ զբանս, ամրացո զմեզ
եւ անԵրկիւղս պահեա յամենայն չարէ»:

Այս դրուագ է՝ գոր ասէ երանելին ՅովՀան, թէ վասն
այսաՀարացն կարդեալ է. քանզի արտաքոյ եկեղեցւոյ կալով
այտոյքն՝ յայսմ ժամու 'ի ներքս ածէին սարկաւագունքն, եւ

106

You hung on the cross, You also poured out the Holy *Spirit on the blessed apostles.* The term *richly* indicates an abundance surpassing that of the prophets and that is why they are called *blessed,* since He *bestowed* the descent of the *Spirit on them* with overflowing exuberance. To this it adds the request:

§9 *"We beseech You, Lord, make us partakers of Your divine gifts."*

To be a *partaker* is to be an equal. The *divine gift* intended is the forgiveness of sins granted by Christ's sufferings and grace from the coming of the Holy Spirit. This is expressed even more clearly by the next phrase. After saying, *"We beseech You, Lord, make us partakers of Your divine gifts"* it adds:

§10 *"The forgiveness of sins and reception of the Holy Spirit."*

It says, I pray that Your precious blood which purified the world would cleanse us too and that Your *Holy Spirit* would come upon us. Then having partaken of these gifts we might be cleansed from sin, filled with the *Spirit* and worthily render thanks for these Your gifts. This is the sense of

§11 *"That we may be worthy with thanksgiving to glorify the Father, Son and Holy Spirit, now and forever and to ages of ages. Amen."*

§12 *"Peace be to all."*

§13 *"With Your peace, Christ our Savior, which is above all thought and word, strengthen and preserve us without fear of any evil."*

This is the portion which the blessed Yovhan says is appointed for demoniacs. The spirit-possessed would stand outside the church, but at this point the deacons would usher them inside and position them in front. When the priest offers his prayer the whole people make supplication for them.

կացուցանէին յառաջ. եւ քանզ(ի)ան ½ զայս մատուցեալ աղօթս,
թովանդակ ժողովուրդն պաղատանս վասն նոցա առնէն:

«Խաղաղութեամբ քով, Քրիստոս փրկիչ մեր»:
Դու ես, ասէ որ փրկեցեր զազգս մարդկան 'ի ծառայութենէ
սատանայի. եւ այժմ փրկութիւն շնորհեա սոցա, ամրա-
ցուցանելով քով խաղաղութեամբդ, որ 'ի վեր է քան զամենայն զմիտս եւ զբանս. զի ոչ իմանի մտոք, եւ ոչ պատմի
բանիւք. այլ քան զգերշտակաց եւ քան զմարդկան իմացումն եւ
ասելութիւն 'ի վեր անցանէ. «Ամրաց, ասէ, եւ աներկիւղ
պահեա յամենայն չարէ». զի ոչ միայն յայնցանէ որ ըլլենն,
այլ եւ յամենայն ազգաց դիւաց աներկիւղ արա զմեզ,
ամրացուցեալ քով խաղաղութեամբդ:

§14 «Հաւասարեցո զմեզ ընդ ձշմարիտ երկրպագու քո,
որք Հոգւով եւ ձշմարտութեամբ քեզ երկիր պագանեն»:

Քանզի որիշ 'ի ժողովրդենէն աղօթել հրամայէ ըլլելոցն 'ի
դիւագ. վասն զի որք թաւիւր ի Հոգւոյ լեալ՝ դիւագ մատնին,
կամ որք մեղօքն մերկացան զՀոգին՝ յուսին իշխանութիւն
հաւասարել նոցա, որք Հոգւովն Աստուծոյ են միացեալք, նուիմք
գերկրպագութիւն Աստուծոյ մատուցանեն. գորոց Տէր ինքնին
ասէ, ձշմարիտքն երկրպագուք երկիր պագանիցեն Հօր՝ Հոգւով
եւ ձշմարտութեամբ. քանզի եւ Հայր այնպիսի երկրպագու
իւր խնդրէ:

Արդ՝ աղաչէ աղօթիցս բան, զի սրբեսցին 'ի պիղծ այսոցն՝
եւ զՀոգին սուրբ ընկալցին, եւ հաւասարորդ լիցին ձշմարիտ
երկրպագուացն, որք հոգւով եւ ձշմարտութեամբ երկիր պագանիցեն Աստուծոյ. Հատտատեալ Հոգւովն 'ի ձշմարիտ հա-
լատան, եւ լուսաւորեալ նովիմբ, բացաւ երեսօք զիւառս Տեառն
իբրեւ ընդ Հայելի տեսանեն, եւ դէմ յամնդիման սուրբ
Երրորդութեանն զերկրպագութիւն մատուցանեն։ Այլ զի հասարակաց ասի այժմ աղօթքն՝ 'ի Հնութենէն յեղեալ են բանքն. զի
յառաջ այսպէս իմանի լեալ, ամրացո զտոս, եւ թէ հաւասարեցո զտոս ընդ ձշմարիտ երկրպագու քո։ Նա եւ որ այժմ
ասէ՝ ոչ ինչ հեռի է 'ի դիտաւորութենէն. զի ամենայն մեղաց
արկածք 'ի չարէն են. եւ թուի թէ որ վասն այասհարացն

108

With Your peace, Christ our Savior, means that You are the One who saved the human race from service to Satan. Now therefore grant salvation to these here present, *strengthening* them with *Your peace which is above all thought and word.* It cannot be comprehended by *thought,* nor described in *words,* but exceeds the perception and powers of expression of both men and angels.

Strengthen and preserve us without fear of any evil means keep us from fear not only of those demons which torment us, but from every sort, having *strengthened us with Your peace.*

> §14 *"Make us equal to Your true worshippers who worship You in spirit and in truth"*

directs those tormented by demons and detached from the people to pray, since those who lack the Spirit are given over to the demons and those who have stripped off the Spirit with sins cannot be on a par with those united to God *in spirit* and thereby offer worship to God. The Lord Himself says of them, "True worshippers shall worship the Father in spirit and in truth; for such are the worshippers the Father seeks" (John 4:23).

Now this section of the prayer implores that they be cleansed from foul spirits and receive the Holy Spirit and become *equal to true worshippers who worship* God *in spirit and truth.* Established by the Spirit in the true faith and illuminated by Him, they see the glory of God with uncovered face as in a mirror and offer worship to the Holy Trinity, face to face (cf. Deut 34:10, I Cor 13:12). However, now this prayer is said of all without distinction, in contrast to ancient practice. Previously it was understood, *strengthen* these people and *make* them *equal to Your true worshippers.* However, the present meaning is not far removed from the observation that every onset of sin is from the evil one and it seems that those who prayed for demoniacs said, *"Strengthen and preserve them without fear of evil",* but now we

109

աղօթիւն՝ այսպէս ասէին. «Ամրացո եւ աներկիւղ պահեա 'ի
չարէն». իսկ այժմ ասեմք յամենայն չարէ. այսինքն յամենայն
նեղից նորա. «Հաւասարել եւ մեզ ընդ ձշմարիտ երկրպագուս
քո, որք Հոգւով եւ ձշմարտութեամբ քեզ երկիր պագանեն». եւ
թէ մեք չեմք արժանի, այլ գի իրաւունք են վայելել է քո տէ-
րութեանդ տալ գիտաս, յայն սակս հաւասարեցո զմեզ ար-
ժանաւորացն. քանզի այս միւռ են որ զկնի դայ բանն։

§15 «Վասն զի ամենասուրբ Երրորդութեանդ վայելէ
փառք իշխանութիւն եւ պատիւ. այժմ եւ միշտ եւ յաւիտեանս յաւիտենից ամէն»:

Յայսմ տեղի աս որպէս յարձակել գժողովուրդն՝

§16 Օրինես տէր.

գի բեմասացութեան տեղի է, եւ աւարտեն գաղօթան օրհնու-
թեամբ.ք, եւ 'ի վարդապետութեանն յունկնդրութիւն տան գանձինս, եւ ապա գխորհրդականն կատարեն։ Բայց գի յայլում
վայրի ասացեալ է մեր վասն որք ոչ կարեւոր համարին
գունկնդրութիւն գրող սրբոց, ասանօր հարկ համարիմ սակաւ
ինչ ասել առ այնոսիկ որք ասենն, գի լսեմ եւ ոչ առնեմ՝ ապա
բնաւ եւ ոչ լսեմ, գի մի' աւելի դատեցայց։ Ի դեպ է ասել
նոցա. ո'վ աներկիւղ երկիւղածութեանդ. պատգամ Աստուծոյ
եկեալ յերկնից, է՞ր իշխես ասել ոչ լսեմ եւ ոչ առնեմ. ապա
ուրեմն առաւել դառնացուցիչ քան գրբեայան գտանիս Աստուծոյ,
գի նոքա ունկնդիր լինելով[8] լսին. Զամենայն գոր ինչ ասացէ
տէր Աստուած մեր լուիցուք եւ արասցուք. իսկ դու եւ լսես
անգամ ոչ: Եւ թէ երկիրաւոր թագաւորի գրող իշխէիր ասել, թէ
ոչ կարդամ, եւ ոչ լսեմ հրամանաց արքային, մահու պարտաւոր լինէիր. Աստուծոյ պատմի հրամանք, եւ դու արհա-
մարհե՞ս. չհամարին գքեզ յաւիտենական ստակմանն արժանի: Վա'յ, ասէ մարգարէն, արհամարհողաց՝ որ արհամարեն, եւ
արհամարհանօք արհամարեն գորենադիրն. գայս եսայի. իսկ
երեմիա՝ որպէս յերեսաց Տեառն. Արք Յուղայ եւ բնակիչք
Երուսաղէմի' դարձուցին յիս գթիկունս եւ ոչ գերեսս. ուսուցի
գնոսա ընդ առաւոտս, ուսուցի եւ ոչ անսացին ընդունել գլսրատ:
Տեսանէ՞ս, քան գչառնելույն գգրամանն՝ գլսելույն առաւել բողոքէ

say, *"from all evil"* i.e. from all its arrows, *"and make us equal to Your true* believers *who worship You in spirit and in truth."* Although we are not worthy, since it is right and fitting to give glory to Your lordship, for this reason *make us equal to* those who are worthy; for this is the sense of the following phrase:

§15 *"For glory, dominion and honor befits the all-holy Trinity, now and ever and to ages of ages. Amen."*[1]

At this point,

§16 *"Bless, Lord"*

is said, as at the dismissal of the people; for it is the occasion for an utterance from the *bema*.[1] Thus the prayer is completed with a blessing and then the people give their attention to teaching before celebrating the mystery.

As I have already spoken elsewhere about those who do not consider it important to give heed to Holy Scripture, I judge it necessary here to address briefly those who say, "Because I listen but do not act, I should not listen at all, in case I am judged more severely."[2] It is fitting to reply to them, "O irreverent reverence! How can you say, 'I neither hear nor do the word of God which came down from heaven'? So you embitter God even more than the Jews; for they gave heed and listened. "Whatever the Lord God says, let us hear and do" (Exod 19:8). But you do not even listen. And if it were possible for you to say of the rescript of the earthly king, "I neither read, nor listen to the king's commands", you would be condemned to death. How then when God's commands are announced do you disdain them? Do you not consider you deserve everlasting death? "Woe", says the prophet, "to disdainers who disdain and with their disdain, disdain the law-giver" (Isa 24:16). Thus Isaiah. Jeremiah says on God's part, "The men of Judah and inhabitants of Jerusalem have turned their backs to me instead of their faces. I taught them in the morning,

Աստուած։ Տեսցուք գի՞նչ եւ Սողոմոնիւ ասէ. Յորժամ գայցէ ճեզ նեղութիւն եւ պաշարումն, իջէ զի կարդայցէք առ իս, եւ ո՞չ լուիցեմ ձեզ։ Եւ վասն է՞ր գայս յառաջ քան զայս, եւ զկնի ասէ զպատմառան.— յառաջ, Փոխանակ զի կոչէի ձեզ եւ ոչ լսէիք ինձ. յերկարէի զբանս իմ, եւ ոչ անսայիք, այլ ապախտ առնէիք. եւ յետոյ՝ ասէ. Անդրիացէն զիս չարք եւ ոչ գտանիցեն. զի ատեցին զիմաստութիւն եւ զերկիւղ Տեառն ոչ խնդրիցին։ Արդ՝ առաջինն է Հնազանդութիւն լսել երկիւղիւ զբանս Աստուծոյ, զոր ընդ մեծ բարեգործութիւնա յարգեցուցանէ Եսայի, այսպէս ասելով. Լուարուք զպատգամս Տեառն՝ որք դողայք 'ի բանից նորա. դարձեալ ասէ. Եթէ ախորժեցիք եւ լուիցիք ինձ՝ զբարութիւնս երկրի կերիջիք, ապա թէ ոչ կամիջիք լսել ինձ, սուր կերիցէ զձեզ։ Տես եւ դու որպիսի՞ բարի ունկնդրացն է յառաջ քան զանհնլն, եւ որպիսի պատիւ. քանզի սիրով խոտորի 'ի չարէն[9], եւ բարւոյն փափաքէ. եւ Հեզութեամբ եւ խոնարհ մտօք դողութեամբ ո՛ւնկն դիր պատգամաց Աստուծոյ, եւ բնակարան Աստուծոյ լիցիս։ Եւ ո՞ ասէ զայդ ասէ. ինքն Աստուած. Երկինք աթոռ իմ, եւ երկիրս պատուանդան ոտից իմոց. եւ ես յո՞ բնակեցայց, եթէ ոչ 'ի Հեզս եւ 'ի խոնարնս, եւ ոյ¬ դողան 'ի բանից իմոց. վասն այնորիկ ոչ տայ թոյլ լսել բանասարկուն, զի զայս եւ նա գիտէ, թէ ախորժութեամբ լսողաց զբանն Աստուծոյ՝ ինքն Աստուած տայ նոցա զերկիւղն իւր, եւ զինքն 'ի նոսա բնակեցուցանէ. եւ յորում Աստուած բնակէ՝ նմա ամենայն դժուարինք դիւրինք լինին, եւ տարժանելիքն ախոր¬ ժելիք, եւ քաղցրանայ նմա լուծն Քրիստոսի, եւ բեռն նորա փոքրոգի լինի նմա. քանզի մեռանի մարմին մեղաց, եւ կեն¬ դանանայ արդարութիւն[10]. ըստ գրեցելումն, Իսկ եթէ Քրիստոս 'ի ձեզ է՝ ապա մարմին մեռեալ է վասն մեղաց, եւ Հոգի կենդանի վասն արդարութեան. ասաց առաքեալ, եւ զայլսն որ զկնի։ Մարիամ՝ ասէ Տէրն, վասն բարի ընտրեաց, որ ոչ բարձցի 'ի նմանէ. զի նստէր առ ուտա Տեառն եւ լսէր զբանս նորա։ Հաւատարիմ համարեա եւ դու զՏէրն, եւ ընտրեա զբարւոք բաժինն զանբառնալին. եւ մի' Հաւանիր բանասկուին խաբէու¬

112

I taught them but they were not interested in adopting my advice" (Jer 32:33). Do you see? God complains more against those who do not listen to the command than those that do not act upon it.

Let us see what He says through Solomon too: "When trouble and oppression come upon you, if you call on Me, shall I not listen to you?" (Prov. 1:26-27). This is clarified by the surrounding context. Previously he writes, "Because I called you and you did not listen to Me, I prolonged my words but you ignored Me and disobeyed" (Proverbs 1:24). Immediately afterwards he says, "Wicked men will seek and not find Me for they hated wisdom and did not seek the fear of the Lord" (Prov 1:28). Now the first is obedience, to hear God's words with fear which Isaiah distinguishes with great benefactions saying: "Hear the counsels of the Lord, you who tremble at His words" (Isa 66:5). Again he says, "If you desire and heed Me, you shall eat the good things of the earth, but if you do not wish to hear Me, the sword shall devour you" (Isa 1:19-20). See then how much good and honor is accorded to listeners before they act, because in love He shuns evil and desires the good. Attend to God's words with meekness and the reverence of a humble mind and you will become God's dwelling. And the One who says this is none other than the God Himself who also says: "Heaven is my throne and the earth my footstool. And where shall I dwell if not in the meek and humble and those who venerate My words?" (Isa 66:1). That is why the devil does not permit them to listen because he is also aware that God Himself gives His fear to those who listen to God's word with pleasure and takes up His dwelling in them. And whomever God makes His dwelling in finds all difficulties become easy and awkward things pleasant and Christ's yoke becomes tender on him and His burden light (cf. Matth 11:30). For the flesh of sin dies while righteousness is made alive according to the verse: "If

թեանն, եւ գրկեր զքեզ 'ի բարւոյն. քանզի իւր սերմանցն կամի առնել զքեզ անդաստան. վասն այնորիկ արգելու առ 'ի յընդունելութենէ ատուածային սերմանցն: Մի՛ հաւանիր օձին՝ որ զԵւայն պատրեաց, զբարւոքն չբարւոք նմա ասացեալ, եւ զիւրան նմա ատուածացուցիցս լուսացուցեալ. լուր Աստուծոյ. Ունկն դիք աստ լսելեօք ձերովք, զեւտ եկայք ճանապարհաց իմոց. լուարուք ինձ եւ կերիչիք զբարութիւնս, եւ վայելեսցեն 'ի բարութեան անձինք ձեր: Այսքան աւետիք աստ եւ 'ի հանդերձելումն, եւ դու ոչ Աստուծոյ՝ այլ սատանայի լսել ախորժես. բանսարկուն զԱստուծոյն ոչ տայ լսել, զի մի՛ եւ 'ի ճանապարծն Աստուծոյ ելանիցեմք, եւ Տեառն բարեացն հասանիցեմք. եթէ 'ի դղրխատէն զմեզ, կամի զի մի՛ եւ աստ Աստուծոյ խնամօքն կեցցուք, եւ մի՛ դարձեալ յանմահական 'ի կեանսն վայելիցեմք: Լուիցուք Աստուծոյ, զի արասցուք զպատուիրանս նորա[11]. իսկ եթէ ոչ լուիցուք՝ ուստի՞ գանելն իմասցուք. զկա՞րդ զԱստուած հայտեցուսցուք, չզխտելով թէ որո՛վ եւ ո՛ր իւիք զնա բարկացուցաք: Արդարեւ եւ 'ի դէպ դաս մեզ ասել զբանն Եսաեալ, որ ասէ. Յայնմ ժամանակի յայոնեսցին՝ որ կնքեացեն զորէնս, զի մի՛ ոք ուսանիցի եւ ասիցէ կացից մնացից Աստուծոյ, որ դարձոյց զերեսս իւր 'ի տանէն Յակորբայ, եւ եղեց յուսացեալ 'ի նա:

Տեսե՞ր զպատճառս չտալոյ լսել զբող, զի մի՛ յուսով 'ի զեղջ եկեալ քաւութեան հասցէն: Եթէ արդար ես՝ լուր պատուիրանացն Աստուծոյ, եւ եւս հատատեսցիս յարդարութեան. եւ եթէ մեղաւոր՝ լուր զապանալեան Աստուծոյ, եւ ասա որպէս Դաւիթն, Մեղայ Տեառն. եւ լսես զնոյն պատասխանի, եւ Տէր անցոյց զքեզ զմեղս քո: Զանաչիր ոչ բարկացուցանել զԱստուած, ապա եթէ վրիպեցիս՝ դեղ լիցի քեզ հանապազորդ մեղանչելոյն հանապազ լսել սատին Աստուծոյ, եւ մեղայ ասել եւ յաճի նորա կալ, քան ամենեւին ապտամբել եւ հեռի 'ի նմանէ լինել: Հայր է, աստ զնեղութիւնն գոր հատուցանէ քեզ չարն եւ որովք խաբէ, եւ ա՛ո 'ի նմանէ իբր ի՛ դժած հօրէ՝ խրատ եւ օգնականութիւն: Իժիկ է հողոց, ծանո գլէրա քո, եւ

114

Christ is in you, then the flesh is dead because of sin, yet the spirit is alive because you have been justified" (Rom 8:10).

So spoke the apostle. Now the Lord says the following, "Mary has chosen the better part which shall not be taken from her; for she sat at the Lord's feet and listened to His words" (Lk 10:42). You should also count the Lord faithful and choose the better part which cannot be taken away. Do not favor the devil's deceit and deprive yourself of the good. For he wishes to make you a field for his seeds. That is why he prevents your acceptance of the divine seeds. Do not favor the snake who seduced Eve, telling her something was good when it was not, and giving her the hope that what he had to offer would make her divine. Listen to God, "Hear", He says, "with your ears, follow My paths. Heed Me and you will eat good things and your souls will rejoice in plenty." There is so much good news both in this life and in the one to come and yet you prefer to listen to Satan rather than God. The devil does not permit us to hear what is of God in case we set out on God's path and reach the good things of the Lord. He wrested us from paradise and does not wish us to be saved by God's care even here so as not to savor paradise again in eternal life. Let us listen to God in order to fulfill His commandments. For if we do not listen, how shall we know how to fulfill them? How shall we placate God, if we do not know in what way or by what means we have angered Him? In that case it is appropriate for us to recall Isaiah's verse: "At that time those who seal the law will be revealed so that no one should learn and say, "I will remain steadfast for God who turned His face from the house of Jacob, and I will hope in Him" (Isa 8:16).

Did you observe the reason for not permitting one to listen to scripture?—in case they repent in hope and obtain atonement. If

գտանես 'ի նմանէ դեղ եւ բժշկութիւն. ոչ բարկանայ երբ
առաջի անկանիս, թէպէտ եւ բիւրապատիկ եւեր գլարատով նորա. միայն[12] տեսցէ զքեզ երթեալ առ նա եւ յուզեալ զվէրան,
չէ յօտարաց բժշկաց՝ եթէ կարէ անտես առնել գվէրա քո. Հայր
է, աղեկէզ լինի 'ի քո արտասուէն վասն ախտից Հոգւոյ, եւ
վազվազակի 'ի բժշկէլն պատրաստի. քանզի եւ Դիւրագայթս
գիտէ գմեր բնութիւնս, եւ ըստ յամախութեան ախտից բազ-
մօրինակապէս դեղա պատրաստեաց գխնարճութիւն, գխստովա-
նութիւն, գանխակալութիւն, գթողութիւն յանցաւորին գողորմութիւն, գպաՀս, գաղօթս, գնուէրս, գարբող կատարէլ չիշատակս,
գճիւրասիրութիւն, գխնամածութիւն որբող եւ այրեաց,
գկարեկցութիւն առ եղբարս, եւ որ սոցին նման են բարեգոր-
ծութիւնք, գորա գոյ յատատուածային խրատուց առնուլ օրինակս
որ ըստ օրէ 'ի բժշկութիւն Հոգւոյ։ Ի վերայ ամենայնի եւ
նախ քան գամենայն, Քրիստոսի Հանապազորդ պատարագին. գի
վասն մեր Հանապազ 'ի յանցանս անկմանն՝ մ]չտ պատարագէլ
առ 'ի քաւութիւն. ոչ չատացեալ որ 'ի խաչին մի անգամ պա-
տարագեցաւ[13], այլ յամախապէս գնոյն գենումն յանդիման
Աստուծոյ վասն Հալատացելոց կենդանեաց եւ ննջեցելոց՝
յամենայն եկեղեցիս սուրբ պատարագաւն մատուցանէ. գի գոր
անձր 'ի վեր 'ի բարձրութեան խաչին գքալութիւն տրեգերաց
չնորՀեաց, գնոյն եւ սուրբ պատարագաւն օր ըստ օրէ չնորՀեացէ։
Վասն այսորիկ պարտիմք Հատատուն Հալատով եւ մեծ յուսով
'ի ժամուն յայնմիկ կալ առաջի Աստուծոյ աՀիւ եւ դողութեամբ. պարկեշտացեալ 'ի կերակրոց եւ չչապելեաց, ըստ կարի գօրութեանն 'ի կարօտան տուեալ տուրս, խատուման լինելով
Աստուծոյ գգործեալն արտաքոյ կամացն Աստուծոյ, եւ ար-
տոսրալից ջերմեռանդն պաղատանօք սուրբ պատարագաւն
Հայցել քալութիւն. գի ամենողորմն Աստուած իւր միածնին
մեռելութեամբն որ վասն մեր՝ սրբեացէ 'ի մեղաց եւ ագա-
տեացէ յամենայն պարտեաց, եւ ամրացուցեալ եւ պարապեալ
գմեզ սուրբ խորՀրդովն, անըմբռնելիս արասցէ 'ի թշնամւոյն,
նաեւ աՀարկու եւս նմին տացէ մեզ լինել, մանաւանդ թէ

you are just, hear God's commandments and you will be further established in righteousness. If you are a sinner, hear God's threats and say like David, "I have sinned against the Lord" and you will hear the same reply: "And the Lord has made your sins pass from you" (2 Sam 12:13). Try not to anger God, but if you fail, let your remedy be always to heed God's reproof whenever you sin and say, "I have sinned and stand in fear of Him," rather than rebelling completely and withdrawing from Him. He is a father; explain the trouble which the evil one causes you and how he deceived you and accept advice and assistance from Him as a compassionate father. He is the physician of souls; show Him your wounds and He will provide you with a remedy and cure. He does not get angry when you fall before Him, although for a myriad times you have deviated from His counsel. Only go to Him, show Him your wounds and let Him see you. He is not like alien doctors that He can ignore your wounds. He is a father and his heart is moved by your weeping for your spiritual malaise and quickly prepares to cure it. He knows our nature is prone to stumble and has arrayed numerous treatments for our recurring ailments, humility, confession, not harboring a grudge, forgiveness of a wrong-doing, pity, fasting, prayer, alms, commemorating the saints, hospitality, caring for orphans and widows, sympathy for our brothers and similar good works as examples of divine counsel which are available to take day by day to heal our souls. First and foremost the frequent celebration of Christ's sacrifice which is always offered to atone for the sins into which we constantly fall. The church does not keep repeating the sacrifice made on the cross, but continually offers the same sacrifice to God in the holy liturgy in all the churches on behalf of the faithful, alive and asleep. This is done that the atonement which He then granted the world high upon the cross may be granted day by day in the

զգլուխ նորա կոխել, եւ անվնաս 'ի նմանէ լինել։ Ցաղագս որոյ
եւ անարգել որ առ Աստուած է մտացն ճանապարհորդութիւն՝
ունել զնացումն, եւ անտի բարիօքն ատատին իսկ բերկրեալ
յուսալից եւ յարագուարծ եղեալ։

Բայց զի չափաւորապէս առ որ բանս էր ասացաւ՝ սկիզբն
արասցուք խորհրդականացն բացայայտել գրանս, օգնական զնոյն
ինքն զպատրագեալն ունելով։ Ի մերձէլ սուրբ խորհրդոյն յա-
ճախին սեղանն՝ առ սարկաւագն։

§17 «Մի՛ ոք յերեխայից, եւ մի՛ ոք 'ի թերահաւատից,
եւ մի՛ ոք յանապաշխարից մերձ կայցէ կամ հաղոր-
դեսցի»[14]։

Հրամայէ թէ երեխայ ոք իցէ, կամ թերի 'ի հաւատոն, կամ
ոչ ապաշխարեալ գմեղս իւր՝ արտաքս գնալ. քանզի յելանելն 'ի
սուրբ սեղանն հացին եւ բաժակին նուիրաց՝ բանին երկինք, եւ
երկնայինքն յերկիր իջեալ՝ զսրբարար սեղանովն բոլորին. վասն
այնորիկ գոչ սրբեալըն աւագանաւն, եւ գոչ մատքրեալըն ապաշխարութեամբ եւ որք ոչ են հաստատեալ 'ի հաւատս՝ արտաքս
վարէ քարոզն։

ՄԵԿՆՈՒԹԻՒՆ ՔԱՐՈԶԻՆ

§18 «Կացցուք առաջի սրբոյ սեղանոյս Աստուծոյ ա-
հիւ»։

Որպէս 'ի քնոյ ընդրատուցանէ քարոզն, զսեղանն՝ Աստուծոյ սեղան կոչելով, զի առաջի Աստուծոյ կայ եւ զորդին Աստուծոյ
'ի վերայ ունի բացմեալ. յաղագս որոյ ահիւ կալ առէ առաջի։

118

holy liturgy. Therefore, we should stand before God at this hour with firm faith and strong hope in fear and trembling. We should abstain from food and drink and give gifts to the needy according to their ability. We should also confess to God what we have done against God's will and seek atonement at the holy liturgy with tears and fervent entreaty. We should ask the all-compassionate God through the death of His only-begotten Son for our sake to purify us with His holy mystery and keep us from the assault of the enemy, drive away our fear of him, and enable us to trample upon his head without being harmed by him. In this way we should have unimpeded access to God in meditation and, encouraged in the here and now by the blessings of the world to come, we should be filled with hope and joy.

But as we have outlined in sufficient detail the addressees for whom the passage is intended, let us begin to interpret the text of the anaphora with the help of the very One who is sacrificed. As the holy mystery approaches the dread altar the deacon says:

§17 *"Let no catechumen,*[1] *no one of weak faith or impenitent* [2]*draw near and communicate."*

He bids any *catechumen,* anyone lacking in *faith* or not repentant of his sins to go out. As the gifts of bread and wine ascend to the holy altar, the heavens open and the heavenly ones descend to earth and encircle the sanctifying table. Therefore, the deacon's proclamation bids depart those not cleansed by baptism, not purified by repentance nor established in *faith.*[3]

Commentary on the Proclamation

§18 *"Let us stand in fear before God's holy altar."*

The proclamation stirs us as from sleep by calling the *altar God's holy altar.* It stands before God and God's Son lies reclining upon it and so it exhorts us to *stand before* it *in fear.*

119

§19 «Մի՛ խղճիլ գայթակղութեամբ»:

Խիղճ գայթակղութեան զգայթակղեալն 'ի մեղս ածէ, զոր թէ ոչ խոստովանութեամբ հանեալ իցէ 'ի սրտէ՝ մի՛ կացցէ առաջի սրբոյ սեղանոյն յահաւոր յայնմ ժամուն:

§20 «Մի՛ նենգութեամբ խորամանկութեամբ»:

Նենգութիւն խորամանկութեան ատ, որ կեղծաւորին սէր եւ խաղաղութիւն ունել առ եղբարս, եւ յանձինս նենգութեամբ գզարութիւն խորհին, զոր ոչ ընդունի աստուածեղէն խորհուրդն, այլ արտաքս հանէ:

§21 «Մի՛ պատրանօք խաբէութեամբ»:

Բազմադիմի են խաբէութեան պատրանք՝ եւ առ Աստուած եւ առ մարդիկ. նախ առաջին, հալատուն կերպարանել ուղղափառութիւն, չարախառ գոլով. կամ յարդար ձեւացեալս՝ մեղաւոր լինելով. կամ առ մարդիկ երեւեալ այն՝ որ չիցէ ստոյզ, կամ սիրուն, կամ պարզամիտ, եւ որ այլ ինչ է խարդախութիւն, ստութիւն եւ խաբէութիւն, զայն ցուցանելով լինէն՝ որ չիցէ, զորա 'ի բաց մերժէ Տէր ասելով. Ի բաց կացէք լինէն ամենեքեան՝ ոյք գործէք զանօրէնութիւն:

§22 «Մի՛ երկմտութեամբ թերահաւատութեան»:

Երկմտութիւն թերահաւատութեան է եթէ յայնցանէ զոր զալանիմք զկնի սուրբ աւետարանին զնալատն՝ երկմիտ եւ թե-րի իցէ ոչ իւիք. կամ 'ի սուրբ խորհուրդն՝ ոչ որպէս յնա-տուծոյ մարմին եւ յարիւն հալատայ, կամ որ ինչ 'ի նմա յոյսն՝ թերացեալ իցէ իւիք. զոր նախ աղօթիւք եւ գրոց խրա-տուք ուղղել պարտ է. զի որպէս գրեալ է, մաքրելի է նախ առաջին եւ ապա 'ի մաքուրն մերձենալի:

§23 «Այլ ուղիղ վարուք»:

Ուղիղ վարք այն է՝ զոր պատուիրանն ասէ, անթիւրն յաջ կամ յահեակ:

§24 «Պարզ մտօք»:

Այն երեւել ցինչ իցէ, եւ ոչ յայլ գունեալ:

120

§19 *"Not with a guilty conscience:"*

A *guilty conscience* means one trapped in sin. Unless one has removed that sin from the heart by confession, one should not stand before the holy altar at that awesome hour.

§20 *"Neither with cunning deceit:"*

Cunning deceit refers to those who pretend to love their brothers and live at peace with them, but inside deceitfully plot their harm. The divine mystery does not admit such people, but dismisses them.

§21 *"Nor with false pretence:"*

There are many kinds of *false pretence* both towards God and men. First of all, affecting a semblance of orthodoxy in faith when one is unorthodox or passing oneself off as righteous when one is a sinner or appearing to people something one is not, either loving or sincere or whatever other form of trickery, delusion or deceit one exposes in oneself which is not genuine. Such people the Lord turns away saying, "Depart from me all you who work iniquity" (Matth 7:23).

§22 *"Nor with ambivalent scepticism:"*

Ambivalent scepticism applies to anyone who is in any way doubtful or uncertain about the faith we confess after the holy gospel, or does not believe in the holy mystery as the body and blood of God or whose hope is in some way lacking. This must first be corrected by prayer and the admonition of scripture for, as it is written, "One must first be cleansed to approach the clean."[1]

§23 *"But with upright conduct:"*

Upright conduct means, as the commandment states, bending neither to right nor left (Deut 5:32).

§24 *"With integrity:"*

Giving a true and not a coloured impression of what something is.

§25 «Միամիտ սրտիւ»:

Ողջամիտ առ Աստուած եւ առ մարդիկ, եւ ոչ ուբեք խոր-
հըրդովն թիւրեալ:

§26 «Կատարեալ հաւատով»:

Այս է կատարումն հաւատոյն, զՀայր եւ զՈրդի եւ զսուրբ Հոգին ճանաչել, երիս անձինս եւ մի Աստուած, ոչ զիտել 'ի նոսա
առաւել կամ նուազ, կամ յառաջ կամ յետոյ, այլ Հարթ Հա-
լասար, եւ միապէս յամենայնի, եւ նոյն բնութեամբ. ծնող
զՀայր, եւ ծնունդ զՈրդի, եւ ելումն զՀոգին[15] եւ ոչ ծնունդ.
անժամանակք երեքեան եւ ի սկզբանէ ընդ Հօր Որդի եւ Հոգին
սուրբ. մարմնացեալ Որդին 'ի Մարիամայ անճառապէս, եւ ան-
փոխխաբկաբար. նոյն ինքն Աստուած ճշմարիտ եւ մարդ կատարեալ. զաստուածութեանն զօրութիւն ցուցանելով՝ որպէս
զՆստուած, եւ զմարդկայինն առանց մեղաց կրելով որպէս
մարդ, միալոր բնութեամբ[16]. նոյն ինքն խաչի եւ մահու համ-
բերեալ եւ յարուցեալ երեքօրեայ, եւ զմերն բարձեալ զանձծա
եւ զմեղս եւ զմաճ։ Մերով մարմնովս Համբարձեալ յերկինս, եւ
դայ դատել զկենդանիս եւ զմեռեալս, եւ Հատուցանել ըստ
իւրաքանչիւր գործոց, արդարոցն՝ կեանս յաւիտենականս, եւ
մեղաւորացն՝ տանջանս յաւիտենականս. խոստովանել եւ
զմկրտութիւնն՝ վերստին ծնունդ 'ի Հոգւոյն սրբոյ, յորդե-
գրութիւն Հօրն երկնաւորի. Հաւատալ եւ գիրկական խորհուրդն՝
ստուգապէս մարմին եւ արիւն Քրիստոսի. որով միանամք 'ի
Քրիստոս, եւ ժառանգակից նորուն լինիմք։ Այսու հաւատով
լինել կատարեալ:

§27 «Լցեալ սիրով»:

Աստուածսիրութեամբ լի եւ եղբայրսիրութեամբ անթերի:

§28 «Առաւելալ ամենայն գործովք բարութեանց»:

Ոչ ինչ յաստուածսիրութենէն եւ յեղբայրսիրութենէն բարիք:

§29 «Կացցուք առաջի սրբոյ սեղանոյս Աստուծոյ»:

Դարձեալ վերստին յիշեցուցանէ զկալն առ սեղանն Աստուծոյ,
զի առաւել ընդ աշիւ փակեցց:

122

§25 *"Singlemindedly:"*

Sound in disposition towards God and man and not distorted in mind.

§26 *"With perfect faith:"*

Fullness of faith is acknowledging Father, Son and Holy Spirit three persons and one Godhead, not accepting more or less, nor before or after, but exactly equal and united in all and of one nature, with the Father as generator, the Son as generated and the Spirit as procession, not birth. All three being timeless, the Son and Holy Spirit being with the Father from the beginning. The Son taking flesh from Mary ineffably and without change. That He is true God and perfect man, as God displaying the power of divinity and bearing the human condition as man, yet without sin, united in nature. He suffered the cross and death and rose on the third day removing our curse, sin and death. Ascending to heaven with our body, He is coming to judge the living and the dead and to reward men according to their works, to the righteous eternal life and to sinners, eternal torment. To confess baptism, regeneration by the Holy Spirit, adoption by the heavenly Father and to confess that the saving mystery is truly Christ's body and blood by which we become one in Christ and joint heirs with Him. This is *full faith.*

§27 *"Filled with love:"*

Full of love for God and not lacking in brotherly love.

§28 *"Abounding in all good works:"*

These are the good deeds that stem from love of God and one's brother.

§29 *"Let us stand before God's altar:"*

Again the deacon mentions *standing before God's altar* in order to close with greater awe.

§30 «Եւ գտցուք ողորմութիւն յաւուր յայտնութեան ՚ի
միւսանգամ գալստեան փրկչին մերոյ»:

Յիշեցուցանէ եւ զահաւոր գալուստն Քրիստոսի, զի մի՛ անփորձ
մատիցուք առ աստուածային սեղանն. զի եթէ խղճիւ կացցուք՝
մեծապէս լինիմք կշտամբեալք, որպէս զագռեդի համեդերձիւք
մտալն ՚ի հարսանիսն. ապա թէ լուացեալ գալստն, եւ հար-
սանեաց զգեցեալ պատմուճանն՝ ըստ խրատու քարոզին, ո-
դորմեալ լինիմք յայնմ աւուր, եւ ողորմութեամբն Քրիստոսի
՚ի նորա բարին վայելեմք. զի թէպէտ բիւրապատիկ լցեալ
իցեմք արդարութեան վաստակոք, սակայն ողորմութեամբ են
պարգեւքն, բազմապատիկ առաւել քան զվաստակն մեր.
աղօթիւք կնքէ զբարոզն ասելով.

§31 «Ամենակալ տէր Աստուած մեր, կեցո եւ ողորմ-
եաց մեզ».

զի թէ ողորմութեամբդ ոչ օգնիցիմք՝ ոչ կարեմք այնպիսի
մաքրութիւն ստանալ՝ մինչ զի խառնումն ընդ քեզ ունել. այլ
ողորմելովդ լիցուք արժանի, եւ Հացուք կենացն յաւիտենից:

ՊԱՏԱՐԱԳԱՄԱՏՈՅՑ

§32 «Տէր Աստուած զօրութեանց, եւ արարիչ ամենայն
լինելութեանց».

Բազում անգամ ասացաք յայլ աղօթսն, թէ տէրն անուն վասն
տիրելոյն է. իսկ աստուածն վասն ստեղծանելոյն եւ յատիս
աձելոյ զեղեալըս: Զօրութեանց, թէ Հրեշտակաց, զի ոչ միայն
երկրի եւ որ ՚ի նմա են՝ տէր Աստուած է, այլ եւ երկնիցն եւ
երկնայնոցն, զոր ասէ մարգարէն. ՕրՀնեցէք զՏէր՝ ամենայն
Հրեշտակք նորա. զօրք զօրութեանց, որ առնէք զկամ նորա: Եւ
արարիչ ամենայն լինելութեանց, թէ որ ինչ լեալք են՝ ամենայն
քո Հրամանաւ են Հաստատեալ. բայց որ ասենն զայս, եւ որ
լսել արժանանան, իմասցին թէ նմա առաջի կամ է՝ որում զօրք
Հոգեղէնք եւ Հրեղէնք են սպասաւորք. որ ասաց ամենայնի եւ
եղեն, Հրամայեաց եւ Հաստատեցան:

124

§30 *"To find mercy at the day of the appearance of our Savior at His second coming:"*

This mentions the dread coming of Christ, in case we approach the divine altar without examining ourselves. For if we stand with something on our conscience, we shall be severely rebuked like the one who entered the wedding feast with filthy clothes (Matth 22:11). But if we wash away the dirt and put on our wedding garment as the proclamation exhorts us, we shall find mercy on that day and through Christ's compassion we shall enjoy His benefits. Though we are full of thousands of works of righteousness, His gifts of mercy are innumerably more than our achievement. The deacon concludes the proclamation with a prayer saying:

§31 *"Almighty Lord our God, Save us and have mercy:"*

For if we are not assisted by Your mercy, we cannot receive cleansing to be united with You. But by Your mercy may we be worthy of this and attain eternal life.

Offertory

§32 *"Lord God of Hosts and Creator of all that exists:"*

We have often said in other prayers that the title *Lord* applies to exercising lordship, whereas *God* relates to the creation and rearing of those creatures which came into existence. *Of Hosts* i.e. angels, for God is *Lord* not only of the earth and everything in it, but of heaven and its denizens. The prophet says, "Bless the Lord, all you His angels, powerful forces that do His word" (Ps 103 [102]:20). *And creator of all that exists* means that whatever came into existence was established at Your command. Now those who say this and those worthy to hear it should understand that they stand before the One who is served by both the earthly and the fiery powers. The One who "spoke to everything and it

§33 «Որ յանէութենէ զբնաւս 'ի ցուցակութիւն ածալ
գոյացուցեր»:

Յանէութենէ՝ է յանլինելութենէ. զբնաւս՝ զամենայնս. 'ի ցու-
ցակութիւն՝ 'ի ցուցումն եւ 'ի տեսութիւն. ածալ գոյացուցեր՝
գոյս արարեր գորս չէինն, զանինչն՝ ինչ արարեր, զչգոյն՝
գոյացուցեր, զոր ոչն էր՝ 'ի տեսութիւն ածեր։ Բանքս սակաւ
են, եւ մտածութիւն անհաս ունի. չէին երկինք եւ ոչ երկնից
երկինք. ոչ վերնոցն զանագան եւ անթիւ բազմութիւնք, ոչ
արեգակն, ոչ լուսին, ոչ աստեղք, ոչ օդ, ոչ ամպք, ոչ անձրեւք,
ոչ երկիր, ոչ հուր, ոչ ալբիւրք եւ գետք եւ ծովք. ոչ ազգի
ազգի բոյսք եւ տունկք եւ սերմանիք, իւրաքանչիւր հոտովք եւ
ծաղկովք եւ պտղովք եւ համովք. ոչ բազմատեսակ անասունք,
եւ գազանք, եւ սողունք եւ թոչունք եւ ձկունք. ոչ պատուական
եւ պտանի նիւթք, ոսկի, արծաթ, պայծառ քարինք, երկաթ,
պղինձ, կապար, ապակի, եւ սոցին նմանք. ոչ ալբիւրք ճարագոյ,
կամ որ զազն բերեն ջուրք եւ լերինք. այլ սոքա եւ որ այլ
եւս են լինելութիւնք՝ յոչընչէ եղեն կամելովն Աստուծոյ, եւ
գործ եղեն եւ տեսութիւնք յանդիմանակաց։ Եւ յայն սակա նախ
զգիր գոհութեանցս գայս եդ, զի ընդ ամենայնի սրբով պա-
տարագաւ գոհացօղ լիցուք. եւ սարսեալք յամենագօր եւ յա-
մենարար Տեառնէն՝ մեծաւ ահիւ յանդիման նորա կացցուք, եւ
զաղօթս մեր մատուցուք, եւ ամենայն սրբութեամբ 'ի սուրբ
խորհուրդն մատիցուք:

§34 «Որ եւ զմեր հոդեղէն բնութիւնս պատուեալ մարդասիրապէս, այսպիսի անպատում եւ ահաւոր խորհըր-
դոյ կարգեցեր սպասաւորս»:

Հոդեղէն կոչէ զմարդկան բնութիւնս. վասն զի 'ի հողոյ ստեղծաւ
մարմին. պատիւ կոչէ զքաՀանայութիւն, եւ մարդասիրապէս,
վասն զի սիրեաց զմարդիկ, եւ զայն պատիւ եա' որում եւ ոչ
Հրեշտակք չէին[17] բանական։ Անպատում աե եւ ահաւոր զուրբ
խորհուրդն. անպատում է, զի ոչ պատմի բանիւ որ ինչ էն, եւ
ահաւոր է՝ վասն ատագին փառացն. զի յորզ տեսանէին[18]՝ թէ
յանմարմնոց Հրեշտակաց եւ թէ 'ի մարմնաւորաց սրբոց,

126

was fashioned, who commanded and they were established (Ps 33 [32]:9).

§33 *"Who brought all things from non-existence into visible reality:"*

Non-existence is non-being. *All things* is everything. *Into visible reality* is into sight and view. *You brought* means You made into beings things that were not, You made into something what was nothing, You brought into objective reality what had no existence. This phrase is short, but the thought it contains is immense. The heavens were not, nor the heaven of heavens, nor innumerable, diverse multitudes of celestial beings. No sun, no moon, no stars, no air, no clouds, no rains, no earth, no fire, no springs, rivers and seas. None of the various kinds of plants, trees and seeds, each with their fragrance, blossom, fruit and flavor. No variety of species of animals, beasts, reptiles, birds and the like. No sources of fat, no salt-bearing waterways and mountains. These and all other existing things came into being from nothing at all at God's will and assumed activity and visible form. This is given prime place among the things for which we should be thankful in order that through the holy liturgy we should give thanks for all and in awe of the almighty, all-creating Lord, we might stand before Him in deep reverence, offering our prayers and approach the holy mystery with all holiness.

§34 *"Who honored our earthly nature through His love for mankind by appointing us servants of such an ineffable, awe-inspiring mystery."*

Our human *nature* is called *earthly* because our body was created from the *earth*. The priesthood is styled *honor* and *through His love for mankind* because He loved humanity and gave them that *honor* for which not even the angels were qualified. The holy mystery is styled *ineffable* and *awe-inspiring* because of its

127

անհանդուրժելի եւ ահեղ նոցա է. բայց որքան է՝ ոչ տեսաւ յումեք. զի զԱստուած ոչ ոք եւս երբէք. արդ զի որդի Աստուծոյ է մարմնին՝ Աստուած է անտես յամենայն բնութենէ եւ սպասաւորի 'ի հոգեղինաց:

Ասաց նախ առաջին զԱստուծոյ մեծութիւնն 'ի տերելոյ վերին զօրացն, ապա յարարչութենէն, իսկ ատանօր աստ յանպատում եւ յահեղ փառացն. եւ թէ որ այսպիսիդ ես՝ առ սեր քո բարերարութեանդ գնողա յայսքան պատիւ վերաբերեցեր, մինչեւ սպասաւոր աննառ խորհրդոյ լինել: Եւ խոսիմք զայս ընդ հոր, պատարագ նմա ընծայեալ գՔրիստոս. յաղագս որոյ աստ բանն. Թէ,

§35 «Դու Տէր, որում պատարագեմք զպատարագիս՝ ընկալ առ 'ի մէնջ զառաջադրութիւնս զայս»:

Պատարագ կոչի ընծայ. դու Տէր, աստմք զՀայր, որում ընծայեմք մեք Մարդիկս այսպիսի պատարագումն, զոր պատարագիս ասաց բանն. եւ դու, ասէ, ընդունիել սովոր ես, այժմ եւ 'ի մէնջ ընկալ զոր առաջի եդաքս:

Յամենայն պատարագամատոյցան, առաջին աղօթքն վասն մատուցանողին արժանաւոր լինելոյ ասի, եւ զգոյն միտս ունի. աղայէ չհամարել խոտան զմատուցօղն. այս է զոր աստէն. Ընկալ առ 'ի մէնջ. Թէ որպէս մեծարեցեր զգնութիւնս մեր, եւ ընդունիս պատարագել քեզ մարդկան զայսպիսի պատարագ, զնոյն արասցես եւ մեզ, անտես առնելով զոր յանցեաքն:

Հանապազ իսկ՝ բայց առաւել առ ահեղ խորհրդոյն՝ յանցանքն մեր առաջի մեր լիցին, եւ յիշեսցին անուղղայ գործեցեալքն 'ի մէնջ. եւ սրանանան յիշմամբ եւ մեր բնութեանս անարգութեամբ՝ զկապարտութիւն զամենայն 'ի բաց ընկեսցուք. զի թէ Հայրապետն Աբրահամ՝ որ ոչ գիտէր զանձին խիղճ ինչ, այլ եւ բազում ուղղութեանց վկայ զԱստուած ունէր, համայն 'ի խոսել անդ ցուցանէր զինքն ոչ հող միայն այլ եւ մոխիր, ապա ո'րքափ եւս առաւել մեզ մեղաւորացս պարտ է բնութեամբս եւ վնասակար գլոյս ցածնուլ. զի եւ պատարագ իսկ խոնարհ հոգին լինի Աստուծոյ, եւ նախ զինքն Աստուծոյ մատուցանէ խոնարհեցուլն եւ սրբելով զսիրտն 'ի խղճէ չարեաց,

128

terrible glory. Whoever saw it, whether bodiless angels or saints in the body, found it unendurable and awesome. But no one has seen its full extent; for "No one has ever seen God" (John 1:18). As the Son of God is in the flesh, God is invisible to all creation and is served by those from the earth.

First the text affirmed God's might from ruling the supernal hosts, then from the process of creation and finally from His *ineffable* and *awesome* glory. And since such is Your nature, out of love of benificence You raise things of earth to such a height of glory as to be a *servant* in this *ineffable mystery*. We say this to the Father as we offer Him Christ as a sacrifice, as the passage continues:

> §35 "Lord, we offer this sacrifice to you. Receive this oblation from us:"

The offering is called a *sacrifice*. By *Lord* we address the Father, to whom we men *offer this oblation* which the text refers to as a *sacrifice*. As You are accustomed to, *receive* now what we have set before You.

In all anaphorae the first prayer pertains to the ministrants being made worthy and has the same signification. The text asks that the celebrant not be counted unacceptable. This is what is meant by *receive from us*. As You honored our nature and permit mankind to *offer* this sort of *sacrifice* to You, allow us to make this offering, overlooking our misdeeds.

Our guilt should be constantly before us, but specially during the awesome mystery when we should recall the wrongs we have done. And we should put aside all our pride by recollecting our mistakes and our dishonor of our nature. If the patriarch Abraham who had no guilty conscience but had God as witness of his many just acts, always when talking depicted himself not only as earth, but ashes (Gen 18:27), then how much more should we

և զիրա սուրբ եւ գծողի խոնարհ՝ Աստուած ոչ արհամարհէ:

§36 «Եւ աւարտեա զաս 'ի խորիրդականութիւն մարմնոյ եւ արեան միածնի քոյ»:

Աւարտ՝ կատարման իրաց սովոր եմք կոչել. ասեմք թէ սորա
կատարումն՝ եղիցի լինել մարմին եւ արիւն որդւոյն Աստուծոյ: Դարձեալ եւ խորհուրդ Աստուծոյ է, զոր յայտնեալ է,
եւ յայտնէ սրբոց իւրոց, եւ ծածուկ է 'ի պղծոց. զի մի' տացի
սրբութիւն շանց, եւ մի' ընկեսցի մարգարիտ խոզաց, զի մի'
առ ոտն կոխեսցի. վասն այնորիկ եւ մի' վայրապար զայսպիսի
խորհուրդ անհաւատից տացուք. զի մի' այպանեալք 'ի նոցանէ
երգիծանիցիմք. այսինքն է, զի մի' կակիծ 'ի սիրտ առցուք. Զի
ճառ խայլին կորուսելոցն յիմարութիւն է: Ոչ վայրապար եւ
զմիածինն բանն եդ 'ի վերայ որդւոյն. այլ զի յուշ լիցի մեզ՝
թէ որպիսի ասէ գտաք յԱստուծոյ, զի մի որդին նորա' որ
միայն է նորա ծնունդ' պատարագեցի վասն մեր:

§37 «Դեղ թողութեան մեղաց պարգեւեա նաշակողացս
զիացս եւ զգինիս. շնորհօք եւ մարդասիրութեամբ
Տեառն մերոյ եւ փրկչին Յիսուսի Քրիստոսի»:

Վասն զի կերակրով մեղաք եւ մահանացուք եղաք, կերակրով
դարձեալ զքաւութիւն եւ զանմահութիւն տանալ մեզ՝ Քրիստոսի չարչարանքն պարգեւեցին. ապաեթ վասն հացիս եւ գին-
լոյս եղելոյ 'ի սեղանն, զի լինելով մարմին եւ արիւն Քրիս-
տոսի՝ լիցի մեզ քաւիչ, եւ կեցուցիչ կենդանեաց եւ մեռելոց.
եւ այս վասն սիրոյն Քրիստոսի, որ մեռաւն վասն մեր, զոր
շնորհ եւ մարդասիրութիւն կոչէ: Զի չիք ոք առանց սխալանաց, եւ բացում են՝ զոր անգիտութեամբ մեղանչիմք. եւ զի
որ խոստովանին եւ զապաշխարութիւն յուցանեն՝ քաւութիւն
սուրբ խորհրդովն առնուն, եւ միաւանգամ 'ի Քրիստոս միանան,
լինել նմա մարմին եւ անդամս, վասն այնորիկ մեծի դեղդն 'ի
խնդիր լինիմք:

sinners be abased since by nature we are prone to cause such harm. Moreover, a humble spirit should be a *sacrifice* to God. First one becomes humble, presents oneself to God and purifies one's heart from a guilty conscience, for God does not despise a pure heart and a humble spirit (cf. Ps 51 [50]:17).

§36 *"And fulfill this as the mystery of the body and blood of Your only-begotten Son:"*

Fulfillment we are accustomed to call the finalization of something. We mean, may the *fulfillment* of this be *the body and blood* of the Son of God. Again, the *mystery* is God's and He revealed it and continues to reveal it to His saints, but keeps it hidden from the impure, not to give something holy to dogs or to let a pearl be tossed before swine and be trampled on (Matth 7:6). Therefore, let us advise unbelievers to good purpose so as not to become a mockery and laughing-stock to them i.e. so as not to be vexed at heart. For talk of the cross is nonsense to those who are lost (cf. 1 Cor 1:18). There was also a good reason for referring to the Son as the *only-begotten* word to remind us of the great love we received from God in that His one Son, His only offspring is sacrificed for us.

§37 *"And grant this bread and wine as a remedy for the atonement of sins to those who taste it by the grace and love for mankind of our Lord and Savior Jesus Christ."*

As we sinned and became mortal by food, Christ's sufferings allowed us again to receive atonement and immortality by food. I pray that the bread and wine set on the table, by becoming Christ's body and blood, may atone for us and save both the living and the dead. This is possible through the love of Christ who died for us, which is called *grace* and *love for mankind*. For no one is without shortcomings and there are many sins we commit in ignorance. Since those who confess and show repentance find *atone-*

131

§38 «Ընդ որում քեզ Հօր ամենակալի, հանդերձ կենդանարար եւ ազատիչ սուրբ Հոգւով՝ վայելեն փառք, իշխանութիւն եւ պատիւ»:

Ամենակալ կոչէ զՀայր, զի ընդ իւրով իշխանութեամբ ունի
զերկինս եւ զերկիր լրիւ իւրեանց. կենդանարար եւ ազատիչ
սաաց զՀոգին սուրբ, զի նովաւ աւազանն զմեզ վերստին ծնանի
որդիանալ Աստուծոյ, ազատելով 'ի մեղաց եւ կենագործելով
յանմահական կեանս. նոյն եւ զսւրբ խորհուրդն՝ զկենդա-
նարարն եւ զազատիչն՝ գործէ: Նա եւ զՀանդերձեալ նորոգումն
յարութեամբ մեզ շնորհէ. վասն որոյ բաբերաքի սւրբ Երրորդութեանն վայելուչ աստ եւ արժանաւոր զփառատրութիւնն
այսպէս ասելով.

§39 «Նմա վայելեն փառք, իշխանութիւն եւ պատիւ.
այժմ եւ միշտ եւ յաւիտեանս յաւիտենից»:

ՔԱՐՈԶ

§40 «Ոչ ոչ տուք միմեանց 'ի համբոյր սրբութեան»:
Համբոյր սրբութեան է՝ որ սուրբ սիրոյն է, եւ ոչ նենդաւոր եւ
ոչ պոռնկական խորհրդով, այլ յստակ մտոք իշչ յեղբայըն:

§41 «Որ ոչ կարող էք հաղորդել՝ 'ի միմեանց ուսարուք,
եւ առ դրունս աղօթեցէք»:

«Պատարագ Քրիստոս մատչի»:

Եւ զի Քրիստոս է որ պատարագին՝ անմաքուրքն եւ աղտեղ-
եալքն ողլով արտաքս ելցեն, զի չեն արժանի 'ի Հոգեւոր
ուրախութիւնն վայելել. խրատեցեն զմիմեանս սւրբ գրովք,
եւ առ դրունս աղօթեսցեն. սպացեալ սրտիւ եւ Ջերմեռանդն
արտասուօք ողբացեն զգրլանսն, զի 'ի Հոգեւոր Հարսանեացն
արտաքս վարեցան, զի չեղեն արժանիք յաճալոր ժամուն՝ մերձենալ առ երկրալոր սեղանն, եւ ոչ երդակիցել Հրեշտակացն
անեղր գումարելոց, եւ ոչ 'ի Քրիստոս միանալ խորհրդովն սըր-
բով, եւ 'ի մի Հոգի նովաւ լինել: Արդ որք ըստ այսմ խոր-
Հըրդոյ ելաննեն արտաքս, երկիւղիւ եւ ամօթով զիւրեանց

132

ment through the holy mystery and are re-united with Christ to be His body and limbs, we should be eager for this great remedy.

§38 *"With whom to You, Almighty Father, with the life-creating and liberating Holy Spirit are fitting glory, dominion and honor:"*

The *Father* is called *Almighty* because He holds the heaven and earth and their fullness under His authority. The *Spirit* is termed *life-creating* and *liberating* because through His agency we are re-born in baptism to become sons of God, freeing us from sin and vivifying us for eternal life. Similarly, He makes the holy mystery *life-creating* and *liberating* and bestows on us the renewal to come through the resurrection. That is why it says that it is *fitting* and worthy to give *glory* to our benefactor, the Holy Trinity in the words:

§39 *"To Him are fitting glory, dominion and honor, now and ever and to ages of ages."*

Proclamation

§40 *"Greet each other with a holy kiss:"*

A *holy kiss* is one given with pure affection, with neither deceitful, nor lustful intent, but with a clear mind as to one's brother.

§41 *"You who are unable to receive communion, learn from each other and pray at the doors. Christ is offered as sacrifice:"*

Since it is *Christ* who is sacrificed, those who are impure or defiled in spirit should leave, for they are not worthy to exult in the spiritual joy. They should admonish one another with the holy scriptures and *pray at the doors*. With mournful heart and fervent tears let them lament their exclusion. They were led away from the holy wedding because they were unworthy to approach the heavenly altar at the awesome hour and join the song of the angels

սխալանսն խոստովանութեամբ առաջի Աստուծոյ ունելով՝ հայտութիւն հայցիցեն յամենդորմն Աստուծոյ՝ ՚ի ձեռն Քրիստոսի զենմանն, փոթով քաւութեան հացնն. իսկ անզգայքն եւ եղեալքն յերեսաց Աստուծոյ եւ մերժեալքն ՚ի սրբութեանցն, որ ոչ եղիցեն յապաշաւանս, այլ սովորական իրս համարելով՝ եղանիցեն խնդամիտ, եւ մնացցեն անտրտում, եւս առաւել չար- ժեն ՚ի ցասումն զանբարկանալին Աստուած. զի եւ ոչ ՚ի պա- տուհասեն եւ յորոչեն ՚ի սրբոցն եւ ՚ի բացեայ առնելն յիմր- մէ՝ հոգացան ինչ, վասն որոյ յիրաւի դատին:

§42 «Ահիւ կացցուք, երկիւղիւ կացցուք, եւ նայեցարուք զգուշութեամբ»:

Չի թէ որ ամենեւին սուրբքն են անմարմին գործք, յլա- կիրգբանչն մինչեւ ցայժմ երկիւղալից ահիւ կան առաջի մեծի փառացն Աստուծոյ, ո՛րչափ եւս առաւել մեք՝ որ հանապազ ՚ի յանցանս ըմբռնիմք՝ դողալ եւ սարսափել պարտիմք. եւ զի՛նչ է նայելն զգուշուեամբ. մի՛ իբր ՚ի լոյ հաց եւ ՚ի գինի նայել՝ որք ՚ի ներքս մնայցեն, այլ մարմին եւ արիւն Աստուծոյ հա- ւատալ զառաջի եղեալն. եւ մեծ ահիւ կալ, եւ որպէս յԱստուած հայել. զորոյ գչետ դաս տունն եւ ուսուցանէ:

§43 «Պատարագ Քրիստոս մատչի ՚ի միջի մերում զառն Աստուծոյ»:

Այս է՝ յորմէ երկնչելն եւ դողալն հրամայիմք. զի նա որ ՚ի կուսական յարգանդին ՚ի Մարիամայ առեալ մարմին՝ մինացալ ՚ի նոյն բովանդակ աստուածութեամբն, այժմ ըստ նմին նմա- նութեան ՚ի հացս եւ ՚ի բաժակս մինայ. եւ որ ՚ի խաչին անհնչացաւ՝ անհնչապէս եւ ՚ի սեղանս յայս զնոյն մետելութիւն ըստ մարմնոյ ցուցանելով, եւ զենումն՝ կենդանի աստուա- ծութեամբն գոլով՝ մատուցանի սուրբ Երրորդութեանն պատա- րագ. գոհացողութիւն տուեցլոյ պատղեցագն, եւ քաւութիւն մեղացն գործելոց, եւ փրկութիւն յարաջիկայն, եւ բարեխոս առ հանդերձեալան կենդանեաց եւ մեռելոց: Չայս օրինակէն ՚ի հնումն օրէնք՝ անասնոն մատուցմամբ, ոմանք գոհութեան նուէրք, կէսք քաւութեան, այլք վասն փրկութեան. ՚ի մի յայս բովանդակեալ ՚ի մեծի պատարագիս խորհուրդ: Արդ յառաջ

gathered there and unite with *Christ* in a holy mystery and be of one spirit with Him.

Now those who go outside for this reason should confess their shortcomings before God in fear and compunction and beg reconciliation from all-merciful God through Christ's sacrifice, soon to obtain atonement. Yet those who are indifferent and go from the face of God, abstaining from the holy things, and will not come to contrition, but regard these as commonplace will leave jocularly and feel no remorse. Such people only move God even more to wrath, although He is by nature slow to anger. They are not in the least concerned at being punished, separated from the saints and taken from God's presence, and therefore are rightly judged.

§42 *"Let us stand with awe, let us stand with fear[1] and look with reverence:"*

If all the holy bodiless powers stand before God's great glory in fearful awe from the beginning until now, how much more should we who are frequently ensnared in iniquity tremble and quiver? And what is *looking with reverence?* Those who remain inside should not *look* at the gifts as mere bread and wine, but believe that the body and blood of God has been set before us and *stand* in great *awe* and view this as God, as indeed the next section explains:

§43 *"Christ is offered as sacrifice in our midst as the Lamb of God:"*

This is what we are commanded to fear in trembling. He is the One who took flesh from Mary's virgin womb and united to this His entire Godhead and now unites with this bread and cup in similar fashion. He who breathed His last upon the cross exhibits the same breath-less mortality according to the flesh upon this altar. A victim made alive by His divinity, He *is offered as sacrifice* to the Holy Trinity. A thanksgiving for the gifts that have been

քան զատ տանն՝ որ զգուշութեամբն ճայել հրամայէ՝ ասեն առաջի կացեալքն, թէ

§44 «Առ քեզ աստուած»:

Այս ինչ է, եթէ առ քեզ ճայիմք՝ եւ ճաւատամք զի յանապա-
կանութիւն աստուածութեանդ քոյ փոխարկես գրնծայումս: Իսկ
այժմ տան ասեն,

§45 «Ողորմութիւն եւ խաղաղութիւն եւ պատարագ
օրհնութեան».

զասացեալն 'ի մէնջ ցուցանելով. զի ողորմութիւն է՝ քաւիչ
մեղաց լինելով. խաղաղութիւն է՝ փրկութիւն եւ խաղաղութիւն
ճոգլող եւ մարմնոց շնորճելով. զի եւ ոմանք 'ի ճնոցն պա-
տարագաց՝ խաղաղականմ անուանին. իսկ պատարագ օրհնութեան է՝ զի ընծայի Աստուծոյ 'ի գոճութիւն ամենայն ե-
րախտեաց նորա, յիսկզբանցն ճետէ առ մեզ եղելոց. եւ օրինեմք
ընդ ամենայնի սուրբ պատարագաւն զՆստուած. որպէս եւ բանք
պատարագամատուցացն յայտ առնեն:

§46 «Շնորհիք, սէր եւ աստուածային սրբարար զօրու-
թիւն՝ Հօր եւ Որդոյ եւ[18] Հոգւոյն սրբոյ եղիցի ընդ
ձեզ ամենեսեան»:

Այս է զոր գրեաց Պօղոս Կորնթացւոյն. «Շնորհք Տեառն մերոյ
Յիսուսի Քրիստոսի եւ սէրն Աստուծոյ եւ ճաղորդութիւն Հոգ-
լոյն սրբոյ եղիցի ընդ ձեզ ամենեսեան». եւ զայս որ զպատարագն մատուցանէ՝ տայ ժողովրդեանն, թէ որ ինչ Քրիստոսի
տնօրէնութեամբն քաւութիւն եղեւ եւ պարգեւք շնորճեցաւ, եւ
սէրն Աստուծոյ Հօր որ որբեգրեաց զնաւատացեալս, եւ Հոգւոյն
կցորդութիւնն որ ընդ սուրբս, եղիցի ընդ ձեզ. զի մաքուրք
լեալք՝ եւ 'ի սէրն Աստուծոյ միացեալք, եւ Հոգւոյն սրբոյ
ճաղորդեալք՝ յառաղաստիս երկնայնում ընդ անմաճ փեսային
իցեմք: Ապա ատ 'ի մերձ կացելոցն, ոչ որպէս 'ի տալն
զխաղաղութիւն յաղօթան, զի անդ ասեն, եւ ընդ Հոգւոյդ քում,
թէ եւ քում Հոգւոյդ. իսկ ատ թէ

136

given, atonement for sins committed, salvation to come and inter-
cessor on behalf of the living and the dead for the next life. This
the law imitated of old by animal offerings, some as a thanksgiving
offering, others for atonement, others for salvation. It is all en-
compassed in the great mystery of the liturgy.

Now before they administer that which it is commanded to *look
upon with reverence*, those standing before the altar say:

§44 *"To You, O God:"*

i.e. that we look to You and believe that You will transform this
offering into the incorruptibility of Your divinity.

Now as they offer it to God, they say:

§45 *"Mercy and peace and sacrifice of praise:"*

indicating what we said, i.e. that it is *mercy* atoning for sin: it is
peace granting salvation and *peace* to our souls and bodies, as some
of the sacrifices of old were styled *peace*. But it is called *sacrifice
of praise* because it is offered to God as thanksgiving for all His
benefits bestowed on us from the beginning and we *praise* God
with all through the holy liturgy, as the celebrant's words make
clear:

§46 *"The grace, love and divine, purifying power of
Father, Son and Holy Spirit be with you all:"*

This is what Paul wrote to the Corinthians, "The grace of our
Lord Jesus Christ and the love of God and the communion of the
Holy Spirit be with you all," (2 Cor 13:14) and is what the celebrant gives to the people. Whatever atonement was effected by
Christ's economy and gifts were granted, and the *love* of God the
Father who adopted believers and the fellowship of the *Spirit* who
is in the saints, *be with you*, that being purified and united to the
love of God and having partaken of the *Holy Spirit*, we may enter
the heavenly bridal chamber to be with the immortal bridegroom.

Then the clerks standing nearby respond

§47 'ի հոգւոյդ քում. զի որպէս 'ի Մովսիսի հոգւոյն՝ եօթանասուն եւ երկու ծերոցն տուաւ հոգին, նոյնպէս եւ 'ի քո հոգւոյդ մեզ պարգեւեսցէ, որ նման Մովսիսի առ Աստուած մտեալ՝ զմերս մատուցանես գոհութիւնս եւ մաղթանս:

§48 «Վեր արարէք զսիրտս ձեր յաստուծային խորհուրդս».

զի թէպէտ եւ յերկրի ատ կատարի՝ յերկինս է պատարագումնս. վասն որոյ աստուածայինն Պօղոս գրէ. Զվերինն խոր-հեցարուք, մի՛ զայս որ յերկրի ատ է: Եւ ասեն առ այս:

§49 «Ունիմք առ քեզ, Տէր ամենակալ».

Թէ առ քեզ՝ Տէր ամենակալ, ամբարձաք զսրդիս մեր. որպէս թէ անդ ոգին բնակէ եւ անդղուստ 'ի յամենայն մարմինն ազդէ:

§50 «Եւ զոհացարուք զՏեառնէ բոլորով սրտիւ».

Վասն զի սկիզբն կամ'ի առնել զոհութեանցն, խրատէ զամենայն սիրտս բոլորովիմբ զկնի եւ զոհացողական բանիցն համբառնալ եւ զոհանալ զԱստուծոյ: Յորոց ասի.

§51 «Արժան եւ իրաւ».

Արժան է գոհութեան, եւ յիրաւի գոհանալ զնորա բարերարու-թեանցն, քանզի պարտապան եմք:

ՄԵԿՆՈՒԹԻՒՆ ԱՂՕԹԻՑ ԶՈՐ ԱՍԷ ՔԱՀԱՆԱՅՆ 'Ի ԾԱԾՈՒԿ

§52 «Արժան է ստուգապէս եւ իրաւ ամենայորդոր փութով, քեզ՝ էն եւ ես եւ էդ Աստուած, անսկիզբն եւ անճնելի, երրեակ միութիւն, միշտ երկրպագել փառա-ւորելով».

Բառ ասելոյն 'ի ժողովրդոցն՝ կրկնէ քահանայն, թէ արժան է ստուգապէս եւ իրաւ. ճշմարտապէս ասէ, իրաւացի է: Ամենա-յորդոր փութով. փոյթ է սրտի մտոք հոգ տանել. իսկ ամենա-յորդոր փոյթն՝ զատտիկ ջերմութիւն ողլուն ասէ, որ յամենայն սրտէ եւ 'ի զօրութենէ եւ 'ի տոաց՝ յորդորի 'ի փոյթն, բառ Պօղոսի խատտուն. Ի փոյթ՝ մի՛ վեսհրուք, հոգւով եռացէք: Արդ

138

§47 *"From your spirit"*
not "and with your spirit"[1] or "and to your spirit" as at the prayer
when giving the peace. Just as the *Spirit* was given to the sev-
enty-two elders from Moses' spirit (Num 11:25), so may God
bestow it on us *from your spirit,* since like Moses you have approached God and offer our thanksgiving and prayer.

§48 *"Lift up your hearts to this divine mystery:"*[1]
for although it is being performed on earth, the sacrifice is in
heaven. Hence the divine Paul writes, "Contemplate what is
above, not that which is on earth" (Col 4:2). And they respond
to this:

§49 *"We lift them up to You, Almighty Lord:"*
i.e. *we* have raised our souls towards You, *Almighty Lord,* as the
soul dwells there and from there influences the whole body.

§50 *"And thank the Lord with all your heart:"*[1]
Because he wishes to begin the *thanksgivings,* he counsels *all
hearts* together to rise after words of *thankfulness* and give *thanks*
to God. They reply,

§51 *"It is worthy and right:"*
He is *worthy* of thanks and *it is right* to thank Him for His
bounties, as we are in His debt.

Commentary on the Prayers which the Priest Says in Secret:
§52 *"It is indeed worthy and right with most ardent devotion always to worship and glorify You, the God who is,
was and is to come, without beginning and inscrutable triune unity:"*[1]

As the people say, so the priest repeats that *it is indeed worthy
and right.* Truly, he says, *it is right. With most ardent devotion:
devotion* is to take pains willingly, while *most ardent devotion*
refers to the passionate fervor of spirit which issues in *devotion*

այապիսի արժան է 'ի քո երկրպագութիւնն վերաբերիլ։

§53 «էն եւ ես, եւ եղ Աստուած»։

որ էիր յառաջ քան գյաւիտեանս, եւ այժմ ես եւ մնաս յաւիտենից յաւիտեանս։

§54 Անսկիզբն.

ոչ ունիս լինելութեան սկիզբն եւ առաջ. եւ

§55 անննանելի,

զի ոչ 'ի Հրեշտակաց եւ ոչ 'ի մարդկանէ քննի քո որպիսութիւնդ կամ գտանի։

§56 Երրեակ միութիւն,

երեք անձն եւ մի բնութիւն ատռուածութիւն։ Քեզ, ասէ անրա-կրզբանդ եւ անքնին մխասնական Երրորդութեանդ՝ արժան է հանապազ ամենայորդոր փութով երկրպագել փառաւորելով. եւ թէ վասն ոյր է փառաւորելի եւ երկրպագելի այապիսի փութով՝ ասէ, 'ի Հայր գբանն ձգելով։

§57 «Որ կոյին, հայր, աննննելի եւ արարչակից բանիդ՝ զանիծիցն բարձեր գկրենիմն»։

Բան կոչէ զՈրդի. զի անալատ ծննդեամբ 'ի Հորէ՝ որպէս բան 'ի մտաց. եւ ծանուցիչ է կամացն Հոր՝ որպէս քան ծանուցիչ կա-մաց խսսողին. եւ զի որպէս քան՝ միով ճայիւ 'ի բազումս՝ բովանդակ եւ ոչ մասամբ մտանէ, եւ զի մարմնացաւ, տեսաւ եւ շօշափեցաւ, անմարմինն՝ ըստ նմանութեան բանի՛ որ 'ի քարունն[19] մարմնանայ եւ տեսանելի եւ շօշափելի լինի. եւ ան-մեկնելի է 'ի ծնողէն, որպէս քանն յայլան Հնչէ եւ 'ի միտ մնայ։ Աննննելի ասէ, վասն զի անեղբունելի եւ անշօշափելի է բնութիւնն Աստուծոյ։ Արարչակից է, վասն զի Հասարակաց Երրորդութեանն է արարչագործութիւնն։ Եւ զի պատուիրանա-զանցութեամբն՝ անէծք կրենիմն եղաւ ընդ մեզ եւ ընդ Աստուած, այսինքն՝ արգել անկաւ եւ որոշաց զմեզ Յաստուծոյ եւ 'ի դրախտէն եւ 'ի կենաց, եւ ողորմեալ մեզ Աստուծոյ 'ի բաց եբարձ որ յանիծիցն էր կրենիմն. եւ զայն ոչ Հրամանաւ կամ Հրեշտակաւ կամ մարդով սրբով, այլ իւր արարչակից Որդւովն. առաւել գերագոյն պատիւ է՝ քան զբաննական զանէծսն. այն զի Որդւովն եբարձ։

140

augmented from all one's heart, strength and mind, according to Paul's counsel, "Do not be lazy in *devotion*, be fervent in spirit" (Rom 12:11). Now the next phrase is worthy to attribute to God in your worship:

§53 *"The God who was, is and is to come:"*
You were before eternity, are now and remain to ages of ages.

§54 *"Without beginning:"*
You have neither *beginning* nor source of existence. And

§55 *"Inscrutable"*
for Your identity cannot be investigated or discovered either by angels or men.

§56 *"Triune unity:"*
three persons and one nature, Godhead. It means *it is worthy always with most ardent devotion to worship and glorify You*, the unified Trinity who are *without beginning and inscrutable*.

And as to who is to be *glorified and worshipped* with such *devotion* it says, referring the passage to the Father:

§57 *"That, O Father, by Your unsearchable and co-creative word, You removed the obstacle of the curse:"*
Word refers to the Son, for He is begotten purely by the *Father* as speech by the mind, and He makes known the *Father's* will as speech makes known the speaker's intention. As speech with one sound penetrates many things whole and not in part, so He who was bodiless took flesh and was seen and touched like speech which becomes embodied and thus visible and tangible on paper. He was also inseparable from the *Father* as speech remains in the mind, though resounding in other places. He is called *unsearchable* because God's nature is inscrutable and intangible. He is *co-creative* since creation is the work of the trinity in common.

And as by transgression of the commandment the curse was set as an *obstacle* between us and God, i.e. a barrier which fell and

141

§58 «Որ ժողովուրդ ինքեան՝ զառ 'ի յեկեղեցւոյ սեպ-
հականացբաց զհաւատացեալս ի քեզ՝ որ յեկեղեցւոյ են քո
հաւատացեալք՝ իւր սեպհական ժողովուրդ արար. սեպհական
ասէ՝ սեռան եւ անհակառակելին. սերտեաց ասէ զմեզ իւր
բնական ժողովուրդ, անքակ յերմէ տէրութեանէ:

§59 «Եւ զննելի բնութեամբ ըստ 'ի Կուսէն մնտեսու-
թեան հանեգաւ բնակել 'ի մեզ»:

Զօր աւետարանիչն Յովհաննէս ասէ, Բանն մարմին եղեւ եւ
բնակեաց 'ի մեզ. այն է զօր ասեւ. քանզի անզննելի է Բանն,
որպէս ասացաւ սմին յառաջագոյն, եւ մարմնանալովն 'ի Կուսէն
զննելի եղեւ. որպէս 'ի կաթողիկէից թղթին գրէ նոյն Յովհաննէս, թէ Զեռք մեր շօշափեցին 'ի վերայ բանին կենաց:
Տնտեսութիւն՝ գործառնութիւն է. վասն զի ա'ո յանձն Որդին
Աստուծոյ զայս գործել, 'ի Կուսէն որդի մարդոյ լինել: Բնակեն
'ի մեզ՝ այն է, ըստ մեզ լինել. զօր մարգարէն Եսայի, ծնի-
ցելոյն 'ի կուսէն ասէ, կոչեսցեն զանուն նորա Էմմանուէլ, որ է
ընդ մեզ Աստուած:

§60 «Եւ նորագործ աստուածապէս նարտարապետեալ
երկինք զերկիրս արար»:

Արդարեւ նորագործեաց, զի զերկիր երկինս արար, որ Աստուծոյ
նարտարապետութեանն միայն է կարելի. զի 'ի չգոյէ գոյացոյց
զերկիրս նախ, եւ արդ՝ յերկրէ երկինք փոխարբեաց. եւ թէ
որո°վ օրինակաւ այս եղեւ, ասէ.

§61 «Զի որում ոչն հանդուրժէին առաջի կալ զուարթ-
նոցն ջոկք՝ զարհուրեալք 'ի փայլականացայտ եւ յահեղ
լուսոյ աստուածութեանն, եղեալ այդպիսիդ մարդ յա-
դագս մերոյ փրկութեան, շնորհեաց եւ մեզ ընդ երկ-
նայինս պարել ընդ հոգեղէն պարս»:

Տեսե°ր, զիա'րդ եղեւ երկիրս երկինք. զի երկնից եւ Հրեշտակաց
տէրն յերկիր էջ, եւ մարդ եղեւ, եւ զմարդիկ Հրեշտակս արար.
եւ զվերին զօրսն եւ զմարդիկ՝ 'ի միմեանս յաբեաց. եւ միաբան ընդ նոսին զնոցայն օրհնութիւնս յերկրի երկրայնոցս
երգել արժանաւորեաց:

142

separated us from God, paradise and life, so God had pity on us and removed the *obstacle* formed by the *curse*. He effected this not by a command, nor an angel or holy man, but by His *co-creative* Son. A much higher honor than His Son's removing the *curse* was:

§58 *"That He made a people for himself from the Church, those who believed in You:"*

Those who believe in *the Church He made* His own *people.* His own means firm and incontrovertible. He confirmed them, it says, as His *people,* unseverable from His rule.

§59 *"And He was pleased to dwell among us in tangible form by economy from the Virgin:"*

This the Evangelist John describes as "The Word became flesh and *dwelt* among us" (John 1:14). This is what it means—the Word is *intangible,* as was stated previously, but in taking flesh *from the Virgin* became *tangible,* as John writes in his Catholic Epistle: "Our hands touched the Word of life" (I John 1:1). *Economy* means undertaking, because the Son of God took upon Himself to do this viz. to be son of man *from the Virgin.* To *dwell among us* means being as we are. The prophet Isaiah says about His birth *from the Virgin* "They shall call His name Emmanuel, i.e. God with us" (Isa 7:14).

§60 *"And He created the earth anew, divinely designing it as heaven:"*

Certainly *He created anew:* for He made *earth heaven,* something only possible for God's *design.* For He first brought the earth into existence from non-existence and then transferred it from *earth* to *heaven* and the continuation clarifies how this occurred:

§61 *"For the one the ranks of angels could not bear to approach for fear of the effulgent radiance and awesome light*

143

Բայց պարտ է՝ նախ քան 'ի գլուխ տանել զգեղեցիկ զայս դրուակ՝ գշրաչալի սորա գյարմարումնս ընդ միտ ածել: Թէ որչափ գմեծութիւն Աստուծոյ չնորհէն՝ գմ'ի քան գմ'ի չարաչ մատուցեալ՝ յոյժ գերագանց ցուցանէ: Եւ այղ տես անդուստ 'ի սկզբանէն: Արժան է ստուզապես եւ իրաւ ամենայորդոր փութով՝ քեզ էն եւ ես եւ էղ Աստուած, անսկիզբն եւ անֆննելի երրեակ միութին, միշտ երկրպագել փառաբանելով. որ կոյին, Հայր, անզննելի եւ արարչակից Բանիդ՝ գանիծիգն բարձեր գկրնիմն: Մեծ էր յոյժ պարզել՝ յանիծիգն ազատել. բայց եւս մեծ է, զի մխածնաւն զայս արար. որ ինքն անէծֆ եղեւ եւ մեզ գորհնութիւն եառ: Եւ չյատացաւ այսու, այլ եւ ժողովուրդ իւր սեպհականեաց գորա ընդ անիծիւքն էաք. եւ այս քան գանիծիֆն ազատելն յոյժ առաւել է:

Դարձեալ այլ եւս առաւելութիւն. որպէս գմեզ լինելն՝ եւ 'ի մեզ ընակելն, որ կարի գերագոյն է քան գժողովուրդն լինել մեզ նման: Եւ քան գայս եւս մեծագոյն է՝ գերկիրս երկին առնել, եւ գմարդիկ հրեշտակս: Եւ 'ի վերայ սոցունց կարի անչափ է գերամբարձութին՝ գի գոր հրեշտակֆ բագում երկիւդիւ պաշտեն, եւ գերգան գոր նոքա մեծաւ ահիւ ադադակեն, գայն մեզ համարձակապես ընդ նոսին երգել չնորհեաց. որպէս ագդակից եւ մարմնակից սիրով վատաչել 'ի պաշտոնն: Արդ գմնացեալ բանն տեսցուֆ մասնաւորաբար:

«Չի որում ոչն հանդուրժէին առաջի կալ գուարֆնցն ֆոկֆ»:

Չուարֆունֆ կոչին վերնֆն, վասն միշտ 'ի գուարֆութեան եւ յուրախութեան գոլոյն աստուածային տեսութեամբֆն, եւ բարեգունֆ նորա խնամովֆն, որֆ գատեալֆ դաս դաս 'ի միմեանց կարգեալֆ կան 'ի պաշտամանն Աստուծոյ. գորա ֆոկա բանն կոչեաց: Եւ գի ասագ՝ թէ ոչ հանդարտէին առաջի կալ, վասն գի Եսայի եւ Եզեկիէլ մարգարէֆ, մին գֆերովֆէֆիգն եւ մ'իսն գֆերովֆէֆիգն գչանդամանանն որչափ կարացին առնուլ՝ պատմեցին մեզ, աճապնեալ գնոսա յոյժ գարհուրանօֆ: Չի Եզեկիէլ պատմէ գֆերովֆէֆիգն գֆֆիւան տարածեալս 'ի վերայ գլխոգն եւ բո-

> *of Your divinity became such a man for our salvation and gave us the possibility of consorting with the heavenly host in their spiritual choirs."*

Did you see how the *earth* became *heaven?* —the Lord of *heaven* and *earth* descended to *earth, became man* and made men angels. He joined mankind with the celestial *hosts* and made us who are earthborn worthy on earth to sing their hymns in union with them.

But before bringing this beautiful piece to its conclusion, it is necessary to consider its splendid composition. Rehearsing them one by one, it reveals extremely well the greatness of God's grace. Just look back at the beginning:

> *"It is indeed worthy and right with most ardent devotion always to worship and glorify You, the God who was, is and is to come, without beginning and inscrutable triune unity, because, Father, by Your unsearchable and co-creative word, You removed the obstacle of the curse:"*

Freeing *us from the curse* was a marvellous gift, but it is even more marvellous that He did this by means of His only-begotten Son who became a *curse* and gave us the blessing. And that is not all—for He appropriated as *His people* us who were under the *curse* and this is much more than release from the *curse*.

A further gain was His becoming as we are and *dwelling among us* which is far superior to our being His *people*. And that was surpassed by making *the earth heaven* and mankind angels. But immeasurably more excellent than all these was that *the one* whom *angels* worship with great *fear* and hymn with much reverence made it possible for us to sing boldly with them, entrusting us the office in love as one sharing our race in the flesh. Now let us look at the rest of the passage in detail:

> *"For the one the ranks of angels could not bear to ap-*

վանդակ անձանցն, զի որպէս ՚ի սատիկ յաչս ընդ թեւօքն աստ սալարէին։ Իսկ Եսայի՝ զաեռովբէից նոյնպէս զվեց թեւան բաժանեալ յերկուս երկուս, կրկնապատիկ զերեսան եւ զոտան ամբրացուցեալ յաստուածային հրոյն, եւ միշտ ընդոստուցեալ ՚ի սատկուԹենէ աՀագին տեսուԹեանցն՝ յերեւրս ծպտեալ՝ եւ երկիւղալից բարբառով աղաղակ առ իրեարս եղեալ. վասն այսր աստ, Ոչ հանդարտէին առաջի կալ. այսինքն Թէ ոչ ժուժէին։

«Ձարհուրեալք ՚ի փայլակնագայտ եւ յահեղ լուսոյ աստուածուԹանդ»։

Բանգի լոյս ահեղ աստուածուԹեանն փայլատակունս ցայտէ անհանդուրժելիս, եւ յար տոսկումն եւ զարՀուրանս եւ պակուցումն նոցա առնէ։

«Եղեալ այսպիսիդ մարդ յաղագս մերոյ փրկուԹեան»։

Թէ որ այլդպիսի ահաւոր եւ անտանելի փառօք էր վասն գմեզ փրկելոյ մարդ եղեւ, ինքն ՚ի մեր աղքատուԹիւնս իջեալ, եւ մեզ զիւր աստուածուԹիւնն շնորՀեաց։ Այլ առ անգամ մի ոչ զայս դնէ, այլ զայն՝ Թէ իրեշտակաց Հաւասարակից արար։

«Շնորհեաց եւ մեզ, ասէ, ընդ երկնայինսն պարել ընդ հոգեղէն պարսն»։

պարելն՝ դասակցել է. զերկրայինսս աստ եւ զՀողեղէնսս՝ ընդ երկնայինսն եւ ընդ Հոգեղէնսն կցորդակցեաց. շնորՀօք զայս՝ եւ ոչ լրատ արժանեաց տուեալ, այսինքն՝ նեըելով, ողորմուԹեամբ, անյիշաչարուԹեամբ, զի այս է շնորՀեաց ասելն։

proach:"

The celestial beings are called *angels*[1] because they are always joyful and glad at seeing God and experiencing His merciful care. They are divided according to class (which the text called *ranks*).[2] With regard to their inability to endure approaching God the prophets Isaiah and Ezekiel have informed us the particulars they were able to obtain (the former about the seraphim, the latter about the cherubim), though inspired with frightful terror. Ezekiel relates that the cherubim spread their wings over their heads and their whole body, for he says they hid themselves under their wings from intense fear (cf. Ezek 1:23ff.). Isaiah mentions that the seraphim similarly divide their six wings two by two, folding them to shield their face and feet from the divine fire and continually recoiling from the intensity of the awesome visions, they cower together and cry to each other in a fearful tone (cf. Isa 6:2ff.). On this our text says: They *could not bear to approach* i.e. they could not tolerate it *for fear of the effulgent radiance and awesome light of Your divinity;* for *the awesome light of divinity* emits unbearable *effulgence* and also causes their trembling, terror and petrifaction.

> *"Becoming such a man for our salvation:"*

He who was of such *awesome* and unbearable glory became man to save us. He descended to our poverty and granted us His divinity, though that is not the point made here, but rather that He made us equal to the *angels.*

> *"He gave us the possibility of consorting with the heavenly host in their spiritual choirs:"*

Consorting means being grouped along with. The earthly and those of clay, it says, He linked with the *heavenly* and spiritual. He granted this by grace and not according to merit, i.e. by for-

§62 «Ընդ սերովբէսն եւ ընդ քերովբէսն միաձայն սրբասացութեամբ յօրինել ունագս»։

Նուագ՝ երգոյ է անուն. միաձայնենՙ զնոյն երգել գոր նոքայն. սրբասացութեամբ, զնոյն ասել զերեքսրբեան օրհնութիւնՙ գոր սերովբէքն երգեն. եւ յօրինելՙ ըստ նոցա յօրինուածութեանն կացմել։

§63 «Համարձակապէս քարրառով ապադակել ընդ ունսին եւ ասել»։

վասն զի եղբայր մեր եղեւ տէրն փառաց, առաւել քան զեերովբէսնՙ ընդ նոսա կալովՙ զսրբասացութիւնն բարբառիմք։

§64 «Սո՛ւրբ սո՛ւրբ սո՛ւրբ, Տէր զօրութեանց»։

Երեք, ըստ երից անձնաւորութեանցն, Հօր եւ Որդւոյ եւ Հոգւոյն սրբոյ. եւ մի Տէր, քանզի մի յերեսին է տէրութիւն աստուածութեանն. տէր զօրութեանց, այսինքնՙ Հրեշտակաց, զի Հզորք են զօրութեամբ, եւ զի զօրք են թագաւորին երկնից։

§65 «Լի են երկինք եւ երկիր փառօք քո»։

Երկինք երկնայնովքն եւ երկիրս երկրայնովքս՝ զքո փառդ քարձրացուցանեն, ոչ միայն ՚ի ձեռն բանաւորաց եւ մտալորացՙ այլ ՚ի ձեռն ամենայն ընութեանց, որք զոյութեամբ իւրեանց պատմեն զփառս Աստուծոյ։

§66 «Օրհնութիւն ՚ի բարունս»

Հօր, որում ասեմք Հայր երկնաւոր. թէպետ ոչ միայն ՚ի բար- ձունս է այլ ամենայն ուրեք, այլ զի որ անդն են՝ կամարարք նորա ամենեքին են՝ վասն այնորիկ անդ լինել ասեմք։

§67 «Օրհնեալ որ եկիր եւ գալոցդ ես անուամբ Տեառն»։

Որդւոյ ասէ՝ որ եկն ՚ի վերկել զարարածս, եւ գալոց է դատել զազգս մարդկան. անուամբ Տեառն, վասն զի յանունն Հօր իւրոյ եկն, որպէս եւ ինքն իսկ ասաց, Թէ ես եկի յանունն Հօր իմոյ. եւ դարձեալ զինքն տէր անուանեալ է, եւ է իսկ տէր։

148

giveness, compassion and not remembering wrongs, for this is what grace signifies.

§62 *"To compose melodies in unison with the seraphim and cherubim in the sanctus:"*

Melody is a term for song. To be *in unison* is to sing the same as them. *In the sanctus* means saying the same thrice-holy hymn which *the seraphim* sing and *to compose* is to create something according to their style of composition.

§63 *"To cry with them with bold exclamation and say:"*

Because the Lord of glory who is greater than *the seraphim* became our brother, we stand among them and proclaim *the sanctus*.

§64 *"Holy, holy, holy, Lord of Hosts:"*

Three according to the three persons Father, Son and Holy Spirit and one *Lord*, since the divine lordship is one in eternal expression. *Lord of Hosts*, i.e. of the angels; for they are strong in power and the forces of the King of heaven.

§65 *"Heaven and earth are full of Your glory:"*

Heaven with the heavenly beings and *earth* with the earthly ones exalt *Your glory*, not only by means of natures endowed with reason and intelligence but by means of all things which by their existence tell out the *glory* of God (Ps 19[18]:1).

§66 *"Praise in the highest:"*

to the Father whom we call heavenly Father. However, He is not only *in the highest*, but everywhere. Yet since those there all fulfill His will, we say He is there.

§67 *"You are blessed who came and are to come in the name of the Lord:"*

speaks of the Son who came to save creation and is to come to judge the race of men. *In the name of the Lord* because He came *in the name* of His Father, as He Himself said, "I have come *in* my Father's *name*" (John 5:43) and again He called Him *Lord* and

§68 «Օրհնութիւն 'ի բարձունս» այսինքն յերկինս՝ Հոգւոյն սրբոյ, որոյ գալուստն, 'ի Տէրն 'ի Յորդանան, եւ 'ի վերնատունն յառաքեալսն 'ի յերկնից ցուցաւ։

Այլ զի Փրկչին ասեմք զօրհնութիւն 'ի բարձունս, որպէս Հօր եւ Հոգւոյն սրբոյ, 'ի խոնարհելոյ նորա առ մեզ՝ յօժարեմք օրհնել զնա, զմանկանցն Հնչեցեալ ձայն. զի որպէս նոքա, 'ի յովանակին (sic) տեսեալ զնա՝ ասէին, Օրհնեալ եկեալ անուամբ Տեառն, զաւթեան ձայնիւն լաւելադրեալ, նոյնպէս եւ մեք 'ի սուրբ սեղանն՝ ականատես նորա լեալ, պատուական նորա մարմնովն եւ սուրբ արեամբն զնա օրհնեմք։

§69 Ճշմարտապէս՝
զատոյգն աւէ, եւ

§70 ամենասուրբն՝
զամենայնիւ սուրբն. եւ սուրբ է փառաւորեալ. զի որ առանց ամենայն պակասութեան ունի զխառն՝ ճշմարտապէս փառաւորեալ է, եւ ամենայնիւ փառաւորեալ։ Ըստ մեզ՝ սուրբն մաքուր աս. այլ երանելի վարդապետուքն մեր յայսմ նուագի՝ փառաւորեալ՝ զատեն 'ի Հրեշտակաց մեզ ծանուցին։

§71 «Եւ ո° ոք պանծացի բանիւ բովանդակել զՔո 'ի մեզ զանբաւ բարեգործութեանդ զեղմունս»։

Զիբ ոք աս՝ որ պանծացի բովանդակել եւ ասէ բանիւ, թէ զամենայն լիով զԲո 'ի մեզ զբարեգործով զեղեալսդ՝ ոչ ոք կարէ պարծել թէ ասիցէ, զի անբաւ եւ անբովանդակ է։ Գործեցն է առաւել քան զգթան, զոր Քերմն սիրով 'ի վերայ ձննդոցն ցուցանեն ծնողքն մեծաւ խանդաղատանօք. զոր ոչ միայն 'ի մարդիկ, այլ բազում անդամ եւ յայլ կենդանիս է տեսանել. որպէս 'ի Հաւուցն՝ առ ինքն եւ առ Երուսաղեմ Տէրն առակէր։ Արդ աս զանչափ զբարեյորդորդ զեղեալսն 'ի մեզ, զի ոչ միայն զի յածախ է գոհանալ պարտիմբ, այլ առաւել զի 'ի Քերմն սիրոյ եւ 'ի սատիկ գթոյ՝ եւ յանպատում գործովոյ զգուեալ յածախեաց զբարին. եւ վասն զի աղքատ էր մեր բնութիւնս եւ յունէր ինչ զի ընդայատուր Աստուծոյ լիցի, եւ առաջի եղեալ Աստուծոյ՝ զբարեբարութեանցն դռնասցի, յաղագս ալ-

150

Lord He truly is.

§68 *"Praise in the highest:"*[1]
i.e. in heaven, to the Holy Spirit whose coming upon the Lord in the Jordan and on the apostles[2] in the upper room (Acts 2:1) was manifested from heaven. But in as far as we say *"praise in the highest"* to the Savior, as well as the Father and the Holy Spirit, in His condescension towards us, we are eager to *praise* Him, echoing the children's chant. When they saw Him on the ass they said, *"Blessed* is the one that comes *in the name of the Lord"* (Matth 23:39). Witnessing Him at the holy altar, we too chant David's psalm (Ps 118 [117]:26) and *praise* Him for His precious body and holy blood.

§69 *"Truly"* means indeed and

§70 *"All-holy"*
entirely *holy* and what is *holy* is glorified; for the One who possesses glory without any deficiency is *truly* glorified and entirely glorified. Among us *holy* means pure, but our blessed vardapets have informed us that it means glorified in this song, as sung by the angels.

§71 *"And who will boast of circumscribing in word the*
overflowing of Your infinite lovingkindness towards us:"
No one can *boast* that he may do so, for it is infinite and uncontainable. *Lovingkindness* is more forceful than tenderness which parents exhibit towards their offspring with warm affection and great fondness which can be observed not only among men, but also on many occasions among other animals such as hens to which the Lord likened Himself and Jerusalem (Matth 23:37; Lk 13:34). Now it says we ought to give thanks for the superabundance of bounties we have received not only for their frequency, but rather for the warm affection, profound tenderness and ineffable *lovingkindness* with which God embraced us in His contin-

սորիկ ոչ կամեցաւ Աստուած չքաւորս յայս լինել մեզ. այլ
անկշռելի եւ անեզրական սիրով պատրաստեաց զիւր միածին
որդին տալ մեզ, զի Հարուստք լեալ նովաւ՝ զնա առաջի դիցուք
Աստուծոյ, եւ նովաւ գբարեացն 'ի մեզ եղելոց՝ գոհասցուք:
Վասն այնորիկ 'ի Հանելն զպատարագն 'ի սեղանն՝ սկիզբն
առնեմք յիսկզբանցն գոճանալ: Բայց նախ խոստովանի բանս,
թէ չկայ յոք կար՝ զզովանդակ բարեբարութիւնն 'ի մեզ
եղեալս՝ բանիւ յառաջ բերել. եւ ապա սկսանի զգոճութիւնս:

§72 «Որ եւ անդէն իսկ 'ի նախնումն զանկեալն 'ի մեղս
զանազան յեղանակօք խնամեալ սփոփեցեր»:

Յառաջինս՝ գոր 'ի նախնումն կոչեաց՝ զբնութիւն մարդկան՝
զանկեալն 'ի մեղս, պէսպէս խնամօք մխիթարեցեր ասէ. զի
սփոփելն՝ մխիթարել է, եւ զանազանն՝ պէսպէս: Իսկ յեղա-
նակօքն՝ դարձուածօք է: զի երբեմն երկայնակեցութեամբ լաւ
եւ պիտանի Հարցն զգնացս արդարութեան ուսուցանէր ծննդոց.
էր զի եւ զՀաճոյս պատուէր չնորշիւ, որպէս զԵնոք փոխամբն.
եւ էր երբեմն՝ զի գյանցուցեալսն պատմէր, որպէս զկային, եւ
որ առ զրՀեղեղեան, եւ զՍոդոմայեցիսն. զի եւ այս խնամք են
Աստուծոյ պատժելն եւ կարճել 'ի մեղաց, եւ այլոցն տալ
զգուշութիւն: Դարձեալ եւ ուխտադիր ընդ արդարսն լինելով եւ
վերկոզ նոցին, որպէս Նոյի, Աբրահամու եւ զաւակի նորա, որպէս
Հովտայ, Յակոբայ, բովանդակ արդարոց եւ որդւոցն Իսրայելի՝
զորս յԵգիպտոսէ վրկեաց եւ յանապատին խնամարկեաց, եւ
որոց գործենան հոտ, յորոց եւ զմարդպարկն յարոյց, որոց եւ
զերկիրն աւետեաց պարգեւեաց, որոց զբաՀանայութիւն եւ
զթագաւորութիւն հոտ, որոց գողջակէզան, զգոՀան եւ զնուէրսն
պարգեւեաց. զի մինչեւ գայցէ ճշմարտութիւնն՝ ստուերական
ճշմարտութեան մխիթարեսցին. նաեւ Հրեշտակօք խոսեցաւ, եւ
ազգի ազգի նմանութեամբք ինքն իսկ Աստուած երեւեցաւ. եւ
զի ընդ ազգաց պաշապանս յիւրոց Հրեշտակաց կարգեաց: Զայս
եւ որ սոցին նման այլ բազում՝ միով բանիւ ընծայեցոյց՝
յասեն, թէ

ual benificence. Moreover, our nature was poor and had nothing to offer God and set before Him in gratitude for His bounties. Yet God did not wish us to go without this and so in His immeasurable and boundless love He arranged to give us His only-begotten Son to become rich through Him and set Him before God and through Him give thanks for the benefits we had received. Hence in placing the sacrifice on the altar we begin to render thanks from the elements. But first the text admits that no one has the ability to enumerate in speech all the benefits done for us. Then it commences the eucharist.

§72 *"You who even in former times consoled those fallen in sin and cared for them in various ways:"*

It says that He comforted human nature which had *fallen in sin* in the first men (whom it calls *old*) in diverse fashion. *Consoling* is comforting and *various* is diverse, while *ways* means responses. For by the longevity of good and valuable fathers He would teach their offspring the paths of righteousness. Sometimes He honored the obedient with grace, as in Enoch's translation (Gen 5:24); on other occasions He would punish miscreants like Cain (ibid. 4:11-12), the generation of the flood (ibid. 7:21) and the people of Sodom (ibid. 19:23). For this is also God's concern to punish and prevent sin by fostering caution in others.

Again He established a covenant with the righteous and saved them e.g. Noah (Gen 5:24), Abraham and his son (ibid. 22:17), Lot (ibid. 19:29), Jacob (ibid. 35:11) and all the righteous and children of Israel whom He saved out of Egypt, cared for in the desert and gave the law. He raised up the prophets from them, proclaimed and bestowed the land on them and gave them the priesthood and kingdom. He bestowed the whole burnt offerings, sacrifices and sacred gifts to comfort them with a shadow of the truth until the truth should come (Heb 10:1). He also spoke by

153

§73 «Զանազան յեղանակօք խնամեալ սպոփեցեր. մար-
գարէիւք, օրինացն տուչութեամբ, քահանայութեամբ, եւ
ստուերակերպ երնչոցն մատուցմամբ».

զի ամենայն մատուցեալքն ՚ի հնումն՝ թէ վասն մեղաց, թէ
վասն փրկութեան, թէ ՚ի գոհութիւն, Քրիստոսի պատարագելոյն
էին օրինակք։ Եւ երինչքն այլբեցեալք՝ որոց մոխիրն սրսկէր
զպղծեցելովքն, զայժմու մաքրութիւնն՝ որ Քրիստոսի մկրտու-
թեամբքն եւ պատարագաւն՝ տպաւորէր. վասն որոյ աւն առաքեալ. Զատուեր հանդերձելոց բարեացն ունէին օրէնքն, եւ ոչ
զնոյն կերպարանս իրաց։ Ստուեր ասէ՝ զոր չուք մեզ կոչեմք,
որ անկանի ՚ի մարմնոյ, եթէ ՚ի կենդանւոյ եւ եթէ յայլ ինչ
իրէ։ Եւ հանդերձեալ բարիս՝ զայժմու ասէ, որ Քրիստոսիւ
յայժմած մեզ հանդերձեալ էր լինել. զոր յայլում թղթի եւս
յայտնապէս ասէ Պօղոս. գործնականն[20] տուեալ՝ որ են ստուերք
հանդերձելոցն, այլ մարմին Քրիստոս է, զի ուսցին ՚ի Քրիստոսէ անկեալ զստուեր օրինացն, որ գործնականն փոփոխեաց.
եւ ծանիցես՝ թէ որչափ ՚ի մէջ է ընդ ստուեր. եւ յորմէ
ստուերն անկանի, այնքան է միջոց օրինացն եւ շնորհացս որ
մեզա պարգեւեցաւ։

§74 «Իսկ ՚ի վախնան աւուրս այսոցիկ գրովանդակ
իսկ զպարտեաց մերոց խզեալ զդատակնիֆ»։

Վախնան աւուրց կոչէ, զի ըստ վեցօրեայ աւուրցն արար-
չութեան վեց հազար ամօք ստոի կեանքս ցուցանի, եւ յեօթ-
ներորդումն լինի հանրդերբեալ կեանքն։ Արդ զի ՚ի վեջին
հազարիս շնորհք Աստուծոյ Քրիստոսի յայտնեցաւ ՚ի վեցե-
րորդիս, եւ այլ լրումն հազարի յետ սորա ոչ է, վասն այսորիկ
վախնան աւուրց հազարամեայ աւուրցն կոչէ, վերջ հազարացն
ցուցանելով. զոր եւ Պօղոսի յայտ արարեալ ասէ. ՚ի վախնան
աւուրցս այսոցիկ խօսեցաւ ընդ մեզ Որդւովն։
«Զրովանդակ իսկ զպարտեաց մերոց խզեալ զդատակնիֆ»։
րովանդակն՝ ամենայն կոչէ. պարտս՝ գյանցանան ասէ. զոր եւ
Տէրն ուսուց՝ յաղօթսն խնդրել, թէ թող մեզ զպարտս մեր.
դատակնիֆ կոչէ՝ զոր գրբն Թագաւորք զվնասակարացն եւ

angels and God Himself appeared in a range of likenesses and appointed His angels as guardians of the various nations (Dan 11:13). These and many other similar cases are alluded to in a single phrase:

> §73 *"You consoled them and cared for them in various ways—by prophets, by giving the law, by the priesthood and by the prefigurative offering of cattle:"*

For all offerings in the Old Testament, whether for sin, salvation or thanksgiving were types of Christ's sacrifice. And the immolated *cattle* whose ashes sprinkled the unclean typified the present cleansing effected by Christ's baptism and sacrifice. Hence the Apostle says, "The law had the shadow of good things to come and not the very form of the things" (Heb 10:1). It says "shadow which we call shade which falls from a body, be it something animate or any other object. And the "good things to come" refer to those now current which then were still to come through Christ. Paul makes this very clear in another epistle, citing the legal regulations which are "shadows of what is to come," whereas Christ is the body (Col. 2:17). From this we should learn that the shadow of the law fell from Christ who transformed the provisions of the law and perceive from the extent comprehended by the shadow and from the source of the shadow the magnitude of the contrast between the law and the grace which was bestowed upon us.

> §74 *"But at the end of these days You tore up the reckoning of all our debt:"*

It is described as *the end of days* because according to the six days of creation, this life is depicted as six thousand years and on the seventh will be the afterlife.[1] Now at the end of this sixth millennium God's grace was revealed in Christ and there is no supplementary millennium after Him. Therefore the millennium of days is styled *the end of days,* indicating *the end* of the millennia.

կնքեալ պահին, մինչեւ հատուսցեն ըստ յանցմանն: Ըստ որում նմանութեան եւ մարդկան բնութիւնս յառաջին մարդոյն մինչեւ 'ի Քրիստոս՝ որպէս գրով եւ կնքով պահիւր յոր վերժխնձրութեան ապատամբութեանցն, խորհուրդք եւ բանք եւ գործք, որ Քրիստոսիւ խզեալ լինէ կնիք դատին: Վերստին արդ գբանէն բուսն հարցուք:

§75 «Իսկ 'ի վախնան աւուրս այսոցիկ գրովանդակ իսկ զպարտեաց մերոց խզեալ զգատականիք, զՔո միածինդ եսուր մեզ պարտապան եւ պարտս»:

խզեցեր ասէ զգատականին՝ ո՛չ բռամբ, այլ իրաւամբք. զի մի՛ վրիպանք արդար դատողութեանդ քոյ լինիցի. այլ կացուցեր մերոց մեղացն պարտականտ՝ ո՛չ 'ի հրեշտակաց եւ ո՛չ 'ի սրբոց, այլ զքո միածինդ: Դարձեալ զառաւել ասէն յիշելով գրճանա, թէ զոր միայն էիր ծնեալ՝ զնա մեզ պարտապան եսուր, որ ո՛չ այլով էիթ՝ այլ ինքեամբ զպարտս մեր հատոյց: Տէր հատուցանող ընդ իմ եղեալ, ըստ Դաւթի. եւ պարտք՝ ըստ Եսայեայ. Տէր մատնեաց զնա առ մեղս մեր. եւ ինքն Տէր ասէ. Այնպէս սիրեաց Աստուած գաշխարհ՝ մինչեւ զորդին իւր միածին ետ: Եւ Պօղոս, թէ Յիւր որդին ո՛չ խնայեաց, այլ վասն մեր ամենեցուն մատնեաց զնա:

§76 «Զքո միածինդ, ասէ եսուր մեզ պարտապան եւ պարտս, զենումն եւ օծեալ, զառն եւ երկնաւոր հաց, քահանայապետ եւ պատարագ»:

Ո՛չ միայն պարտապան եւ պարտք զքո միածինդ ասէ եսուր, այլ զենումն եւ օծեալ, զի փոխանակ օծեալ քահանայապետիցն՝ զգա եսուր մեզ լինել՝ օծեալ եւ քահանայապետ, եւ զենումն եւ զառն պատարագի, եւ հաց առաջաւոր. քանզի յորինականն իմն քահանայապետք ընդ առաւոտս եւ ընդ երեկոյս զախինս հանապազորդա մատուցանէին, եւ ըստ աւուրց զառաջաւորաց 'ի սեղանն կարգէին. եւ զժողովրդոցն զիւրաքանգիւրոցն մատուցանէին զնուէրս. եւ անասնոցն արեամբ՝ զմարմնոցն աւետաւորէին զարբութիւն: Իսկ քո միածինդ մեզ՝ ամենայն ինքն լեալ, ո՛չ զմարմնոյ եւեթ մաքրէ զպղծութիւն, այլ բովանդակ զհոգի եւ զմարմին մաքրէ, ո՛չ առակաւ եւ ստուերաւ, այլ ճշմար

156

Paul too signifies this: "At the end of these days He spoke to us through His Son (Heb 1:2).

Tearing up the reckoning of all our debt: All means every, *debt* means wrongdoing, as the Lord taught us to ask in prayer, "Forgive us our debts" (Matth 6:11), *reckoning* is what kings draw up against criminals and keep sealed until they repay them as their crime requires. Similarly, human nature from the first man until Christ was held in custody by a writ sealed till the day of retribution for disobedience in word and deed, so that the judgment seal might be *torn up* by Christ. Now let us return our attention to the text.

> §75 *"But at the end of these days You tore up the reckoning of all our debts and gave us Your only-begotten Son as debtor and debt:"*

You tore up, it says, *the reckoning* not in violation of justice, but rather in fulfillment of it, to obviate any departure from Your just judgement. Yet You appointed *debtor* for our sins not one of the angels or saints, but Your *only-begotten* Son. Again the priest gives thanks, commemorating God's great love. *You gave us Your only Son* as *debtor* for us who paid our debts by no other means than Himself. "The Lord has become my recompenser," as David put it (Ps 18 [17]: 21, 25) and *debt* according to Isaiah, "The Lord gave him over to our sins" (Isa 53:6) and the Lord Himself said, "God so loved the world that He gave His only-begotten Son" (John 3:16) and Paul "He did not spare His own son, but gave Him up for us all" (Rom 8:32).

> §76 *"You gave Your only-begotten as debtor for us and debt, victim and anointed one, lamb and heavenly bread, highpriest and sacrifice: "*

Not only did *You give Your only-begotten as debtor and debt*, it says, but *victim and anointed*; for instead of the *anointed* high-

157

տութեամբ. որպէս եւ ինքն իսկ ասաց. Ի վերայ նոցա ես սուրբ առնեմ զանձն իմ, զի եղիցին եւ նոքա սրբեալք ճշմար֊ տութեամբ. եւ յասիյն ճշմարտութեամբ՝ յայտ արար թէ առա֊ ջին սրբիչն օրինակօք էին եւ ոչ ճշմարտութեամբ:

Արդ ասացեալ թէ զքո միածինդ խաւր մեզ պարտապան եւ պարտս, զենումն եւ օծեալ, որ զզենումն զենոյր, զանն եւ երկնաւոր հաց, քահանայապետ եւ պատարագ, յարէ ՚ի նոյն.

§77 «Վասն զի դա է բաշխող եւ նոյն ինքդ բաշխի ՚ի միջի մերում՝ միշտ եւ անծախապէս»:

Չայս ամենայն Պօղոս յանապաղէս յեղյեղէ թէ Քրիստոս եղեւ քահանայապետ, եւ թէ ինքն մատոյց պատարագ, եւ իբրով արեամբն եմուտ ՚ի սրբութիւնն յաւիտենական, եւ թէ ունիմք մեք սեղան՝ ուստի ոչ ունին իշխանութիւն ճաշակել որք զխո֊ րանին պաշտեն զպաշտօն. յայսմ սեղանոյ է բաշխիչն Քրիստոս, եւ ինքն է որ բաշխին. զի որպէս ՚ի վերնատանն յառաքեալն բաշխեցաց եւ բաշխեցաւ, նոյնպէս եւ յայսմ օրէ մինչեւ ցայսօր՝ յամենայն եկեղեցիս ամենայն հաւատացելոց նոյն ինքն բաշխէ եւ բաշխի եւ ոչ սպառի. վասն այնորիկ ասէ թէ բաշխի ՚ի մեզ անծախապէս: Ապա եւ զօրինակն եւս այսպիսի շնորհաց յայտ աձեալ ցուցանէ, թէ զիա՞րդ է քահանայապետ եւ պատարագ եւ օծեալ եւ երկնաւոր հաց, եւ բաշխիչ եւ բաշխումն. այսպէս ասելով.

158

priests *You gave* Him to be *for us* both *anointed and highpriest* as well as *victim,* sacrificial *lamb* and showbread. For the highpriests of the law regularly offered lambs in the morning and evening (Exod 29:39, 41) and set the showbread on the table from day to day and offered each of the people's gifts and proclaimed purity by the blood of animals. But *Your only-begotten,* being all Himself, not only purifies the pollution of the body, but cleanses all the spirit and flesh not by semblance and shadow, but in truth, as He Himself said, "I consecrate Myself for them, that they too may be truly consecrated" (John 17:19). In saying "truly" He demonstrated that the first means of purification were types and not the reality.

After saying *You gave us Your only-begotten as debtor and debt, victim and anointed one* who sacrificed the *victim, lamb and heavenly bread, highpriest and sacrifice,* the priest adds:

§77 "For He is the one who distributes and is Himself distributed among us always without being consumed:"

All this Paul frequently rehearses. Christ became *highpriest,* He offered the *sacrifice* and by His blood entered into the eternal sanctuary. Thus we have an altar from which those who officiate at the altar may not eat. Christ distributes from this altar and He is the One distributed, so that as in the upper room He *distributed and was distributed* to the disciples, so from that day to this in all churches of all the faithful He it is who *distributes and is distributed* and is never depleted. That is why it says "He is distributed among us without being consumed" (cf. Heb ch. 9).

Then the means of such grace are indicated, how He is *highpriest and sacrifice, anointed and heavenly bread, distributor and distributed* in what follows:

159

§78 «Վասն զի եղեւ հաւաստապէս եւ առանց ցնորից
մարդ»։

Ոչ ցնորիւք ասէ, այսինքն կարծեօք, այլ ստուգապէս մարդ
եղեւ։

§79 «Եւ անշփոթ միութեամբ մարմնացաւ 'ի սուրբ եւ
յաստուածածին Կուսէն Մարիամայ»։

Միացաւ ասէ 'ի մարտին անշփոթաբար. զի ոչ փոխարկումն
կամ 'ի բաց բարձումն արաբ աստուածային կամ մարդկային
բնութեանցն, այլ միացոյց զբնութիւնսն, զնոյն գոլ Աստուած եւ
զնոյն մարդ. որպէս զի բանն Աստուած` մարմին[21], որ 'ի կուսէն
մարմնացաւ` Աստուած, եւ նոյն ինքն Աստուած եւ մարդ, եւ
Մարիամ` որ ծնաւն զԱստուած Բանն` աստուածածին եւ Կոյս։

§80 «Ճանապարհորդեցաւ ընդ ամենայն կիրս մարդկային կենցաղոյս առանց մեղաց»։

Ճանապարհի` զկենցաղս կոչել սովոր են գիրք, ընդ որոյ Քրիստոս
ընդ վարան անց ասէ, եւ ոչ մեղաւ, զբռոյանդակ զմարմնոյ
կրեալ զկիրս. այս է` ծնաւ, սնաւ, քաղցեաւ, ծարաւեցաւ, աշ-
խատ եղեւ, եկեր, արբ, զզեցաւ, հոգաց, տրտմեցաւ, ար-
տասուեաց, եւ որ այլ եւս 'ի մարմնի բերի` յանձն էառ. եւ
ազատ 'ի մեղաց մնալով` յաղթող մարմնականաց սխալմանցն
արար։

§81 «Եւ յաշխարակեցոյցն եւ յառիթն փրկութեան մերոյ եկեալ կամաւ 'ի խաչն»։

առիթն պատճառ է, եւ զխաչելութիւնն` կենաց աշխարհի եւ
փրկութեան մարդկան պատճառ Տէրն եցոյց. վասն որոյ եւ
գոհանալով` բանն աշխարհակեցոյց եւ առիթ փրկութեան մերոյ
զխաչն կոչէ։

§82 «Առեալ զիացն յամենասուրբ 'ի կենդանարար 'ի
ձեռն իւր»։

Ամենասուրբ արդարեւ էին ձեռքն աստուածային. եւ կենդանարար, զի 'ի ստեղծմանն կենդանութիւն յայնմանէ մարդկան տուաւ. եւ որ 'ի նորոգումն կենաց եղեւ նորոգումն` նովին
շնորհեցաւ։ Զի նոյն ձեռք է որ զԱդամն գոյացոյց. թէ եւ ան-

160

§78 *"Because He became man assuredly without illusion:"*
Without illusion means without appearance, but really became man.

§79 *"And was incarnate in a union without confusion of the holy Mother of God and Virgin Mary:"*

It says He united with the flesh *without confusion* for He effected no change or diminution to either the divine or human nature. Rather He united the natures to be both God and man, so that God the Word might be flesh and that which was incarnate of the Virgin might be God and He Himself both God and man and *Mary* who bore God the Word be *Mother of God and virgin.*

§80 *"He passed through all the passions of human life without sin:"*

Scripture is accustomed to call life *passage* and so Christ lived out His life but committed no sin, bearing *all the passions* of the flesh, i.e. He was born, nourished, hungered, thirsted, grew tired, ate, drank, felt, became anxious, sorrowed, wept and took upon Himself all else entailed by the flesh. And remaining free from *sin,* He became victorious over fleshly shortcomings.

§81 *"And willingly came to the cross which saves the world, the occasion of our salvation:"*

Occasion means cause and the Lord revealed the *crucifixion* to be a cause of life for *the world* and for the *salvation* of mankind. Rendering thanks for this, the text calls the cross *that which saves the world, the occasion of our salvation.*

§82 *"Taking bread into His all-holy and life-creating hands:"*[1]

Truly the divine *hands* were *all-holy* and *life-creating* since in creation mankind was given vitality by them and our regeneration, effected in the regeneration of *life* was granted by the same means. For if the same *hand* brought Adam into existence, fleshless then,

161

մարմին յայտժամ՝ որ այժմս մարմնով. նոյն ամենակար եւ
ամենակեցոյց ձեռք՝ որ զՂողն մարդ հոգելոր եւ բանական
փոխադրեաց, զՃացն առնելով՝ մարմին աստուածային փո-
խարկեաց. անդ զմարդկայինն միացուցեալ գոգի, եւ 'ի սա՝
զաստուածայինն միացուցեալ բնութիւն. անդ աստ փչել զգոգին
լերեսսն, որ է Հոգին սուրբ, ստեղծու 'ի մարդումն զկեն-
դանական շունչն. եւ աստ աստ, Առալ զիացն օրհնեաց. եւ է
օրհնելն՝ զՀոգին սուրբ տալ 'ի նա. որ 'ի Մարիամն առաքեալ
զանճառելի տնօրէնութիւնն 'ի նմա գործեաց, եւ միացոյց 'ի
Բանն Աստուած զմարմինն՝ որ 'ի կուսէն, զի ըստ այնմ եւ
զիացին միութիւն յորդին Աստուծոյ՝ Հրաշագործեացէ:

§83 «Օրհնեաց, աստ, զոհացաւ». քանանայապետ մեր
եղեալ, եւ զիւր մարմինն մատուցեալ պատարագ, իբր զմի 'ի
մարդկանէ գոհանայ զԱստուծոյ բարերարութեանցն՝ որ առ
ազգս մեր 'ի սկզբանէ մինչեւ ցյաւիտեան. եւ որպէս 'ի մարդ-
կութենէս՝ զայապխի ընդայ տուեալ նմա տրիտուր:

§84 Ապա աստ. «Ետ իւր ընտրեալ աշակերտացն ասելով.
Առէք կերայք 'ի դմանէ ամենեֆեան, այս է մարմին
իմ, որ վասն ձեր եւ բազմաց բաշխի»:
էին եւ այլ աշակերտք Տեառնն, բայց Գլխաւորք երկոտասանքն
էին, զորս եւ ընտրեալս բանն կոչեաց, նոցա նախ զաւրբ խորհուրդն շնորհեաց: եւ զի ամենայն Հաւատացելոց պարգեւելոց
էր՝ վասն այնորիկ յաւել զկ
 նելով զոր զոր
անսպառութեամբ տալոց էր կերակուր ճշմարիտ Հաւատացելոց:

§85 «Ըստ նմին օրինակի եւ զբաժակն առալ օրհնեաց,
զոհացաւ, ետ իւրոց ընտրեալ աշակերտացն ասելով.
Առէք արբէք 'ի սմանէ ամենեֆեանն. այս է արիւն իմ
նորոյ ուխտի, որ վասն ձեր եւ բազմաց հեղու 'ի քալութիւն մեղաց»:
Սկիզբն արար Տէրն մեր պատարագիս, եւ ուսոյց, թէ որպէս
պարտ է զսա գործութեամբ կատարել. զի ոչ միայն զբարա-
չունէնս, այլ եւ զՃատարակաց մարդկան խնամոց եւ զիրկու-
թեան գոՃացուք. այլ ընդ Հասարակացն եւ վասն իւրաքան-

162

though now in the flesh, it is still the same almighty and all-saving *hand* which transformed earth into man, both spiritual and rational, and took bread and transformed it into a divine body. In creation it united man's spirit to his body, but now it unites the divine nature with the human. At creation, it says, He breathed the spirit upon their face, i.e. the Holy Spirit and created a living breath in man (Gen 2:7) and here it says *taking bread, He blessed it: Blessing* refers to the gift of the Holy Spirit upon it, which was sent to Mary, effected the ineffable economy in her and united to God the Word the flesh from the Virgin, so that in the same way He might miraculously bring the *bread* into unity with the Son of God.

§83 *"He blessed it and gave thanks:"*

Having become our highpriest and offered His body as a sacrifice, as a human representative He thanks God for His bounties bestowed on our race, which have been from the beginning and will continue for ever. He also gives Him such an offering in return on mankind's behalf.

Then it continues:

§84 *"He gave it to His chosen disciples[1] saying, "Take, eat of this all of you.[2] This is My body which is distributed for you and for many:[3]"*

There were other disciples of the Lord, but the principal were the twelve, whom the text calls *chosen.* To these He first granted the holy sacrament which He was to bestow upon all believers. That was why He added *for many*, indicating that from that day till the end of the world He would give food to true believers which would not fail.

§85 *"Having taken the cup in the same way, He blessed it, gave thanks,[1] gave it to His chosen[2] disciples and said, "Take,[3] drink of this all of you. This is My blood of the*

163

չերոց առանձինն բարեաց դտելոց յԱստուծոյ՝ սուրբ պատա
րագաւն երախտահատոյց լիցուք շնորհակալութեամբ. զի ոչ
միայն վրկել եւ կեցուցանել գՏեզ եկն, այլ եւ ամենայն
կարդաց եւ կրօնից Տէրն մեր վարդապետ մեզ լինել։ Եւ արդ
միտ դիր յիսկզբանցն. ծնաւ, աղքատ գմայրն իւր ընտրեաց, զի
դու մի՛ փախչելի համարեսցիս գաղքատութիւնն՝ զոր ամենեց
ունն Թագաւորն ախորժեաց. Հալածեալ եղեւ յԵգիպտոս՝ տղայ
գլով, եւ բազում անզամ յորժամ աքանչելեցոքն երախտագործէր՝
Հալածեալ լինէր. զի դու մի՛ տաղտկայցես ընդ Հալածանս, եւ
մի՛ գայրասցիս Թէ եւ յերախտառուաց եւս նեղիցես. քանզի ոչ
երրէք այնքան բարեգործել կարես՝ որքան նա որ Աստուածն եւ
վրկիչն էր. եւ դարձեալ՝ ոչ այնչափ ազատ ՚ի պարտեաց՝ որ
չափ նա որ անմեղն ամենայնիւ էր. այլ եւ ոչ պատուի եւ մե
ծարանաց՝ աւելի քան գորդին Աստուծոյ՝ զանձն արժանի
մարթասցիս համարել։ Զզեցաւ Հանդերձ՝ ոչ ՚ի պաձուճանս, այլ
՚ի ծածկութիւն մարմնոյ. զի դու մի՛ աւելորդացն այլ Հար
կաւորացն գքեզ տայցես։ Կերակրեցաւ եւ արբ, որպէս եւ զզեց
ցաւ, ոչ փափկութեան զինքն տուեալ, այլ չափաւորապէս զգէտա
մարմնոյն Հատուցանէր։ Եմուտ ՚ի Հարսանիս, եւ գլնդութեանն
պայման եցոյց Համեստութեամբն եւ աքանչելի ընձայատրու
թեամբն։ Յայտ արար եւ գարտասուաց եւ զոզոյ որքանութիւն,
գսիրելին սպալով գՂազարոս։ Նա եւ ուղեգնացաց ետ օրինակ,
Թէ որպիսեօք գրաստուք գաչխատութիւնն Հանդուցանել պատ
շաճ է. վասն զի ՚ի վերայ իշոյ եւ ոչ ՚ի ձիոյ ոսկեսանձն երե
լեելիս նստաւ։ Վարդապետեցաց դարձեալ՝ Թէ որպէս ՚ի փոր
ձութիւնս պարտ իցէ աղօթել, կամ որպիսի Հեզութիւն աո
փորձողան ցուցանել, եւ բարիս ընդ չարի փոխաորել, որպէս եւ
ինքն գունին ծառային բժշկեաց։ Եւ արդ՝ որպէս այտքիւք եւ
այլովք ամենեքումբք իւր կենցաղականօք եւ մանաւանդ
խոնարհութեամբն ազդի ազդեօք՝ որ մինչեւ յոտից աշակեր
տացն լուացումն ուսուցանել կամեցաւ, այսպէս եւ գխորՀուրդն
ուսոյց, Թէ որպէս պարտ է կատարել, օրՀնութեամբ եւ գոՀա
նալով. եւ գի գինքն մնալ մեզ պարտական աախորժէ, եւ ոչ գմեզ
իւր, յայն սակս ՚ի գոՀանալն մեր գԱստուծոյ՝ տայ մեզ փոխա

*new covenant which is shed for you and many to atone[4] for
sin:"*

Our Lord instituted the liturgy and instructed that it should be
celebrated with thanksgiving, offering thanks not only for creation, but for the care and salvation of all mankind, and in addition to general benefits, also for those which everyone individually
receives from God. For He not only came to rescue and save us,
but to be our teacher as the Lord of all rites and usages. And now
pay attention to these principles. He was born and chose a pauper
as His mother, so that you should not regard poverty as something
to avoid, when the King of all was satisfied with it. He was pur-
sued into Egypt as a baby and persecuted many times when He
performed a miracle at someone's request so that you should not
complain about persecution and not become exasperated despite
harrassment by those you have assisted, since you can never be as
beneficent as our God and Savior. Neither can one be as free
from debt as He was who was completely sinless, nor worthy of
honor and respect greater than the Son of God. He wore clothing
not as adornment, but to cover His body to prevent you from allo-
cating yourself more than is necessary. He ate and drank as He
dressed, not abandoning Himself to delicate living, fulfilling the
needs of the body in moderation. He attended the wedding feast
(Jhn 2:1-10) and showed how to enjoy oneself with temperance
and presented a marvellous gift. He demonstrated our capacity for
tears in mourning His friend Lazarus (Jhn 11:35). He set an example for travellers, indicating the sort of animal suitable for re-
lieving one's fatigue by sitting in a donkey and not a horse with
imposing golden saddle. Again, He taught how to pray in temptation (Lk 22:40), the sort of meekness to show tempters and to return good for evil, as He healed the servant's ear (ibid. 22:51).
And so, just as these and all the other events of His life, espe-

դարձեալ 'ի նոյն մեծաւ պատարագաւն. զի մեռելոց եւ կենդանեաց Հատուցզին պարտքն նովաւ, եւ պարտաառւս եւ պարտական մեզ նոյն ինքն Աստուած լինիցի։

Արդ 'ի տալ գրամական ցաշակերւանն ասէ. Այս է իմ արիւն նորոյ ուխտի, որ վասն ձեր եւ բազմաց հեղու 'ի թողութիւն մեղաց. զայն յայլ առնէ որ 'ի խաչին Հեղլոց էր, եւ բեւեռին եւ կողին խոցելն. եւ ոչ ասաց միայն արիւն իւր, այլ նոր ուխտո զնա անուանեաց. քանզի Հին ուխտոն որ ընդ Հրեական վասն պարզեւական երկրին` անասնոց էր արեամբ. իսկ այս նոր ուխտո` իւրով պատուական արեամբն. յաղագս որոյ նախասաց եղեւ Երեմիայիւ` ուխտել ուխտ նոր, տալով գործես իւր 'ի սիրտս եւ 'ի խորհուրդս մեր, Աստուած մեր լինել, եւ ժողովուրդ իւր զմեզ առնել, եւ այլ ոչ եւս յիշել զմեղս մեր եւ զանօրէնութիւն։ Իսկ աստ իւր սուրբը բերանովն` ոչ այսքան միայն ասաց` զուխտոն իւրով արեամբն, այլ զայն եւս յաւել, թէ ուխտոմ ձեզ ես եւ Հայր զարքայութիւնն, եւ գլինեն ինձ ուրախակիցս. զի զուրախանայն ընդ եմին յայր առնէ յաւելն։ Ուտիջիք եւ ընպիջիք 'ի սեղան իմ` յարքայութեան Հօր իմոյ։

§86 «Որ զոյն միշտ 'ի յիշումն իւր առնել մեզ պատուիրանադրեաց, բարերար եւ մարդասէր Տերդ»։

Քանզի ասաց կենարարն, թէ Քանիցս անգամ թէ ուտիցէք զհացս եւ զրամակս ըմպիցէ` զմահ իմ յիշեչիք մինչեւ եկից ես. այս է զոր ասեմքն թէ զոյն զայս խորհուրդ զոր ինքն կատարեաց` եւ մեզ Հրամայեաց առնել յիշատակ մահուան իւրոյ. միշտ, այսինքն հանապազ։

cially the various acts of humility right down to washing His disciples' feet, had a didactic purpose. Thus He indicated that it was necessary to celebrate the sacrament with praise and thanksgiving.

As He desires to remain our debtor and not that we be His when we give thanks to God, He gives it back, returning it to us in His great sacrifice so that the debts of the living and dead should be repaid by Him and God Himself be both our creditor and debtor.

Now in giving the cup to His disciples He says: *This is my blood of the new covenant, which is shed for you and for many to atone for sin:* Thereby He alludes to the *blood* He was to shed on the cross as He hung there and they pierced His side. However, He not only referred to it as His *blood,* but also as a *n e w covenant*; for the old *covenant* with the Jews over the land they were given was sealed with the *blood* of animals, whereas this *new covenant* with His precious *blood.* Moreover, He foretold this through Jeremiah: "Establishing a *new covenant,* putting His law in our hearts and thoughts, being our God and making us His people, no longer remembering our sin and iniquity" (cf. Jer 32:38-40). But here by His holy mouth He did not only say that He was establishing a *covenant* with His own *blood,* but added, "I and My Father covenant the kingdom to you and you shall be partakers of My joy." This is implicit in His saying: "You will eat and drink at My table in My Father's kingdom" (Lk 22:30).

> §86 *"The beneficent, man-loving Lord laid down a command that we should do this always in remembrance of Him"*

The Savior said, "As often as you eat this bread and drink this cup, you commemorate My death until I come" (I Cor 11:26). This is the point I am making. This very same mystery which He performed, He also ordered us to celebrate as a commemoration of

167

§87 «Եւ իջեալ 'ի ստորին վայրս մահու»:

ստորին՝ ներքին է վայր. զգերեզմանն կոչէ զայս, յորում ասառւածային մարմինն եդաւ՝ զոր ա'ռ 'ի Մարիամայ. քանզի աստ:

§88 «Եւ իջեալ 'ի ստորին վայրս մահու՝ իւրով մար-մնովն, զոր ընկալաւ 'ի մերմէս յազգակցութենէ»:

Ազգակից զսուրբ Աստուածածինն զՄարիամ անուանէ. եւ որպէս մարմնովն 'ի գերեզման էջ՝ ըստ այլոց մարմնոց, նոյնպէս եւ ոգւովն առ այլոց մեռելոց ոգիս չոգաւ, եւ յարութիւն բազում սրբոց ընորհեաց, եւ զզօրութիւն մահու ելոյծ: Վասն որոյ յարէ 'ի նոյն.

§89 «Եւ զնիգս դժոխոցն ապարտեալ հզօրեղապէս, ծառնոյց զինքն հաւասատեալ Աստուած կենդանեաց եւ մե-ռելոց»:

զի որպէս արդելանաւ փակեալ ողւոցն 'ի մարմիններն դարձ, եւ մարմնոցն յարութիւն: Թանզի սպառնացաւ մահ Ադամայ, թէ ճաշակեսցէ 'ի պտղոյն. եւ զի յանցաւոր պատուիրանին գտաւ՝ 'ի մահ եւ 'ի մեղս գրաւեցաւ զաւակօք. եւ ոչ գտաւ ոք 'ի մարդկանէ որ անմեղութեամբ զմահուն վճարէր զպարտս, եղեւ որդի Ադամայ՝ որդին Աստուծոյ՝ անպարտն մեղաց, եւ փո-խանակ մեղաւորաց մեռաւ եւ պարտաւորաց. ապա արկ գիշխանութիւն 'ի վերայ մահու, խորտակելով զզօրունս նորա, եւ հանելով 'ի նմանէ զըմբռնեալսն: Կարէր զայս եւ առանց իւրն մահու, որպէս զօրեաց առ Ղազարն, այլ ոչ կամեցաւ իշխա-նութեամբ փրկել միայն, այլ եւ իրաւապէս. որպէս ասաց ոմն 'ի մարգարէից. Թէ Իրաւամբք փրկեսցի գերութիւն նորա եւ ողորմութեամբ. ողորմութեամբ՝ զի մարդ եղեալ մեռաւ վասն մեր. եւ իրաւամբք՝ զի անմեղին մահ մեղուցելոցս կենդա-նութիւն իրաւացուսցէ: Այլ զի 'ի դժմս աճ գբանն 'ի դրանցն արգելարանէ, զոր խորտակեալ աստ, զի ցուցցէ թէ որպէս 'ի բանտէ՝ որ խորտակին դրունքն եւ փշրին նիգքն, որպէս ասաց ապարտեալ. եւ մանաւանդ որ եւ 'ի վերայ թռնացեալն կապի անլոյծ կապանօք, չիք այնուհետեւ արգելականացն առ 'ի յար-տաքս ելանելն խափան. ըստ նմին օրինակի եւ ոչ մեր

His death *always*, i.e. at all times.

§87 *"And descending to the nether regions of death:"*

Nether means the place is lower. This refers to the tomb in which the divine body was laid which He assumed from Mary, as it says:

§88 *"And descended to the nether regions of death in the body which He assumed out of kinship with us."*

It calls Mary the holy Mother of God His *kin* and as He *descended* to the grave in a body like other bodies, so also in the spirit He went to the spirits of the other dead and granted resurrection to many saints and dissolved the power of death.

Hence it continues:

§89 *"And mightily breaking asunder the bolts of hell, He demonstrated conclusively that He[1] is God of the living and the dead"*

so that as the souls shut up in detention might return to their bodies, so the bodies would experience resurrection. Under threat of death if he ate of the fruit, Adam violated the commandment and was given over to death and sin along with his offspring. Since no human could pay the debt owed death by not sinning, the Son of God who owed sin nothing became the son of Adam and died in place of us sinners and debtors. Then He wielded His authority over death, trampling down its gates and releasing its captives. He could have achieved this without giving Himself over to death, as when He raised Lazarus, but He did not wish to save merely by authority, but rather by justice, as one of the prophets said, "His captivity will be delivered by justice and mercy (cf. Hos 2:19). "By mercy because He became man and died for us and by justice, in that the death of the sinless one might restore sinners' right to life. The image of the prison gates being trampled down is employed to signify that when the doors in a prison are smashed

169

յարութեանն լինիցի, Քրիստոսի գմաճ լուծանելով։ եւ յաւմ ամենայնէ ծանուցաւ Հաւատեալ, այսինքն ստուգութեամբ, թէ որ մեռաւն՝ Աստուած է կենդանեաց եւ մեռելոց. որպէս եւ ասէ առաքեալ. Քրիստոս մեռաւ եւ եկեաց, զի մեռելոց եւ կենդանեաց տիրեսցէ։

§90 «Եւ արդ մեք, Տէր, ըստ դորին հրամանատուութեան յառաջ բերեալ զայս խորհուրդ փրկական մարմնոյ եւ արեան միածնիդ քոյ»։

վասն զի հրամայեաց ասէ դա՝ գոր ինքն արաբ զնոյն եւ մեզ առնել. այն է գոր ասեմք՝ թէ ըստ դորին հրամանատարութեան յառաջ բերեմք. յառաջ բերելն՝ դնելն է 'ի սեղանն զշագն եւ զբաժակն, որ խորիւրդ է մարմնոյ եւ արեան որդւոյն Աստուծոյ. այս է խորհուրդն՝ զի ոչ ըստ տեսանելոյն այլ իմանալոյն է Հաւատալն. զի տեսանի Հաց եւ գինի, եւ իմանի մարմին եւ արիւն որդւոյն Աստուծոյ. եւ փրկական կոչի, վասն զի փրկեցաւ նովաւ եւ փրկիմք, 'ի կեալ եւ 'ի մեռանել։

§91 «Յիշեմք զդորին որ վասն մեր՝ գփրկութիւնագործ գչարչարանսն»։

Արդ յասեն՝ թէ յիշեմք որ վասն մեր չարչարեցաւ դա, գմաւ ածցուք՝ զի կապեցաւ որդին Աստուծոյ վասն 'ի կապանաց մեղաց զմեզ արձակելոյ. դատապարտեցաւ 'ի պղծոց, զի գմեզ անդատապարտս արասցէ 'ի դատեն գերկիր. Թուք ընկալաւ յաստուածային դէմսն եւ ապտակ 'ի ծնոտսն, զի նորոգեսցէ զպատկերսն իւր գապականեալս 'ի մէնջ. կրունկս յանարատ 'ի գլուխն ընկալաւ ծածկութիւ, զի բարձցէ յոցլոց մերոց գառասաստն խաւարի, եւ զագզի ազգի չարչարանս ախտից. կատակեցաւ 'ի գինուորացն ծիրանեաւ, փշեայ պսակաւն, եղեգամբն, ընդ խաղ երկրպագութեամբն, զի գմեզ Թագաւրեցուցց ճշմարտապէս եւ աստուածացուցց, չնորՀեսցէ մեզ Հանդերձ փառաց, Թագ արքայութեան, գաւազան զորութեան. անարգեցաւ 'ի Հերովդէէ, մօրակեցաւ 'ի Պիղատոսէ, զի պատուլականս գմեզ արասցէ, եւ գանցաւորութիւն կենացն յաւիտենականաց մեզ պատրաստեսցէ:

170

and its bars splintered (or *broken asunder* as it puts it) and one has forced open the fetters with their securely fastened shackles, there is nothing further to obstruct the detainees' escape. On the same analogy, there can be no obstruction to our resurrection since Christ has annulled death. And from all this it emerges convincingly i.e. with certainty that the one who died is God of the living and the dead. As the apostle says: "Christ died and came to life again to rule over the dead and the living" (Rom 14:9).

§90 *"Now therefore, O Lord, according to His command, we offer this saving mystery of the body and blood of Your only-begotten Son:"*

It says He told us to do the same as He did. That is what is meant by *according to His command we offer. Offering* refers to placing on the altar the bread and cup which is the *mystery of the body and blood of* the *Son* of God. It is a *mystery* for the bread and wine are seen, but *the body and blood of the son* of God are perceived. And the *mystery* is called *saving* because we were saved and continue to be saved by it in life and death.

§91 *"We commemorate His salvific suffering on our behalf:"*

As we say *we commemorate* that He *suffered on our behalf,* let us ponder that the Son of God was bound in order to free us from the bonds of sin. He was condemned by reprobates to cancel our condemnation when He judges the earth. He endured spittle on His divine face and a blow to His cheeks to renew His image in us which we had defaced. Blindfolded, He tolerated buffets on His stainless head to withdraw the mantle of darkness from our souls and similarly underwent the various other vicious torments. He was made a laughingstock by the soldiers who dressed Him in purple, with a crown of thorns and a cane, making mockery of vener-

§92 «Չկենդանարար խաչելութիւնն»:

Վասն զի մեռեալ էաք ՚ի մեղս, մեռաւ ՚ի խաչին եւ կենդանացոյց զմեռելութիւնս մեր. վասն որոյ եւ կենդանարար
կոչեմք զելումն նորա ՚ի խաչն:

§93 «Զերեքօրեայ զանապական գթադումն».

զի ըստ մարգարէին՝ ոչ թողաւ ոգի նորա ՚ի դժոխս եւ ոչ
մարմին նորա ետես ցապականութիւն, այլ եւ զմեր հոգիս եւան
՚ի դժոխաց, եւ զմարմինս փրկեաց յապականութենէ:

§94 «Զերանելի գյարութիւնն».

երանելի ասէ ՚ի գրոց ամենայն բարեաւ բովանդակեալն. որ է
երանելի ամենայնիւ, որպէս նոյն ինքն Աստուած, որ ոչ միայն
երանելի է այլ եւ ամենայն երանութեանց տուօղ. զի մարդ եւ
մարմին գոլով՝ Աստուած ճշմարտապէս ցուցաւ յարութեամբն:

§95 «Զաստուածապէս համբարձումն·

զի չհողեղէն բնութիւնս յաստուածական աթոռն վերացոյց, եւ
զմեզ ընդ իւր յարոյց եւ նատոյց յերկնաւորսն:

§96 «Զահաւոր եւ զփառաւորեալ զմիսանգամ գալուստն»:

Ահաւոր է արդարեւ եւ աճագին եւ փառաւորեալ եւ սոսկալի
գալուստն այն. զի փառօք Հօր գայցէ եւ ամենայն հրեշտակօք,
եւ ՚ի դատաստան ժողովեսցէ զամենայն բնութիւնս մարդկան.
եւ հատուսցէ ըստ իւրանքանչիւր գործոց, փառս անպատումս
արդարոցն չնորհելով մշտնջենաւորապէս, եւ խոշտանգանս դա-
ռինս յաւիտենականս՝ մեղաւորացն:

Արդ աստէք թէ յիշեմք զայս ամենայն եւ գոհանամք. նուէր
այսպիսի եւ ընծայ բարեաց փոխադարձեալ զգատարագս
սուրբ. եւ սովաւ աղաչեմք ապրիլ ՚ի հանդերձեալ դատաս-
տանացն: Վասն որոյ եւ Համաձայնեն առաջի կացեալքն, թէ

172

ation to make us truly kings and divine, granting us a glorious robe, royal crown and sceptre of office. He was dishonored by Herod and scourged by Pilate to endow us with honor and prepare a path for us to life eternal.

§92 *"His life-giving crucifixion:"*

Since we were dead in sin, He died on the cross and revivified our mortality. That is why we call *His crucifixion life-giving.*

§93 *"His incorrupt burial for three days:"*

According to the prophet, His spirit was not left in hell and His body did not see corruption (cf. Ps 16[15]:10). Furthermore, He snatched our souls from hell and preserved our bodies from corruption.

§94 *"His blessed resurrection:"*

Scripture calls *blessed* everything that contains good. He is fully *blessed* as God Himself who is not only *blessed,* but bestower of all blessings. For being man and flesh, He was revealed to be truly God by the *resurrection.*

§95 *"His divine ascension:[1]"*

He exalted our earthly nature to the divine throne and raised us with Him and seated us among the heavenly host.

§96 *"His awesome and glorious second coming:"*

That *coming* is certainly *awesome,* awe-inspiring, glorious and terrible; for He will come with His Father's glory and all the angels and will summon all the human race to judgement and reward, each according to His deeds, granting ineffable glory to the righteous for ever and severe eternal torments to sinners.

We say then that we commemorate all this and give thanks, rendering the holy sacrifice as a token and offering in return for these. Thereby we implore to be saved from the impending judgement. Therefore, those at the altar chant together:

§97 «Յամենայնի գովեմք զքեզ».

այսինքն թէ ընդ ամենայնի գովեմք զքեզ։

§98 «Օրհնեմք զքեզ, գոհանամք զքէն, աղաչեմք զքեզ, Տէր Աստուած մեր»:

Զայս բանս զոր երդով ասէ ժողովուրդն՝ կրկնէ քահանայն, եւ ցուցանէ զմիտսն, այսպէս ասելով:

§99 «Զքեզ արդարեւ Տէր Աստուած մեր գովեմք, եւ զքէն գոհանամք, որ զօրհանապազ զանց արարեր զմեղրովք չարագործութեամբք»:

Գովեմք, *ասէ, զքո քաղցր եւ զանխաբել եւ զբազմագեղ եւ զբազմազուրդ ներողութիւնդ, եւ զոհանամք զառատապարգեւ բարերարութեանցդ քոց. զի մեք հանապազ յանցանեմք խորհրդովք, բանիւք եւ գործովք, եւ դու ոչ հայելով յայն՝ վրէժս հատուցանես, այլ զանց առնես, որպէս թէ ոչ տեսանելով՝ այնպէս ներես. եւ ոչ միայն գյանցանօքն եւ զչարն գործովքն զանց առնես, այլ եւ խնամս եւ ողորմութիւնս ցուցանես. եւ ոչ 'ի մարմին միայն այլ եւ յոգի. ոչ փոքումբք՝ այլ եւ մեծամեծօք. զոր եւ ցուցանէ յաջորդաւս*.

§100 «Որ այսպիսի ահաւոր եւ անպատում խորհրդոյ կարգեցեր սպասաւորս».

անպատում ասի սուրբ խորհուրդն, վասն զի բան չկարէ որպէս էն յայտնել. եւ ահաւոր է՝ ոչ միայն մարդկան այլ եւ հրեշ- տակաց:

§101 «Ոչ յաղագս մերոց ինչ բարեգործութեանց՝ յորոց յոյժ թափուր միշտ եւ ունայն գտանիմք հանապազ, այլ 'ի քո բազմազեղ ներողութիւնդ ցանկ ապաւինեալ՝ համարձակիմք մերձենալ 'ի սպասաւորութիւն մարմնոյ եւ արեան միածնի քոյ»:

Եւ վասն զի ահաւոր է՝ եւ մեք սպասաւորել համարձակիմք[22], ոչ զի բարիս ինչ գործեցաք՝ վատահանամք, այլ 'ի բազում եւ 'ի լցեալ եւ 'ի զեղեալ բարերարութիւնդ ցանկ ապաւինեալ. այսինքն հանապազ համարձակիմք մերձենալ 'ի սպասաւորու- թիւն մարմնոյ եւ արեան միածնիդ քոյ:

174

§97 *"In everything we praise You:"*
i.e. *we praise You* for *everything.*

§98 *"We bless You, we give You thanks, we implore You, O Lord our God:"*

This text which the people sings, the priest repeats and develops the thought as follows:

§99 *"We praise You as truly the Lord our God and we give You thanks for overlooking our wrongdoings every day:"*

It means *we praise* Your sweet, ungrudging, abundant and merciful forgiveness and *we give thanks* for Your generous benefits; for we continually transgress in thought, word and deed, but You do not inspect them and take vengeance, but overlook them and forgive them as if You had not noticed them. And not only do You pass over our transgressions and wicked actions, but exhibit care and compassion, not only to the body, but also the soul, not in small ways but in major, as indicated in the continuation:

§100 *"You appointed ministers for such an awesome and ineffable mystery:"*

The holy *mystery* is called *ineffable* because speech cannot express it in its reality and it is *awesome* not only to man but also to the angels.

§101 *"Not on account of any good works of ours of which we are always found utterly deficient and constantly empty, but continually taking refuge in Your abundant forgiveness, we dare to approach the ministry of the body and blood of Your only-begotten Son:"*

Because it is *awesome,* we also *dare to minister.* We do not trust in any good we have done, but *take refuge in Your* great, ample and *abundant* beneficence and thus constantly *dare to approach the ministry of the body and blood of Your only-begotten Son.*

Եւ ընդէ՞ր հանապազ 'ի սպասաւորութիւն խորիրդոյն առ. վասն զի կատարել զխորհիւրդն չէ մեր, այլ որպէս Յովհան երանելին ասէ, մեք սպասաւորաց ատինան ունիմք. եւ սբբէ եւ վերստին կազմէ նա. գՔրիստոսէ ասէ. քանզի մեք հանեմք 'ի սեղանն եւ 'ի սպասու կամք, գոհանալով զբարեբարութեանցն Աստուծոյ. իսկ միացուցանել ընդ ինքեան զշացն եւ կենատու առնել՝ Քրիստոսի է գործ:

§102 «Խաղաղութիւն ամենեցուն. Աստուծոյ երկրպա- գեսցուք»:

Ապա ասէ քահանայն:

§103 «Երկիր պագանեմք եւ աղաչեմք եւ խնդրեմք 'ի քէն, Տէր, առաքեա 'ի մեզ եւ յառաջի եղեալ յլնծայս յայս՝ գՇֆտնՇշեՇաւորակից քո եւ զեակից սուրբ Հոգիդ»:

Երկիր պագանեմք եւ աղաչեմք եւ խնդրեմք 'ի քէն, Տէր. վասն է՞ր ասէ 'ի քէն, այսինքն թէ 'ի քէն խնդրեմք երկրպագու- թեամբ՝ եւ աղաչեմք, որ աբարիէղ եւ Հայր, որ յափ- տեանցն մարդասէր եւ բաբերար եւ գթած մարդկութեանս եղեր, որ ոչ միայն գաբաբածս 'ի պետս մեր հաստատեցեր, այլ եւ զքո մի եւ սիրելի որդիդ՝ եւոււր մեզ փրկանք եւ փոխանակ. եւ զնոյն ինքդ 'ի սեղան դնես եւ կերակրես գմեզ դովիմք. վասն որոյ ապաւինեալ յանբաւ քո բաբերարութիւնդ՝ գշոգիդ սուրբ առաքել խնդրեմք՝ 'ի մեզ եւ 'ի պատարագս, զի եւ զմեզ Հոգիդ սուրբ սբբեսցէ:

§104 «Որոյ զհացս օրհնեալ՝ մարմին ստուգապես արաս- ցէ Տեառն մերոյ եւ փրկչին Յիսուսի Քրիստոսի. եւ զբաժակս օրհնեալ՝ արիւն ստուգապես արասցէ Տեառնն մերոյ եւ փրկչին Յիսուսի Քրիստոսի»:

Զի մարմնացաւ փրկիչն 'ի Մարիամայ կուսէն. Հոգին սուրբ առաքեալ 'ի Հօրէ՝ առ մարմին 'ի յարգանդէն Մարիամայ, եւ խառնեաց եւ միացոյց 'ի Բանն Աստուած, որ եւ մի որդի եւ Աստուած ծնեալ 'ի նմանէ յայոնեցաւ. զնոյն եւ յեկեղեցւոջ եւ 'ի սուրբ սեղանն գործէ Հոգին սուրբ. առեալ զշացն միա- ցուցանէ յորդին Աստուծոյ, նոյնպէս եւ զբաժակն, եւ լինի մարմին եւ արիւն Քրիստոսի անշարտապես:

176

Why does it say *continually* at the *ministry of the* mystery? Because it is not for us to perform the mystery, but, as the blessed Yovhannēs says, "We possess the rank of *minister*, while He [sc. Christ] purifies and recreates."[1] For we present it on the altar and stand in service, rendering thanks for God's bounties. It is Christ's work to unite the bread with Himself and render it life-giving.

§102 *"Peace to all. Let us bow before God."*[1]

Then the priest says:

§103 *"We bow before You, ask and beseech of You, Lord, send upon us and the gifts set forth here Your eternal, consubstantial Holy Spirit:"*

We bow before You, ask and beseech You, Lord: Why does it say *of You? We ask of You* in worship and implore You as creator and father, who from everlasting have been lover of man, beneficent and merciful to us men, who not only established creation for our needs, but gave us Your one and only-beloved Son as a ransom and a substitute. And You lay Him upon the table and feed us with Him. Therefore, taking refuge in Your boundless beneficence, *we beseech You to send the Holy Spirit upon us and upon* the sacrifice, that the *Holy Spirit* sanctify us also.

§104 *"To bless this bread and make it truly the body of our Lord and Savior Jesus Christ and bless this cup and make it truly the blood of our Lord and Savior Jesus Christ"*[1]

For *the Savior* became incarnate of the Virgin Mary. The Holy Spirit sent by the Father took flesh from Mary's womb and mingled[2] and united it to God the Word who was revealed as one Son and God, born from her. The Holy Spirit acts in the same way in church at the holy altar. Taking the bread He unites it to the Son of God and likewise the cup to become *truly Christ's* body

177

Զորչն գայս հայցեմք եւ հաւատամք լինել, զի անսուտ է
բանն Քրիստոսի. որ ասաց մինչեւ ՚ի գալուստն իւր առնել յիշ
յիշատակ գայս սկզբնաւորեալ յեւրմէ։ Այլ զի ասեմք զՀոգին
սուրբ մշանջենաւորակից եւ յաւիգ, խոստովանիմք միշտ առ
Հոր եւ ընդ Հոր։ Որպէս Հայր՝ էր եւ է եւ միշտ է, եւ չիք
ժամանակ զի չէր, նոյնպէս եւ Հոգին սուրբ միշտ ընդ Հոր եւ
ընդ Որդւոյ էր եւ է մշանջենաւոր եւ յաւ. որ եւ զայսպիսի
մեծամեծ հրաշագործէ. զլով Հացն եւ զգինին՝ յանապա-
կանութիւն մարմնոյ եւ արեան որդւոյն Աստուծոյ փոխելով։

§105 «Որպէս զի եղիցի սա մերձեցելոցս՝ յանդատապար-
տութիւն, ՚ի քաւութիւն եւ ՚ի թողութիւն մեղաց»։
Հաւատով Հայցեալ գտջա Հոգւոյն սրբոյ ՚ի սուրբ պատարագն,
ըստ տեբունեան բանին, կենդանարար մարմին եւ արին խոստովանիմք, եւ աներկբայ սրտիւք սկանիմք ՚ի խնդրուածն.
զորդին Աստուծոյ ՚ի վերայ սրբոյ սեղանոյն՝ աներկբայ եւ
աներկիւան մտոք գիտացեալ, զմեռելութիւնն իւր՝ որ վասն
մեր՝ ականատես մեզ առնելով. քանզի այսուհետեւ այն մարմինն լինէ՝ որ ՚ի խաչին եւ ՚ի գերեզմանին։ Որով եւ զկեն-
դանեաց եւ զմեռելոց Հայցեմք զիրկութիւն. նախ առաջին
գայս խնդրելով, զի անդատարակարտ մնացեմք սպասաւորելով
աչաւրացն. եւ զի ՚ի թողութիւն մեղաց լիցի մեզ մերձեցումն
՚ի նա. վասն այնր ասէ, թէ մեծեցելոցս. զի անարժանիցն եւ
կայն մերձ եւ Հաղորդին՝ դատաստան է. եւ յաղագս այնորիկ
արտաքս ելանէն անպատրաստն, զի մի՝ դատապարտեցին՝
աղտեղի հոգւով յատուծայինն մօտելով յառագաստ։ Եւ
քանզի անբիծ ոչ ոք գտանի՝ ադաշեմք զի թողցին յանցանքն
մեր՝ գիտութեան եւ անգիտութեան, Քրիստոսի պատարա-
գելով։ Չի որք խիղճ զանձանց գիտեն, եւ ոչ էին խոստովանութեամբ եւ ապաշխարութեամբ սրբեալ՝ զնոսա առաջին քարոզն տրոչեաց. իսկ որ չար խղճիւ ոչ էին եւ կամ ապաշխարեալ ըստ գրոց, եւ ՚ի ներքս մնացին, եւ նոքա յանին եւ ՚ի
դողման պարտին լինել. վասն զի Հանապազ ընդ սխալանօք
ըմբռնիմք, խորհրդով, բանիւք, գործով, կամաւ եւ ակամայ,
գիտութեամբ եւ անգիտութեամբ. եւ յաղագս այսորիկ պաղա-

178

blood.

This is what we pray for, believing it takes place, since Christ's word is not false when He told us to perform this following His institution as a memorial of Him until His coming. But by saying the Holy Spirit is co-eternal and consubstantial we confess that He is always beside the Father and with the Father. As the Father was and is and always will be and there was no time when He was not, similarly the Holy Spirit was always with the Father and the Son and subsists for ever. He also effects such prodigious miracles, transforming the mere bread and wine into the incorruption of the body and blood of the Son of God.

§105 *"To be to us who have approached for acquittal from judgement, atonement and remission of sins:"*

Beseeching in faith the descent of the Holy Spirit upon the holy sacrifice according to the word of the Lord, we confess the life-creating body and blood and with trusting hearts we begin our intercessions. With undoubting and unfearing minds we acknowledge the Son of God on the holy altar, making visible to us His mortality for our sake, so that hereafter it may become the body which hung on the cross and lay in the tomb. Hereby we beseech salvation for the living and the dead, first asking to be spared condemnation for administering the awesome gifts and to approach them for the remission of sins. That is why it says *to us who approach*, since for the unworthy it is judgement to come close and communicate.

That is why the unprepared go out, so as not to be condemned for entering the divine bridal chamber with impure spirit. And since no one is without stain, we implore the remission of our transgressions committed in knowledge and ignorance, through Christ's sacrifice. The deacon's first proclamation debarred those who were aware their conscience testified against them and had

տանս Հառաչանօք եւ չերմեռանդն արտասուօք մատուցանելի է, զի մաքրեսցին յամենայնէ՝ եւ սուրբք 'ի մաքուրն տերձեսցին:

§106 «Սովաւ շնորհեա գեր, գիաստատութիւն եւ զղղձալի գիսագոութիւն եկեղեցւոյ քում սրբոյ»:

Սովաւն՝ զպատարագէն աս. շնորհել աս եւ ոչ՛ տալ. զի մի՛ որպէս թէ Հատուցումն ընդ բարւոյ իրիք Հատուցանել ասիցեմք, այլ բարեբարութեան պարգեւ ձրի: Սէր Հայցեմք լինել եկեղեցւոյ, այսինքն Հաւատացեալ ժողովրդոյ՝ առ Աստուած եւ առ միմեանս. եւ հաստատութիւն 'ի Հաւատս եւ 'ի բարի գործս, եւ խաղաղութիւն յարտաքին թշնամեաց, եւ անսասանելի մնալ յամբարշտաց եւ 'ի Հերձուածողաց. եւ փափաքելի եւ ցանկալի խաղաղութիւն ամենայնիւ ունել, զոր եւ ըղձալի ասաց: Ցարէ 'ի նոյն վասն ամենեցունց Հայցել առանձնակ ըստ կարգի, այսպէս ասելով:

§107 «Եւ ամենայն ուղղափառ եպիսկոպոսաց»,

թէ որք ուղիղ են Հաւատով:

§108 «Քահանայից, քագաւորաց, իշխանաց, ժողովրդոց, նանապարհորդելոց եւ որք 'ի պատերազմունս բարբարոսաց».

ամենեցուն՝ Քրիստոսի պատարագաւն օգորմութիւն Հայցելով: Վռանգաւորք են՝ որք յինչ եւ իցէ նեղութիւնս, եւ 'ի պատերազմունս բարբարոսաց են, որք ընդ այլագդիս եւ այդ այլ անՀաւատս մարդ եղեալ կռուին, պարապել յանդորրութեան գեկեղեցի Քրիստոսի:

§109 «Սովաւ եւ օդոց շնորհեա բարեխառնութիւն, եւ պտղոց առատութիւն, եւ ախտացելոց 'ի պէսպէս ցաւոց՝ փութապէս առողջութիւն»:

Բարեխառն օդ այն են՝ որ ոչ վնասեն բուսոց եւ տնկոց, այլ բարիոք սնուցանեն, եւ պտղաբերս առնեն: Ախտացելոց 'ի պէս-պէս ցաւս, աս գշիւանդացեալս յայլ եւ այլ գունակ ցաւոց, փութով առողջութիւն գտանել Հայցելով, թէ մարմնով եւ թէ Հոգւով, թէ մտօք վռանգեալ ոք իցէ:

180

not been purified by confession and repentance. But those who did not have a bad conscience or had repented according to the scriptures and remained inside should also stand in fear and trembling; for we continually detect ourselves off guard in errors of thought, word and deed, voluntary and involuntary, in knowledge and in ignorance. Therefore this supplication should be offered with sighs and fervent tears to be cleansed from everything and draw near pure and clean.[1]

§106 *"Hereby grant Your holy Church love, stability and desirable peace:"*

Hereby means through the sacrifice. It says *grant* and not give since it is not as if we were seeking recompense for some obligement we had done, but rather a free gift of charity. We implore *love* for *the Church*[1] i.e. the faithful peoples both towards God and one another and *stability* in faith and good works and *peace* from external enemies and to remain unshaken from the impious and schismatics, to enjoy to the full coveted *peace* (which is called *desirable* in the text). The continuation offers supplication for all individually in order:

§107 *"And for all orthodox bishops,"*
i.e. those upright in faith.

§108 *"For priests, kings, princes, peoples, travellers[1] and those involved in war with barbarians:"*

Imploring mercy on all through Christ's sacrifice. Those in any kind of trouble are endangered and *those* at *war with barbarians* refers to those who engage in conflict with Muslims and other infidels to preserve Christ's church in tranquility.

§109 *"Hereby grant also temperate weather and abundance of fruit and swift recovery of those suffering from various ailments."*

Temperate weather is that which does not harm plants and

§110 «Սովաւ հանզր զամենեսեան գյառաջագոյն ՚ի Քրիստոս զննջեցեալսն».

Թէ որ յԱդամայ հետէ հաւատով աննջեցեալք են ՚ի Քրիստոս, վասն զի ոչ զկնի գալստեանն միայն՝ այլ եւ յառաջ քան զգալուստն Քրիստոսի հաւատացեալքն յԱստուած՝ ՚ի Քրիստոս աննջեցին. զի նա էր ՚ի սկզբանէ առ Աստուած, եւ Աստուած էր. սուրբքն նախածանօթք իսկ նորա էին. որպէս եւ աստ իսկ եբանելին Գրիգոր աստուածաբան՝ վասն կատարելոցն. իսկ անկատարքն Աստուած դալանելով զոր ՚ի մարգարէիցն եւ յարդարոցն քարոզիւր, սուրբ Երրորդութեանն զերկրպագութիւնն մատուցանէին, թէ եւ առանձնաւորութեանցն անծանօթ հանդիպէին. վասն որոյ եւ նոքա իսկ ՚ի Քրիստոս աննջեցեալք ասին: Յաղագս որոյ ասելով, թէ հանզր զննջեցեալսն ՚ի Քրիստոս, ոչ միայն զորս ՚ի նորումս թուէ՝ այլ աստ զսուրբք հարսն՝ որք յԱդամայ մինչեւ ցնկբրաճամ, եւ որք ՚ի նմանէ:

§111 «Զմարգարէս, զառաքեալս, զվկայեալս, զեպիսկոպոսուս, զերիցունս, զսարկաւագունս, եւ զքնաւ ուխտ եկեղեցւոյ ֆում սրբոյ»:

Այս է, կես սարկաւագքն, զպիրքն, զրրակարդագքն, սամոսեղքն. բնաւ ասեն զրրովանդակն ցուցանէ՝ որ ՚ի կարգի եկեղեցւոյ, ուխտ ասելով եկեղեցւոյ. զի ամենեքին նուիրեալ են ՚ի սպասաւորութիւն եւ ՚ի կարգաւորութիւն եկեղեցւոյ սրբոյ:

§112 «Եւ յաշխարհական կարգէ զարս եւ զկանայս հաւատացեալս ՚ի քեզ»:

Աստանօր զհամօրէն զաշխարհականաց հաւատացելոց՝ որք ՚ի հնումն եւ որք ՚ի նորումս հաւատով վախճանեցան՝ յիշատակէ. զի որպէս զարբրոցն զաղօթս եւ զբարեխօսութիւն մեզ կոչեմք յօդնականութիւն, նոյնպէս եւ մեք պարտիմք առաջնոց աննջեցելոցն օգնել աղօթիւք, մանաւանդ սուրբ պատարագաւն, որ յոյս եւ կենդանութիւն եւ փրկութիւն է աննջեցելոց: Զի զմեր աննջեցեալսն եւ զգերելիան եւ զգանօթան մեր՝ յանուանէ յիշել ունիմք, թէ թերանով եւ թէ մտօք. իսկ զայլսն հայցեմք յիշել Աստուծոյ՝ որ զամենայն գիտէ, եւ կարզ ըստ կարգի յիշելով զսուրբան, եւ ընդ նոսա զամենայն հաւատացեալս ՚ի միմեանս

182

trees, but richly nourishes them and makes them fecund. *Suffering from various ailments* means those sick with different kinds of *ailments*, beseeching that they find a speedy recovery, whether afflicted in body, soul or mind.

§110 *"Hereby give repose to all those who have previously fallen asleep in Christ:"*

Those with faith from Adam on *have fallen asleep in Christ,* since not only those after Christ's coming but also those who trusted in God before it *fell asleep in Christ.* From the beginning He was with God and God (John 1:1). The saints were prescient of Him, as the blessed Gregory the Theologian says concerning the perfect. The imperfect confessed God as He was proclaimed by the prophets and righteous, offering worship to the Holy Trinity although unaware of the distinction of persons. Therefore, they too are said to have *fallen asleep in Christ.* And so the petition *Give repose to those who have fallen asleep in Christ* not only enumerates those of the new dispensation, but includes the holy fathers from Adam to Abraham and those descended from him.

§111 *"Prophets,*[1] *apostles, martyrs, bishops, priests, deacons and the whole covenant*[2] *of Your holy Church:"*

The latter embraces sub-deacons, clerks, readers and psalmodists. The term *the whole* means all and *covenant of the Church* means those in ecclesiastical orders.

§112 *"And men and women who believe in you:"*

This comprises all lay believers, who have died in faith under the old and new dispensations. As we invoke the prayers and intercessions of the saints to assist us, likewise we should help those who have fallen asleep before us by our prayers, but especially through the holy liturgy which is hope, life and salvation to those who have fallen asleep. We ought to commemorate by name those

յարելով՝ իբրև զմի մարմին Քրիստոսի՝ հասարակաց գլխովն
Քրիստոսի պատարագաւն, յիշատակելով առաջի Աստուծոյ Հօր,
յայս գրանն աւարտեմք։

§113 «Ընդ որս եւ մեզ այզ արասցես, բարերար եւ
մարդասէր Տէր»։
Թէ ընդ նոսա ամենեսին՝ գորս յիշատակեցաք՝ եւ մեզ այցե-
լութիւն արասցու․ այսինքն թէ ընդիր արա, եւ խնամածու
ընդ քոյան եւ մեզ լիցիս։ Զառ յա գայս գոր յիշատակէ քահանայն՝
սարկաւագն դարձեալ յիշատակէ բարձր ձայնիւ, ուրոյն ուրոյն
տունս գատուցեալ․ եւ ըստ իւրաքանչիւր տան՝ ժողովուրդն որ
'ի խորՀրդին՝ ասեն ձայնիւ․ «Յիշեա Տէր եւ ողորմեա»։ Որ
բուն քարոզն է բազում տունս ունի․ նախ վասն Աստուածածնին,
եւ ապա ուրոյն ուրոյն սրբոցն ըստ կարգի, նախահարցն,
մարգարէիցն, առաքելոցն, եպիսկոպոսաց, մարտիրոսաց, քահանայից, սարկաւագաց, կանանց ընտրելոց, կանանց մարտիրոսաց,
թագաւորաց սրբոց, իշխանաց սրբոց, վարդապետաց սրբոց,
Հարց առաքինեաց եւ մարտիրոսաց, առաջնորդաց, եւ ամենայն
ճգնաւորաց, եւ որ այլ ինչ օրինական Հաճոյացեալ են Աստուծոյ. զի ըստ իւրաքանչիւրոցն է յանուանէ գոմանս յիշեալ
յամենայն գունակէ, եւ գՀամօրէն կարգակցիսն 'ի նոյն յարեւ.
գորս 'ի տոսա գատկաց ասէն՝ որք բարեկարգութեան Հոգ
տանին։ Իսկ գոր Համառօտիւք Հարկ է ասէլ 'ի ժամ սուրբ
պատարագին՝ է այս։

§114 «Աստուածածնին կուսին Մարիամու, Յովհաննու
Մկրտչին, սրբոյն Ստեփանոս, յիշատակ եղիցի։ Առա-
քելոց սրբոց, մարգարէից, մարտիրոսաց, Պետրոսի Պօղոսի, եւ ամենայն սրբոցն, յիշատակ եղիցի։ Հայրա-
պետաց սրբոց, երանելւոյն սրբոյն Գրիգորի եւ ամենայն սուրբ եւ ուղղափառ եպիսկոպոսաց եւ քահանայից, եւ բոլոր ուխտի եկեղեցւոյ յիշատակ եղիցի։
Եղիցի յիշատակ արանց եւ կանանց հաւատով 'ի Քրիստոս ննջեցելոցն»։
Այլ թէ որպիսի մտօք յիշատակէս այս են՝ ըստ իմում տկար
Հատողութեանս քանացայց ցուցանել։ Բազում եւ ազգի ազգի

184

of our own family, as well as our friends and acquaintances, both verbally and silently, while beseeching omniscient God to commemorate the others. The way to fulfill this is by remembering the saints, class by class, and uniting with them all believers as the one body of Christ, commemorating them before God the Father through the sacrifice of Christ, the head of all.

§113 *"With them visit us also, beneficent Lord who love mankind:"*

i.e. with all those whom we have commemorated. *Visit us also* means tend and watch over us along with Your own. Everything the priest commemorates the deacon commemorates again aloud, dividing the text into separate phrases which the congregation at the mystery punctuate by the response aloud *Remember, Lord, and have mercy*. The Litany itself contains several petitions. First concerning the Mother of God and then different saints in order, the patriarchs, prophets, apostles, bishops, martyrs, priests, deacons, chosen women, women martyrs, saintly kings, saintly princes, holy vardapets, virtuous fathers and martyrs, abbots and all ascetics and those who in any other way were pleasing to God. For in each case one should commemorate several by name from each category and unite all those in the same order together. Those concerned about good order follow this practice at the feast of Easter, but those which it is necessary to mention briefly during the holy liturgy are the following:[1]

§114 *"The Mother of God, Virgin Mary, John the Baptist, St. Stephen. Let there be commemoration of the Holy Apostles, prophets, martyrs, Peter, Paul and all the saints. Let there be commemoration of the holy patriarchs, blessed St. Gregory and all the holy orthodox bishops and priests and all the clergy of the church. Let there be commemoration of men and women of faith who have fallen asleep in*

երախտեացն Աստուծոյ, առաք ՛ Աստուծոյ չնորչ՛ փոխադարձել նմա գալրբ պատարագին Քրիստոսի ընծայումն. որով եւ զամենայն զարարեալ բարերարութիւնն Աստուծոյ յիշելով՛ վասն ամենայնի գոհացողք լինիմք: Եւ ՛ի վերայ ամենայնի վասն ընտրելոցն ՛ի նմանէ գոհանամք սուրբ խորՀրդովն. վասն զի ամենեքեան մի եմք ՛ի Քրիստոս, եւ փառաւորութիւն եղբարցն՛ մեզ է փառ. զմեծ նուէրն յիշատակ գոհութեան նոցա առնեմք, որ այսպիսի լաւ եւ պիտանիս գնաց արար, եւ յաղօթս առ ամենայն մարտս բանաքկուՆ: Եւ ոչ միայն վասն սրբոգն գոհանամք, այլ եւ վասն ամենայն ՛Աստուած Հալատացելոգ արժանացելոգն. քանզի որպէս ասացն Սողոմն, թէ ճանաչելն գԱստուած բուվանդակ արդարութին է. եւ լինել նորա ժողովուրդ եւ սուրբ աւագանին ծնունդ, եւ սուրբ Հաղորդութեանն ընդունող, եւ սուրբ անուամբն Քրիստոսի գչրաժարումն առնուլ՛ պարդեւ մեծ է: Եւ յայտոսիկ ամենեգուն եւ սոլնպիսեաց պարգեւառուագն գոհութին՛ աւարտի սրբով պատարագաւն: Որով ոչ միայն գոհացողութիւն նոլաւ Աստուծոյ մատուցանեմք ընտ իւրաքանչիւրոգն՛ այլ եւ մաղթանս, յիշելով գսրբոգն գնաճատակութիւնս եւ գառաքինի վարս. գոհանամք սուրբ խորՀրդովն, եւ ադաեմք գՔրիստոսի մաՀն՛ որ վասն մեր, եւ գսրբոգն գնգնութիւնս բարեխոս առ երկնաւոր Հայրն ունելով՛ յաղագս ամենայն Հալատացելոգ, կենդանեաց եւ ննջեգելոգ. քանզի որպէս մեզ բերկրեալգ ընդ սուրբսն՛ Աստուծոյ ընդայ եւ գոհութիւնս մատուցանեմք՛ մեզ գնոգայն համարեալ պաալումն[23], նոյնպէս եւ նոքա որպէս իւրեանգ անդամող խնամակալուք լինին բարեխոսութեամբ առ Տէր, մանաւանդ ՛ի ժամ ստկալի պատարագին: Եւ մեք գոհանալով նոքօք ընտ իւրաքանչիւր տանգ ասեմք,

§115 Յիշեա Տէր եւ ողորմեա.

այսինքն թէ յիշեա գոր սրբոգն առ քեզ սէր եւ վատակ եւ ողորմեա մեզ, գի մեր ՛ ունկա, եւ ՛ի մէնջ են. եւ միոյ եկեղեցլոյ ամենեքին մեք, եւ միոյ Քրիստոսի որ գլուխն է մեր՛ բոլորեթեան մարմին եւ անդամք եմք, վասն որոյ եւ յիշատակօք սրբոգն դարձեալ սկիզբն առնեմք մաղթել ողորմութիւն

Christic."

Now, according to my weak ability, I shall strive to explain the sort of reflections which should accompany these commemorations. In return for His many and various benefits to us, we have received grace from God to make Him the offering of Christ's holy sacrifice. Commemorating all God's bounties, we render thanks for everything. Above all we thank God through the holy liturgy for those He has chosen. For we are all one in Christ and the glorification of our brothers is our glory. We present Him the great offering as commemoration of thanksgiving for making them good and profitable, victorious over all the assaults of the devil.

We thank God not only for the saints, but for all those worthy of believing in God; for as Solomon said, "To know God is the sum of righteousness" (Wisd 15:3). Moreover, to be His people, offspring of the holy font and recipients of holy communion and to depart this life bearing Christ's holy name is a great gift. Thanksgiving for all these and similar beneficiaries is offered through the holy liturgy.

Thereby we not only thank God for each individually, but also pray, commemorating the saints' spiritual labors and virtuous life. We offer thanks through the holy liturgy, upholding Christ's death for us and the saints' asceticism as intercessors before the heavenly Father and supplicate for all believers, the living and those who have fallen asleep. For as we rejoice with the saints, offering God gifts of thanksgiving and regarding their crowning as ours, they too act as guardians of their members through intercession to God, especially during the dread liturgy. Giving thanks through them we say after every phrase:

§115 *"Remember, Lord, and have mercy,"*
i.e. *remember* the love the saints had towards You and their labor and *have mercy on us, as they are of us and from us.* We are all

'ի ձեռն սուրբ պատարագին, կարգ ըստ կարգէ. այսպէս անելով.

§116 «Յիշեա, Տէր, եւ ողորմեա, եւ օրհնեա զսուրբ
Սիոն՝ զկաթողիկէ առաքելական եկեղեցի քո, զոր փրկեցեր պատուական արեամբ միածնի քոյ եւ ազատեցեր,
եւ տուր սմա զանշարժ զքո զխաղաղութիւնդ»:

Սիոն մայր է 'ի մեր լեզուս. եւ թէ զերուսաղէմ'ի եկեղեցւոյն է
մաղթանքս վասն սուրբ տեղեացն Երուսաղէմ'ի պատճառ է. զի
նախ զնա դնելի է եւ ապա զամենայն զտիեզերական եկեղեցիս.
եւ թէ զամենայն եկեղեցիք՝ մայր Սիոն կոչէ, եւ այս չէ հեռի 'ի
ճշտաւորութենէն. զի սուրբ եկեղեցի ծնանի սուրբ աւազանաւ
զմեզ, եւ սնուցանէ հոգելոր սննդեամբ զմեզ: Կաթողիկէն՝ տիե-
զերական է. Հայցեմք ողորմութիւն ամենայն եկեղեցեաց՝ որ
յամենայն սիեզերս ըստ քարոզութեան առաքելոցն շինեալ են,
վասն որոյ առաքելական կոչեմք. իսկ որբ Թիւրեալը են յա-
րաքելոցն դաւանութենէ՝ նոքա ոչ եւս առաքելական կոչին: Իսկ
առաքելական եկեղեցիք Թէպէտ եւ ընդ բազում տեղիս են՝
սակայն մի ասի, վասն միասնական հաւատոյն. վասն որոյ որպէս զմիոյ ասի եկեղեցիք ամենայն: «Զոր փրկեցեր պատուական արեամբ միածնի քոյ եւ ազատեցեր». քանզի սուրբ արեամբն Քրիստոսի փրկեցաք յանիծից եւ 'ի մեղաց եւ 'ի
մահուանէ, եւ ազատեցաք 'ի ծառայութենէ սատանայի: Արդ
ասէ, ոչ բազմանունաբար եկեղեցիս այլ եկեղեցի, եւ ոչ զորս
փրկեցեր, այլ զոր փրկեցեր. եւ ոչ ասէ տուր սոցա, այլ թէ
տուր սմա զանշարժ քո զխաղաղութիւն:

§117 «Յիշեա Տէր, եւ ողորմեա եւ օրհնեա զամենայն
ուղղափառ եպիսկոպոսունս, որք ուղիղ զնացիւք հա-
մառօտեն զբանն ճշմարտութեան»:

Զի՞նչ է համառօտելն. այսինքն է՝ ճիշդ զուլիղն եւ զատոզ
վարդապետութիւնն, յոր ոչ յարի ինչ Թիւրութիւն կամ խո-
տորումն յաջ կամ յաձեակ. վասն որոյ եւ յարէ 'ի նոյն՝ թէ
զբանն ճշմարտութեան. զի ճշմարտութիւն մի է, ստուԹիւն 'ի
բազումս բաժանի: Վասն այսր համառօտ բանի ենայի յառաջագոյն զուշակեաց եւ Պաւղոս մեկնէ, Թէ Բան մի հակիրճ եւ

188

one church, and of one Christ who is our head (ICor 11:3). We are all the body and limbs. And so with the saints' commemoration we begin to pray for *mercy* anew through the holy liturgy in order as follows:

> §116 *"Remember, Lord, and have mercy and bless holy Zion, your catholic, apostolic Church which You have saved and delivered by the precious blood of Your only-begotten Son and give it Your boundless peace:"*

Zion means mother in our language and if this petition concerns the church of Jerusalem, then it is fitting because of Jerusalem's holy places that it should be placed before all the churches of the world. However, if it calls every church Mother Zion, this too makes perfect sense. For the holy church bore us in holy baptism and nourishes us with spiritual nourishment. *Catholic* means universal. We implore *mercy* on all the churches which have been erected in the entire world according to the preaching of the apostles, and so we call it *apostolic*. But those who have diverged from the confession of the apostles are no longer called *apostolic*.

Now the *apostolic* churches, though found in many places, are said to be one because of their uniform faith, with reference to which the churches are said to be one.

Which You saved by the precious blood of Your only-begotten Son: By Christ's holy *blood* we have been *saved* from the curse, sin and death and have been *delivered* from service to Satan. Now it says not churches in the plural but *Church* and not those which *You saved*, but *that which You saved* and it does not say *give them*, but *give it Your stable peace.*

> §117 *"Remember, Lord and have mercy and bless all orthodox bishops who with straight approach define the word of truth:"*

համառօտ արդարութեամբ, գրանն Հակիրճ արասցէ Տէր 'ի վերայ երկրի. զի ոչ իբրեւ զորինացն բազմակատկաբար է, այլ Հաւատովք 'ի սուրբ Երրորդութիւնն եւ ի' Քրիստոսի տնօրէնութիւնն` արդաբանամք:

Արդ խնդրեմք ողորմութեամբն Աստուծոյ զաղղաբարդ զեպիսկոպոսունս զօրացուցանել յարաջնորդութեան վատական. զտասրականգն Հայցելով` առաւել պաղատիմք վան որ մեզն առաջնորդէ, այսպէս ասելով.

§118 «Եւ եւս առաւել զվարդապետն մեր եւ զվերակացու, եւ զտեսուչ ոգւոց մերոց, զայն անունն եպիսկոպոս. եւ շնորհեա մեզ, Տէր, ընդ երկայն աւուրս».

Է՞ր ապագաւ չչաւտացաւ եպիսկոպոս միայն ասել, այլ յաւել թէ զվարդապետս մեր եւ զվերակացու եւ զտեսուչ ոգւոց մե-րոց. զի չերմ եռանդն սրտիս, եւ սեր սիրով վան նորա խնդրեցուք. մեզ առաւելագոյն գիտելով քան եպիսկոպոսին` զՀայցուածն. զի թէ փոյթ 'ի վարդապետութիւն լինիցի, եւ զվերակացութիւն քաջապէս կատարեսցէ, եւ զամենեցուն ողիս տեսանիցէ թէ որպէս իցեն, եւ թէ այս անուն կամ այն անուն Հեղզ իցեն 'ի բարեգործութեան, կամ արատ ինչ եւ բիծ 'ի Հոգին ունիցին, եւ չՀեղգայցէ վան նոցա աղօթիւք եւ խրատու, եւ զգուշանայցէ ամենայն արթնութեամբք, Հօտին առաւել քան անմինն գշանն Համբարէ: Եւ մեր գայս գիտելով, ամենայն Հա-լաստութեամբք խնդրեցուք վան առաջնորդաց մերոց. զի ընդ այս եւ զայս ածցուք զմտաւ. թէ պարտական եմք փոխարէն Հատուցանել նոցա աղօթելոյն վան մեր` մերովք աղօթիւք վան նոցա. զի այսպէս առաւել որ վան մեր խնդրուածք նոցա իցեն` լին ա Աստուած` յորժամ մեք վան նոցա աղապիցեմք: Այսպիսեաւ Պաւղոս տայ խրատ Կորնթացւոցն. Բերանք մեր բացեալ առ ձեզ, ասելով, եւ սիրոք մեր ընդարձակեալ. ունինք նեղիք 'ի մենջ. այս ինչ է, թէպէտ եւ բազումք էք զուք, եւ այլք եւս Հոգք են մեզ, այլ չնեղին սիրոք մեր մոռանալ գոք եւ անտեսել 'ի խրատուք եւ յաղօթից. բայց զուք, ասէ, 'ի գուֆսա ձեր նեղիք. եւ ոչ այնչափ վան իմ միոյս Հոգայ, որպէս եւս վան ձեր եւ ամենեցունց. եւ յարէ 'ի նոյն. Արդ

190

What is *defining?*[1] It means precise, straight-forward and accurate teaching in which there is no perversion or deviation to right or left. And so it leads to *the word of truth;* for *truth* is one, while falsehood is divided into many. Isaiah foretold this succinct word (Isa 10:22) and Paul interprets it "A word brief and succinct with justice. May the Lord make the word brief upon the earth" (Rom 9:28). For we are justified not by the multiple regulations of the law, but through faith in the Holy Trinity and in Christ's economy.

Thus we beseech God in His mercy to strengthen right-preaching *bishops* in their supervisory activities. Among our general petitions we pray especially for our own *bishop* as follows:

§118 *"Again especially our teacher and overseer and spiritual director, bishop (name) and grant him to us, Lord, for long days:"*

Why was it not sufficient simply to say *bishop,* without adding *our overseer and spiritual director?* In order to supplicate for him with fervent heart and sincere affection, aware that the petitions are really for ourselves more than the *bishop.* For if he is diligent in teaching, exercises oversight with integrity and observes the condition of everyone's soul (e.g. that some people are lazy in good works, or have a stain or spot on their souls) and is not lazy in praying for them or giving them advice, fully alert to take appropriate precautions, he provides more profit for his flock than for himself. Realizing this, let us supplicate for our prelates with all assurance, bearing in mind also that we are bound to recompense them for praying on our behalf by our prayers for them, since their supplications for us are heard more by God when we pray for them. This is the sort of advice Paul gives to the Corinthians: "We have opened our mouths to you and extended wide our hearts. You are in no way shortchanged by us" (2Cor 6:11-12a).

զնոյն հատուցումն՝ իբրեւ ընդ որդեակս ունիմ, ընդարձա
կեցարուք եւ դուք. զի օրտեցուցէք զնոսա հատուցանողն լինելով,
ասէր զայս. ոչ զիւր օգուտն միայն խնդրելով, որպէս ասաց
ինքն, այլ զբազմաց։ Վասն այնորիկ եւ յամենայնի ՚ի թուղթան
աղօթս հրամայէ իւր առնել. զնոցայն առաւել օգուտ քան զիւրն
հոգալով՝ պէտս առնէր նոցա աղօթից՝ Պաւղոս. այլ կամէր զի
ընդ իւր օգտելոյն ՚ի նոցանէ՝ եւ նոքա օգտեսցին. եւ վասն
այնոսիկ ոչ ասէր զաղօթիցն՝ թէ զի եւ շահեցայց, այլ թէ
բանին լիցի առաւելութիւն՝ առ ՚ի մարդկան փրկութիւն:

§119 «Ցիշեա, Տէր, եւ ողորմեա, եւ օրհնեա զմեզ եւ
զառաջի կացեալ քո ժողովուրդս, եւ զպատարագիս
մատուցօղս, եւ պարգեւեա իրաքանչիւրոցն զպիտոյսն
եւ զօգտակարսն»:

Մեզ *ասաց՝ որք ՚ի խորհրդեանն իցեմք* առաջի կացեալք. եւ
ժողովուրդ՝ *բովանդակ ժողովրդեանս* ասէ. պատարագին մա
տուցօղն, *յայտ է որ զխորհուրդն կատարէ*: «Եւ պարգեւեա
իրաքանչիւրոցն զպիտոյսն եւ զօգտակարսն». *մեք ասէ, բա
զում անգամ լինի զի զանօգուտն խնդրեմք, այլ դու որ գիտես
զմեր պէտան եւ զօգուտն՝ շնորհեա հայրաբար եւ արաբշապէս
իրաքանչիւրոց, այսինքն ամենեցուն մեզ՝ ըստ օգտի*:

§120 «Ցիշեայ Տէր եւ ողորմեա, եւ օրհնեա զպտղաբեր
րիչս եկեղեցւոյ քում սրբոյ, եւ զայնոսիկ որք յիշեն
զաղքատս ողորմածութեամբ. եւ հատո զպարտս հայց
մանց նոցա ըստ ընդարոյս առատութեանդ քոյ՝ հարիւ
րապատիկ, աստ եւ ՚ի հանդերձելումդ»:

*Ոմանք սպաս նուիրանաց ընծայեն եկեղեցւոյ, ոմանք գիրա
ատուածաշունչս, պաղարբերեն եւ ՚ի կալոյ եւ ՚ի Հնձանէ եւ
յանասնոց. այլ եւ ՚ի տօնս փրկականս եւ ՚ի յիշատակս սրբոցն
ընծայաբերեն ըստ կարի. եւ մեք խնդրեմք վասն նոցա, եւ
վասն ողորմածացն՝ որք զաղքատս ընդունին՝ յիրբանց գոյիցն:
Բայց ոչ վայրապար յաճել զողորմածութեամբն այլ գի ծա
նիցուք թէ դբութեամբ եւ ողորմութեամբ եւ ցանկութեամբ
զաղքատն յիշելն՝ Հաճոյ է Աստուծոյ, քան զյորրան. զոր եւ
առաքեալ ասէ. Ողորմութիւնն ՚ի կամաց է, եւ առնեն՝ ըստ*

192

The gist of this is that though you are many and we have other concerns too, still our hearts are not so distracted as to forget or overlook anyone in counseling and prayer. But you are constricted in your affection and you do not care so much for me who am one as I for all of you. He proceeds: "Now I have the same recompense as among sons, open yourselves wide to me too" (ibid. v.13). He said this to benefit them as their remunerator, not seeking his own advantage alone, as he himself said, but that of the many. And so he bids them pray for him in all his epistles. Concerned more with their benefit than his own, Paul availed himself of their prayers, but his intention was that while he was assisted by them, they too should benefit from this. Consequently, his advice on prayer was not for personal gain, but "To advance the word for the salvation of mankind" (cf. 1Cor 2:1).

> §119 "Remember, Lord, be merciful and bless us and the people standing before You and me who offer the sacrifice and bestow on each what is needful and beneficial:"

Us refers to those who stand before you in the mystery, while people means all the people. Clearly the one who offers the sacrifice is the celebrant. And bestow on each what is needful and beneficial: In other words, we frequently ask for what is not beneficial, but You know our needs and best interests. As father and creator bestow on each (i.e. on us all) what is to our advantage.

> §120 "Remember, Lord, be merciful and bless those who bear fruit for Your holy Church and those who mercifully remember the poor and grant their requests according to Your innate generosity a hundredfold in this life and in the world to come:"

Some dedicate liturgical vessels to the church, others divinely inspired books. Others bear fruit from the threshing floor, the

193

գոյին. իսկ ապա պարտական ունին այնպիսիքն զՄատուած։
Աղաչեմք հատուցանել ըստ ընդարոյս առատութեանն իւրոյ.
ընդարոյս է՝ ինքնարոյս, այսինքն՝ թէ բոյս բնութեանդ քոյ է
ողորմութիւն. հարիւրապատիկ աստ Հատո, միոյն հարիւր, եւ
որ ՚ի հանդերձեալսն՝ անպատում պատրաստութիւնք:

§121 «Յիշեա Տէր եւ ողորմեա, եւ օրհնեա զհոգիս հանգուցելոցն»:

որպէս թէ ասիցեմք՝ յիշել յիւր արքայութիւնն, որպէս զա-
լագակն, եւ ողորմութեամբ օրհնել ընդ աջեայան, որք զերա-
նալիցն լսեն գձայն, Եկայք օրհնեալք Հօր իմոյ, ժառանգեցէք
զպատրաստեալ ձեզ զարքայութիւն:

§122 «Յիշեա Տէր եւ զայնոսիկ որք յանձնեցին մեզ
զինքեանս ՚ի յաղօթել, եւ կառավարեա զկամս հայց-
մամց նոցա եւ զմերս՝ ընդ ուղղորդն, եւ որ լին է
փրկութեամբ»:

Զոր օրինակ կառավարն զկառավիգն ուղղէ եւ չտայ թոյլ խո-
տորել ՚ի պողոտայէն, այսպէս եւ Դու մերոց աղօթիցն լիցիս
ուղղիչ, զի մ՚ի՛ վրիպեսցեն ՚ի կամաց քոց, կամ երկրաւոր ինչ
խնդրել կամ թշնամեացն չարի հատուցումն, կամ զմիտան հա-
նել յաղօթիցս իմացուածոց, եւ այար անդր յածեցուցանել. այլ
յերկինս գողիան ամբառնալ, եւ սուրբ մտօք զպիտոյսն եւ զոգ-
տակարան ՚ի նմանէ հայցել, եւ որ ընու զամենայն զմեր փրր-
կութիւն:

194

harvest and from their livestock. They also bring dedications at the salvific feasts and saints' days according to their means. We supplicate for them and for those who *mercifully* provide for *the poor* our of their substance. The inclusion of the adverb *mercifully* is not accidental, but is there to instruct us that the compassion, pity and willingness we exhibit is more pleasing to God than what we give, as the apostle says (2 Cor 9:7). Mercy comes from the will, while the specific form it takes depends on one's substance. But then they have someone in their debt, i.e. God. We ask Him to reward them according to His *innate generosity; innate* means inherent i.e. that mercy is intrinsic to Your nature. A *hundredfold in this life,* a hundred for one, and *in the world to come* with untold provision.

§121 *"Remember, Lord, be merciful and bless the souls of the departed:"*

As if we were to ask God to *remember* them in His kingdom, like the thief and *mercifully bless* them with those at Your right hand who hear the call of the blessed: "Come, blessed of my Father, inherit the kingdom prepared for you" (Matth 25:34).

§122 *"Remember, Lord, also those who have committed themselves to our prayers and steer the intentions of their petitions and ours on a straight course, abounding in salvation:"*

As a coachman steers the horses and does not allow them to veer from the highway, so may You *steer our prayers* so as not to diverge from Your will either seeking something earthly or repaying our enemies with evil or distracting our mind from the import of the prayer, driving it hither and thither but to raise our spirit to heaven and with pure thoughts to beseech from Him what is needful and beneficial and brings about all our *salvation.*

§123 «Եւ վարձատրեա բոլորեցունց».

Թէ ամենեցուն տուր *վարձս․– գո՛ր․– քանանց եւ զերանելի* բարութիւնսն. *Թէ որ ոչն անցանէ, եւ երանելի եւս առնէ* գլխունեօղան:

§124 «Չտեալ զխորհուրդս մեր».

սրբեալ 'ի խղճէ եւ 'ի չար գործոց:

§125 «Տաճարացդ յընդունակութիւն մարմնոյ եւ արեան միածնիդ քոյ տեառն մերոյ եւ փրկչին Յիսուսի Քրիստոսի».

բնակարան աստ եւ տուն քո միածնիդ պատրաստեա զմեզ վէր֊ *լական պատարագաս:*

§126 «Ընդ որում քեզ, Հօր ամենակալիդ».

այսինքն ընդ Որդւոյ քեզ Հօր ամենակալի, «հանդերձ կեն֊ *դանարար եւ ազատիչ սուրբ Հոգւովդ՝ վայելեն փանք, իշ*֊ *խանութիւն եւ պատիւ․ այժմ եւ միշտ եւ յաւիտեանս յաւի*֊ *տենից. ամէն»:*

ՔԱՐՈԶ

§127 «Քեզ Հօր ամենակալին՝ զոհութիւն եւ փառա֊ բանութիւն մատուցանեմք, վասն սուրբ, անմահ՝, աս֊ տուածային պատարագիս՝ որ 'ի վերայ սրբոյ սեղա֊ նոյս»:

Հայր է *միածին որդւոյն եւ ամենայնի տէր է. Աստուած գոլով՝* ամենակալ է. զոհութիւն եւ փառս փաս տալոյ՝ *մատուցանեմ*ք *աս*֊ *է, վասն արժանի առնելոյ զմեզ այսպիսի պատարագ յա*֊ *հազին սեղանս դնել, ոչ յերկրէ յանասնոց, այլ յերկնուստ ատուածային. զի Աստուծոյ որդի է զենումնն, անարատն, ան*֊ *մեղն, զոր սուրբ կոչէ. եւ Թէպէտ մահու է նշանակ՝ այլ կեն*֊ *դանարար է, վասն որոյ եւ անմահ կոչէ: Քանզի որպէս յաւանդելն Քրիստոս զոգին մարդկային՝ աստուածութեամբ քն կենդանի էր մարմինն, վասն զի Աստուած մարմին էր, ընդ Աստուած միացեալ, եւ մի լեալ խառնմամբն, եւ 'ի կամելն յառնել՝ ինքն զինքն յարոյց. նոյն կենդանութիւն ատու*֊

196

§123 *"And reward all:"*
i.e. give *all rewards*. What sort? *Your blessed bounties that do not pass away:* What *does not pass away* renders recipients even more blessed.

§124 *"Purifying our thoughts:"*
cleansing them from a bad conscience and wicked deeds.

§125 *"Make us temples for the reception of the body and blood of Your only-begotten Son, our Lord and Savior Jesus Christ:"*
This means fit us by the saving sacrifice as a dwelling and house for *Your only-begotten Son.*

§126 *"With whom to You, Father Almighty,"* i.e. to You, Father Almighty with the Son. *"Together with Your life-creating and liberating Holy Spirit befit glory, dominion and honor, now and ever and to ages of ages.*

Proclamation

§127 *"To You, Father Almighty, we offer thanksgiving and glory for this holy, immortal, divine sacrifice upon the holy altar:"*
He is *Father* of the only-begotten Son and Lord of all. As God He is *Almighty.* It says *we offer thanksgiving and glory* for making us worthy to place *on the altar* such a *sacrifice,* not of animals from the earth, but heavenly, divine. For God's Son is the *sacrifice,* stainless and sinless, which the text calls *holy.* Although it signifies death, it is life-creating and thus called *immortal.* For as Christ gave up His human spirit (Lk 23:46), His body was enlivened by His divinity, since it was God's body, united with God and not a mixture and when He wished to rise, He raised Himself. The same vivification of divinity united to the bread and cup is *immortal* and gives immortality to those who ap-

197

ծութեան եւ 'ի հագն եւ 'ի բաժակն միացեալ՝ անմահ է, եւ
անմահութիւն մերձեցելոցն տայ։ Զոր օրինակ մարմինն 'ի
մեռանելն՝ զբազումս 'ի մեռելոց կենդանացոյց, այնպէս եւ 'ի
լինել պատարագին տէրունական մահուն յիշատակ՝ զսրբեալսն 'ի
խղճէ կենդանի առնէ, որք նմայն հաղորդին. քանզի զայս
գուշակելոյ վասն՝ յարեան որք մեռելութեամբն Քրիստոսի
յարեան կենդանացեալք։ Եւ արդ տես զայս ժամու զխսաքն եւ
հաւատա թէ այժմ նոյն լինի, զի չէ նուազ այմ քան զայս
մարմինն. այն նոյն է, եւ այն իսկ է։ Վասն որոյ եւ Տէրն
խոստացաւ զսա ճաշակողացն՝ յաւիտենական առնուլ զկեանս.
այլ որպէս անդ ոչ ոք յանսրբոյն կենդանացաւ, նոյնպէս եւ ոչ
այժմ առանց սրբութեան ոք, կամ անապաշխարքն՝ կենդանութիւն գտանեն. այլ թէ լրբին երբէք՝ որպէս զՅուդաս՝ նմա-
նութեամբ նորին դատապարտին։ Այլ յետ գոհանալոյ զայսպիսի
մեծապարգեւութեանց՝ խնդրուածս առնէ.
§128 «Զսա մեզ 'ի փրկութիւն եւ 'ի կենդանութիւն
պարգեւեա»։
եւ զսոյն՝ որ 'ի սեղանս է՝ արասցես պատարագաւ։
§129 «Սովաւ շնորհեա զսէր, զհաստատութիւն եւ զղղձալի զիսպաղութիւն եկեղեցւոյ քում սրբոյ, եւ ամենայն ուղղափառ եպիսկոպոսաց։ Եպիսկոպոսապետին
մերոյ, եւ քահանայիս՝ որ զպատարագս մատուցանէ»։
Արդ՝ թէպէտ եւ միանգամ Հայցեաց քահանայն, սակայն կրկնէ
սարկաւագն բարձր ճայնիւ, զի լսելի ամենեցուն լիցի, եւ
ամենեքեան միաբան պաղատեսցին. եւ զի ունանիցիմ՝ է թէ որքան պիտանացուք են պարգեւք սիրոյ որ առ Աստուած եւ առ
միմեանս, եւ հաստատութեան եւ խաղաղութեան, նոյնպէս եւ
վասն առաջնորդաց խնդիրք։ Յաւելու եւս, թէ
§130 «Վասն որոյ, Տէր, զմատուցօղս անմոռաց զբու-
թեամբդ քո յիշեա»։
Քանզի արաբշական զուրկ Աստուծոյ զամենայն եղելովքս է,
ապաւէ՝ մատուցողացն՝ զարաբշական զուրկ չմոռանալ առ իւր,
այլ յիշել եւ այցելել Հանապազ։

proach. As in death His body revived many from the dead, so the commemoration of the Lord's death during the liturgy enlivens those cleansed from the twinges of conscience who communicate. This was what was prefigured by those who arose, enlivened by Christ's death (cf. Matth 27:52-53). And now observe the cross of that time and believe it now to be the same, for this body is no less than that was. It is identical and in fact it is that body! That is why the Lord promised that those who taste it would receive eternal life (John 6:51). But just as then none of the unclean became alive, so now no one without cleansing or repentance finds life. But rather, if they are ever insolent like Judas, they suffer the same condemnation.

After giving thanks for such acts of generosity, the priest makes petitions:

§128 *"Bestow it on us for salvation and enlivenment:"*
and make that which is on the altar the same through this sacrifice.

§129 *"Through this grant love, stability and desirable peace to Your holy Church[1] and all orthodox bishops, to our chief bishop and to me, the priest who offer this sacrifice:"*

Now although the *priest* has prayed this once, the deacon repeats it aloud so it is audible to everyone and all supplicate in unity and it teaches us the utility of the gifts of *love* to God and one another and of *stability* and *peace*, as well as petitions for prelates.

The text continues:

§130 *"Therefore, Lord, remember the celebrants in your ever-mindful compassion:"*[1]

Since God's *compassion* as creator embraces all that come into being, the deacon implores *Him* not to forget His *compassion* as

199

§131 «Յիշեա Տէր զհոգիս հանգուցելոցն 'ի քեզ յուսա-
ցելոց»։

Վասն զի յաղագս հաւատոյ եւ յուսով ննջեցելոցն հրամայիմք
խնդրել, վասն այնորիկ ասէ յիշել զհոգիս հանգուցելոց յուսա-
ցելոցն 'ի նա։

§132 «Քո Տէր, զգործութեամբ եւ անմահ պատարագաս
կեցդ եւ ողորմեա մեզ»։

զի վասն մեր է, ասէ, պատարագս, արդ վասն սուրբ պա-
տարագիս՝ կեցուցանօղ, ասէ, զգործ-իւն քո ողորմեցի մեզ։

ԱՂՕԹՔ

§133 «Աստուած ձշմարտութեան եւ հայր ողորմութեան»։

Աստուած՝ բնութեամբ ես, ասէ, վասն զի արարիչ ես, իսկ Հայր՝
ողորմեցար եւ եղեր. յայն սակս եւ ձշմարտութեամբ ասէ
զայն՝ որ սերտուն է, եւ ողորմութեամբ զայն՝ որ խնամա-
ծութեամբն։

§134 «Գոհանամք զքէն, որ 'ի վեր քան զերանելի նա-
հապետացն զմեր պարտաւորելոցս առաւել մեծարեցեր
զբնութիւն. քանզի նոցա Աստուած կոչեցար, իսկ մեզ
հայր հանեցար անուանիլ»։

Ասաց Աստուած, ես եմ Աստուած Աբրահամու, Սահակայ,
Յակովբայ, իսկ զՀաւատացեալս՝ որդիս ասաց իւր լինել. վասն
որոյ եւ Քրիստոս յաղօթելն՝ Հայր կոչել զԱստուած մեզ հրամայեաց. եւ առաքեալ ասէ, Այսուհետեւ չես ծառայ՝ այլ որդի։
Արդ զոհանայ զԱստուած զանչափ մարդասիրութեանցն, զի քան
զարբողն՝ զմեր բնութիւնս զպարտաւորեալս 'ի մեղս՝ առաւ-
լապէս մեծարող արարեր գթալով։

§135 «Եւ այժմ զայսպիսի զատ 'ի քէն զնորոգ եւ
զպատուական անուանադրութեան շնորհս՝ պայծառացեալ
օր ըստ օրէ ծագեցդ յեկեղեցւոչ քում»։

Որովհետեւ, ասէ, այսպիսի սիրոյ արժանի արարեր զբնութիւն
մեր՝ մինչեւ որդիս կոչել եւ Հայր մեր անուանիլ, մի' երբէք

200

creator towards the celebrants, but to keep in mind and constantly visit them with His aid.

§131 *"Remember, Lord, the souls of the departed who put their hope in You:"*

We are commanded to offer petitions for those who have fallen asleep in faith and *hope,* and so it says *remember the souls of the departed who put their hope in* Him.

§132 *"Lord, by Your power and this immortal sacrifice, save and have mercy on us:"*

Because the *sacrifice* is for us, it says, for the sake of the holy *sacrifice* let Your *saving power have mercy on us.*

Prayer

§133 *"O God of truth and Father of mercy:"*

You are God by nature as creator, but became Father by showing *mercy.* Thus by *truth* means steadfastly and by *mercy* is equivalent to by caring.

§134 *"We give You thanks for exalting us sinners above the blessed patriarchs, since to them You were called God, but by us You deigned to be called Father:"*

God said, "I am the God of Abraham, Isaac and Jacob," (Exod 3:6) but He said believers were His sons. And so Christ instructed us when praying to call God *Father* (cf. Matth 6:9) and the apostle says "Hereafter, you are not a slave but a son" (Gal 4:7). Now the priest gives God *thanks* for His countless acts of love for man, since though our nature is more a debtor to sin than that of the saints, You have made it more honorable by Your compassion.

§135 *"And now make the grace of such a new and precious name you gave us to flourish in Your Church, making it more radiant from day to day:"*

201

Մոռացիս զգթալն իբրեւ Հայր յորդիս, թէ եւ մեղանչիցեմք, եւ մի՛ արտաքսիցես զմեզ յայսպիսի մեծապարգեւ շնորհէ. այլ չերմագուն գորովով՝ որպէս նորոգեցեր 'ի մեզ զպատուական անուանադրութեան շնորհս, որ ըստ օրէ պաշծառացեալ եւ ծաղկեալ պահես յեկեղեցւոչ քում, այսինքն 'ի Հաւատացեալս 'ի քեզ:

§136 «Եւ տուր մեզ համարձակաձայն բարբառով բանալ զբերանս մեր, կարդալ առ քեզ՝ Հայր երկնաւոր, եւ ասել»:

Շնորհօք ողորմութեան քո տացես մեզ Համարձակել եւ ապալինել 'ի քաղցրութիւն քո եւ 'ի գթութիւն եւ յանբաւ ներողութիւնդ, եւ կոչել զքեզ հայր հողեղինացս եւ մեղաւորացս, զսուրբ եւ զերկնաւոր Հայրդ. եւ ոչ վայրապար յաւելու զայն՝ թէ բանալ զբերանս մեր. այլ քանզի փակէ զբերանս մեր Հանապազորդ սխալանք բերանից մերոց, վասն այնր ադաչեմք զաւլութիւն առնել եւ սրբել զբերանս մեր, եւ տալ վատա-Հութիւն բանալ զբերանս մեր եւ կոչել համարձակութեամբ հայր՝ զԱստուած:

Ջհայր մեր որ յերկինսն՝ Նիւսացին սուրբն Գրիգոր եւ սուրբն Ցովհան Ոսկեբերան յածախական բանիւք մեկնեալ են, անտի ստուգագոյն ուսցին կամեցողք:

§137 «Հայր մեր որ յերկինս ես»:

Քանզի ըստ մարմնոյ ծննդեանս՝ երկրաւորս ունիմք հայրս[24], իսկ յաւազանէն սուրբ Հոգւովն ծնեալ, եւ Քրիստոսի մարմնովն եւ արեամբն 'ի նա կցորդեալ՝ ունիմք մեզ հայր զերկնաւորն Հայր, զՔրիստոսի ծնօղն, յոր միացաքն մեք. վասն այսորիկ այսպէս ուսոյց Տէրն ասել. «Հայր մեր որ յերկինս, սուրբ եղիցի անուն քո». եթէ վասն մեր՝ սուրբ եւ փառաւոր լիցի անուն քո:

§138 «Եկեսցէ արքայութիւն քո».

արքայութիւնն Թագաւորութեան կոչումն է: Խնդրեմք տիրել մեզ Քրիստոսի Թագաւորութեանն՝ նորուն շնորհօքն, զի մի՛ Թագաւորեալ մեղքն մեր՝ ծառայեցուսցեն զմեզ սատանայի.

202

Because You made us worthy of such love as to call us sons and to be *named* our father, never forget to show compassion as father to sons, although we sin, and do not exclude us from such generous *grace*. But with warm tenderness, as You renewed in us the *grace* of this *precious name, make it more radiant, flourishing from day to day in your Church* i.e. among those who trust in You.

§136 *"And grant us with boldness to open our mouths and cry to You, heavenly Father, and say:"*

By the grace of Your mercy grant us to be bold to take refuge in Your sweetness and compassion and boundless forgiveness and call You the *Father* of us earthly sinners, who are the holy and heavenly *Father*. Nor is the insertion of the phrase *to open our mouths* accidental, since the constant offences of our mouths close *our mouths*. And so we beseech God to grant atonement and cleanse *our mouths* and give us confidence *to open our mouths and boldly* call *Him Father*.

The *our Father in Heaven* both St. Gregory of Nyssa and St. John Chrysostom have commented on in great detail and those who wish may learn from them with great precision.[1]

§137 *"Our Father who are in Heaven:"*

Since in accordance with our fleshly birth we have earthly *fathers*, so when we were born of the Holy Spirit from the font and united with Christ through His body and blood, we have as *Father* the *Heavenly Father* who begat Christ in whom we are one. This is why the Lord taught us to say *"Our Father who are in Heaven, may Your name be Holy"* (Matth 6:9ff.) which means *may your name be holy* and glorious for us.

§138 *"May Your kingdom come:"*

Kingdom is a title of royalty. We ask Christ's *Kingdom* to reign over us by His grace, so that our sin does not dominate us

ցանկամք եւ հանդերձեալ թագաւորութեան նորա գալ, որ
խափանէ զսատանայի եւ զմեղաց իշխանութիւն:

§139 «Եղիցին կամք քո, որպէս յերկինս եւ յերկրի».
որպէս յերկինս չէ մոլորութիւն եւ մեղք, այլ ամենայն ինչ
ըստ կամաց քոց է, այսպէս եւ յերկրէ բարձցի ամբարշտու-
թիւն, եւ հրեշտակացին մարդիկ, ամենեքին լինել կամարարք
քո:

§140 «Զհաց մեր հանապազորդ՝ տուր մեզ այսօր».
զՀարկաւոր պէտս մարմնոյ օր ըստ օրէ պարգեւեա մեզ:

§141 «Եւ թող մեզ զպարտս մեր».
զոր ինչ մեղաք եւ պարտապան պատճog գտաք՝ թող մեզ.

§142 «Որպէս եւ մեք թողումք մերոց պարտապանաց».
այնoցիկ՝ որ մեզն պարտիցին:

§143 «Եւ մի՛ տար զմեզ 'ի փորձութիւն».
կամ 'ի սատանայէ փորձել կամ 'ի մարդկանէ, մեղoք կամ
վտանդիւք իւիք:

§144 «Այլ փրկեա զմեզ 'ի չարէն».
յամենայն սատանայական որոգայթից:

§145 «Տէր տերանց, Աստուած աստուծոց».
ամենայն տերանց եւ աստուածոց Աստուած եւ տէր. Աստուած
եւ Հրեշտակաց եւ քահանայից:

§146 «Հայր երկնաւոր, ազաչեմք զքեզ, մի՛ տար զմեզ
'ի փորձութիւն. եւ մի՛ 'ի դատապարտութիւն, այլ
փրկեա 'ի չարէ, ապրեցո 'ի փորձութենէ».
Հայրաբար, ասէ, փրկող լեր 'ի փորձութենէ. եւ անդատապարտ
պահեա, եւ գերծո 'ի չարէ քանզի կարող ես յամենայնի, եւ
յաղթող է տէրութիւնդ քո ամենեցուն: Եւ վասն այար յաւել
զայն.

§147 «քո է զօրութիւն եւ արքայութիւն. եւ քեզ վայելեն
փառք իշխանութիւն եւ պատիւ. այժմ եւ միշտ եւ յաւիտեանս յաւիտենից»:

204

and enslave us to Satan. We look to the *coming* of His future *Kingdom* which thwarts the power of Satan and sin.

§139 *"May Your will be on earth as in Heaven:"*

As in Heaven there is no deviation and sin, but everything is according to *Your will,* so may impiety cease from the *earth* and men become angels and perform *Your will.*

§140 *"Give us today our daily bread:"*

Grant us from day to day the essential needs of the body.

§141 *"And release us from our debts:"*

Release us from the punishment we deserve for whatever sins we have committed.

§142 *"As we release our debtors:"*

i.e. those who stand in the same position towards us.

§143 *"And do not give us over to temptation:"*

i.e. either to be *tempted* by Satan or by men through sin or any dangers.

§144 *"But free us from evil:"*

from all Satanic snares.

§145 *"Lord of Lords, God of Gods:"*[1]

of all *Lords* and *Gods* God and *Lord.* You are God of angels and priests.

> §146 *"Heavenly Father, we beseech You, do not give us over to temptation, nor to condemnation, but free us from evil, save us from temptation:"*

As a *Father,* be our rescuer from *temptation* and preserve us *free* from *condemnation* and keep *us from evil,* since You are capable of all things and Your lordship rules over all. Consequently, it continues,

> §147 *"Yours is the power and the kingdom and to You the glory, dominion and honor are fitting, now and ever and to ages of ages."*[1]

ԱՂՕԹՔ

§148 «Որ աղքիւրդ ես կենաց եւ փրկութեան եւ բղխու-
մըն ողորմութեան»։

կեանէ եւ ողորմութիւն 'ի քէն է աղբերաբար։

§149 «Ողորմեա ժողովրդեանս՝ որ խոնարհեալ երկիր
պագանէ աստուածութեանդ քո»։

Վայելեացէ յայդմանէ՝ 'ի մշտնջենահաս աղբերէ՝ ժողովուրդս քո,
որ երկիր պագանէն աստուածութեանդ քոյ. եւ 'ի խոնարհեալս
առաջի քո։

§150 «Եւ պահպանեա զսասա ամբողջս»։

Ամբողջ է՝ զոր մեզ համբողջն[25] սահմէ. բովանդակ, ասէ, ամենեքեան ամբողջ պահեացին։

§151 «Տպաւորեա յոգւոջ սոցա զգեւ մարմնոյ ցուցակի»։

զի որպէս մարմնոյ աչաց մերոց ցուցական խորՀուրդս մարմնա-
տեսակ, այսպէս եւ յոգիս մեր օրինակեցի աստուածավայելուչ
փառաց խորՀրդոյս անաւորութիւն. զի տեսան՝ օրինակ է։ Արդ
որպէս վասն Աստուծոյ ասէ առաքեալ, իբրեւ ընդ հայելի
տեսանել զգաաւ նորա, սոյնպէս եւ մեք աղաչեմք անեբեւոյթ
փառաց պատառագին տեսող լինել։

§152 «Առ 'ի ժառանգութիւն եւ 'ի վինակ հանդերձելոյ
քարեացն»։

վինակեցաք, ասէ առաքեալ, յառաջագոյն Հրաւիրեալք. զայն
աղաչեմք՝ զի մ՛ խոտան գոցի ոք. այլ բոլորեքին ժառանցք
հանդերձելոյ քարեացն լիցուք, եւ վինակաւորք եմին։ Յաւելու
եւս.

§153 «Քրիստոսիւ Յիսուսիւ տերամբ մերով»։

Թէ շնորՀօք նորին օժանդակութեամբ հանդերձելոյ քարեացն
արժանասցին, զոր Քրիստոսիւ Յիսուսիւ տերամբ մերով
ընկալան զգրաւականն։

§154 «Ընդ որում քեզ Հոգւոյդ սրբոյ եւ Հօր ամենա-
կալի՝ վայելեն փառք, իշխանութիւն եւ պատիւ. այժմ եւ
միշտ եւ յաւիտեանս յաւիտենից. ամէն։

206

Prayer

§148 *"Fountain of life and salvation and source of mercy:"*
Life and mercy have You as their *source.*

§149 *"Have mercy on this people who bow in worship before Your divinity:"*
May Your *people* which *worship your divinity* and *bow before* You enjoy that everflowing fountain.

§150 *"And preserve them intact:"*
Intact *(ambotĵ)* is what we call *hambotĵ.*[1] It means may all be preserved intact.

§151 *"Impress upon their soul the form of the fleshly sign:"*
For as this mystery is exposed to the eyes of the *flesh,* so may the awesomeness of this glorious mystery which is pleasing to God be imaged in our *souls.* For the *impression* is an image. Now as the apostle describes seeing God's glory as in a mirror (1 Cor 13:12), similarly we ask to view the invisible glory of the sacrifice.

§152 *"For an inheritance and portion of the good things to come."*
The apostle says, "We have as our lot to be invited first" (Eph 1:11). We beg the same, that no one be found unworthy, but all of us be heirs *of the good things to come* and share the lot of the apostle.

It continues:

§153 *"Through Jesus Christ our Lord:"*
Thanks to His help they will be worthy *of the good things to come* which they have received as a pledge *through Jesus Christ our Lord.*

§154 *"With whom glory, dominion and honor befit You, Holy Spirit and the Father Almighty, now and ever and to*

207

§155 «Հայր սուրբ, որ կոչեցեր զմեզ յանուն միածնի Որդւոյ քում քրիստոնեայս»։

Դլխաւորելով որ ինչ վասն մատուցման պատարագին գոհութիւն եւ աղօթք, եւ աւարտեալ զայն առանձնաբար օրհնութեամբ ՚ի սուրբ Երրորդութիւնն, եւ դարձեալ գործնութիւն եւ գիտաս միաւորութեամբ, սկսանի գոհութիւն դարձեալ եւ մաղթանս, որ ոչ բնաւ մարդկութեանս՝ այլ որ Հաւատացելոց միայն։ Եւ քանզի ատգ մեծամայնութեամբ, թէ սրբութիւնՆ սրբոց վայելիցն, եւ յայտնեաց թէ որպիսիք են սրբութիւնՆ, յասեն՝ Հայր սուրբ, Որդի սուրբ, Հոգի սուրբ, եւ սուրբ պատարագն քրիստոսեան՝ վայելէ սուրբ Երրորդութեանդ ընծայ։ եւ թէ որք հաղորդին սրբութեանցն՝ եւ նոքա մաքուր եւ սուրբ պարտին լինել։ եւ զի մարդկային բնութիւնս միշտ աղտեղանայ ՚ի սխալանաց, եւ ոչ կարէ ամենեւին անախտ լինել, կոչէ տկարութեանս մերոյ օգնական զգթութիւնն Աստուծոյ. որով մաքրութիւն ստացեալ՝ ՚ի մաքուրն մերձեցուք։ Եւ նախ առաջին Հայրն ասելով՝ չարժէ ՚ի գթութիւն զմարդասիրութիւնն Աստուծոյ, ապա այնու գոր ՚ի Հայրն յարէ. «Որ կոչեցեր զմեզ յանուն միածնի Որդւոյ քոյ քրիստոնեայս»։ Զի այսպիսի աստ չնորհ եռուր մեզ, զԻո միածնի Որդւոյդ առնուլ զանուն[26]. քանզի դա կոչի Քրիստոս, իսկ մեք քրիստոնեայք, այսինքն քրիստոսեանք. այսու եւ գոհանամք եւ ՚ի գորով ածեմք. զի թէ միՆչ օտարք էաք՝ այսպէս սէրդ քո ստիպեաց դԹալ, մինչեւ միածնիդ քո առնել բաժին եւ ժառանգութիւն, եւ դովիմք անուանիլ, ապա ո՞րչափ քրիստոնեայցս գոլով՝ աղեկէց լինիցիս ՚ի մեզ, վասն քո միոյ միածնիդ եւ սիրելի Որդւոյդ քո՝ մեր լեալ, եւ կոչեցեալ մեր՝ յանուն դորա։

§156 «Եւ շնորհեցեր մեզ մկրտութիւն հոգեւոր աւազանւ ՚ի թողութիւն մեղաց»։

Ոչ, աստ, բաժին միայն եւ ժառանգութիւն եռուր զմեզ միածնի Որդւոյդ քո, ըստ խոստանալոյ մարգարէին՝ թէ տաց քեզ զհեԹանոս ՚ի ժառանգութիւն, այլ եւ եղբարս եւս կամեցար առնել զմեզ սիրելի եւ համագոյ Որդւոյդ քո. զի եղիցի դա ան-

ages of ages. Amen."[1]

§155 *"Holy Father*[1] *who called us Christians by the name of your only-begotten Son:"*

This phrase recapitulates the whole prayer of thanksgiving on offering the sacrifice and concludes it with praises to each person of the Holy Trinity separately. Again offering praises and glory in unity it begins again thanksgiving and petition not for all humanity, but only for believers. And as the priest said with a loud voice that *holy things befit the holy* and demonstrated what is *holy* saying *the Father is holy, the Son is holy, the Spirit is holy and Christ's holy sacrifice is fitting as an offering to the Holy Trinity.* Those also that communicate the *holy things* must be clean and pure, and since human nature always becomes sullied from offences and cannot be completely free from vice, he invokes God's mercy to assist our weakness. Obtaining purification thereby, let us approach the pure one. Opening with the *Father,* it then moves God to compassion through His love for man by the following phrase *who called us Christians by the name of your only-begotten Son.* For You gave us such grace to assume *the name of your only-begotten Son,* (i.e. those belonging to Christ). By this we both render thanks and move God to tenderness, since while we were still strangers, Your love constrained You to show compassion and make us the portion and inheritance of *Your only-begotten* and to be called after Him, now that we are Christians, how much warmth of affection should You show us for the sake of *Your only-begotten* and beloved *Son,* since we are His and are called by His *name.*

§156 *"And You granted us baptism in the spiritual font for the remission of sins:"*

Not only did You give us to *Your only-begotten Son* as a portion and inheritance, as You promised by the prophet: "I will give

209

դրանիկ 'ի մէջ եղբարց բազմաց. յաղագս այնորիկ գազդե-
ղութիւն մեղաց մերոց լուացեր մկրտութեամբ աւազանին. եւ
վերստին ծնընդեամբ Հոգւոյն սրբոյ զմեզ որդիս վերածեր: Այսու
եւս ասէ չերոլւցանել զՀայրական սիրոյ բորբորբոււմն. զի ելողդ
'ի քէն սուրբ Հոգիդ` որ եկնեացն զմեզ` եւ քեզ որդեգիրս
վերածեաց, արժանաւորս արասցէ զմեզ Հաղորդիլ մարմնոյ եւ
արեան միածնիդ քոյ: Եւ քանզի առաւել յոյժ սաստկացաւ սէր
քո 'ի մեզ` ոչ ժուժեցեր` ա՛յլ Որդի ունել զբնութեամբ[27] քո
զՈրդիդ` եւ ա՛յլ զմեզ որ չնորՀօք որդիացաքս. այլ յաղթեալ 'ի
մարդասիրութենէդ` խառնել զնա ընդ մեզ կամեցար. որպէս զի
նա գլուխ մեր լինիցի եւ մեք մարդմին եւ անդամք նորա, եւ
մի լիցուք մարդնով եւ արեամբ Քրիստոսի` 'ի նա յօդեալ եւ
պատշանեալ. Որպէս զի բազումքս մի մարմին եմք 'ի Քրիստոս, ասաց առաքեալ. եւ ըստ այսմ` մի որդի ամենեքեան: Արդ
այապիսի անպատմելի սիրոյ յիշատակ առնելով` ապա զգաձանս
առաջի արկանէ, չընկենուլ 'ի պատուոյն եւ 'ի չնորՀացն` վասն
սխալանաց մեղանաց մերոց. այլ որպէս ասէ, յայնժամ յարա-
ջին վատթարութեանցն` յայապիսի աձեր 'ի լաւութիւն,
մաքուրս եւ այժմ արասցես, եւ այնպէս 'ի մարդմին եւ յա-
րիւնս Քրիստոսի մերձեցուսցես: Ապա ասէ.

§157 «Արա եւ այժմ արժանի ընդունիլ զհաղորդու-
թիւնս զայս 'ի մեղաց թողութիւն»:

Եւ հաղորդութիւն կոչէ` զի կցորդի նա մեզ եւ մեք նմա: Յա-
ղագս որոյ եւ զայապիսի չնորՀէ` գրՀանալ արժանապէս պարտ է.
այապէս ասէ.

§158 «Եւ յամենայնի անդադար փառաւորել զՀայր եւ
զՈրդի եւ զսուրբ Հոգիդ. այժմ եւ միշտ եւ յաւիտեանս
յաւիտենից»:

§159 «'Ի սուրբ[28] պատուական մարմնոյ եւ յարենէ
Տեառն մերոյ եւ փրկչին Յիսուսի Քրիստոսի` որ բաշխի
'ի միջի մերում. սա է կեանդ, յոյս յարութեան, եւ
քաւութիւն եւ թողութիւն մեղաց մերոց»:

'Ի ժողովուրդն դարձուցանէ զբանն` զգուշացուցանելով, թէ առ ո

You the heathen as an inheritance" (Ps 2:8), but You also willed to make us brothers of Your beloved consubstantial *Son that* He might be the first among many brothers (Rom 8:29). Therefore, You washed the stain of our sin by baptism in the font and constituted us sons by rebirth in the Holy Spirit. This passage also indicates the fervor of Your paternal love was so ardent that the Holy Spirit who proceeds from You and who conceived us and adopted us for You would make us worthy to partake of the body and blood of *Your only-begotten Son.* So intense was Your love towards us that You could not be content with having one Son of Your own nature and us whom You adopted by grace. Instead, overcome by Your love for man, You wished to unite Him to us to be our head and we His body and limbs and thus to be the one through Christ's body and blood, joined and conformed to Him. As the apostle said, "We are one body in Christ" (Rom 12:5) and accordingly all one son. Having commemorated such ineffable love, the priest then addresses pleas not to fall from that honor and grace because of our sinful errors. *You have guided us,* it says, *from the depths of abasement to such a state of wellbeing. Preserve us still in that purity and thus grant us to approach Christ's body and blood.*

Then it continues:

§157 *"Make me worthy now to receive this communion for the remission of sin:"*

It calls it *communion* because He is united to us and we to Him. Hence it is necessary worthily to give thanks for such grace, as expressed in the doxology:

§158 *"And to glorify unceasingly in everything the Father, Son and Holy Spirit, now and ever and to ages of ages."*

§159 *"Of the holy, precious body and blood of our Lord and Savior Jesus Christ[1] who is shared among us. This is*

211

մերձին եւ ընդ ում հաղորդին. 'ի սուրբն սրբոց, 'ի պատուական քան զերկինս եւ քան զերկիր, եւ քան զամենայն արարածս. յարաքիչն ամենեցուն, յամենայն պատուական գոյից հատիչն: Նորա է ատ մարմինս այս եւ արիւնս՝ առ որ մեք հպիմք. որ Տէրն մեր է եւ փրկիչն Յիսուս Քրիստոս. որ փրկեաց զմեզ 'ի սատանայէ, եւ ազատեաց 'ի ծառայութենէն մեղաց մերոց, եւ տիրեաց մեզ: Սա 'ի խաչելն վասն մեր՝ անեղծրելի ոսկերօք 'ի խաչին մնաց. իսկ այժմ բաժանի եւ բաշխի 'ի մեզ՝ վասն յամենեսինս խառնման: Սա է կեանք. վասն զի ասաց Տէրն մեր, Որ ուտէ զմացս զայս՝ կեցցէ յաւիտեան: Եւ յոյս է յարութեան. քանզի եւ զայս ասաց Տէրն մեր, Թէ Յարուցից զնա յաւուրն յետնում, որ ուտէ 'ի սմանէ. ոչ Թէ որ ոչ ուտեն 'ի հացս յայսմանէ՝ ոչ յառնեն, այլ զի ոչ վասն կելոյ՝ այլ վասն դա- տելոյ յառնեն, վասն այնորիկ էչ պարգեւ այն յարութիւնն՝ այլ պատիժք. քանզի ասաց Տէրն. Որոց բարիս գործեալ իցէ՝ յա- րութիւն կենաց, եւ որոց զչար արարեալ իցէ՝ յարութիւն դատաստանաց: Յաղագս որոյ գվայելողան չիւր մարմնոյ՝ ատ, սերտիւ յարուցեալ. եւ զայս յոյս զգեցուցանէ քահանայն ժողովրդեանն յասելն, Սա է կեանմ, յոյս յարութեան:

Այլ եւ Քաւութիւն, ատ, եւ թողութիւն մեղաց մերոց. զի յետ ասացանին՝ զախտան խոստովանութեամբ եւ ապաշխա- րութեամբ 'ի սա մերձումն սրբէ. զի ասացանին մաքրութիւն՝ լուացման տարագաւ մաքրէ, եւ խորհրդոյս հաղորդութիւն՝ հա- լոցաց օրինակեալ: Քանզի յախագան՝ 'ի լուանալի անկանիմք նիւթ, որ անտի փոխարկիմք 'ի բնութիւն ոսկւոյ եւ արծաթոյ, որում ոչ լուացման պէտք է այնուհետեւ առ 'ի զգղտն սրբել, այլ հալոցաց կարօտանայ: Վասն այնորիկ 'ի հուրն յայն յաճագին մտանելն առնէ զմաքրումն: Եւ զոր օրինակ անդ 'ի գտումն ոսկւոյ եւ արծաթոյ՝ պիտոյանան եւ այլ ինչ նիւթք, եւ ապա սրբի 'ի նոցունց աղտն հրովն, նոյնպէս եւ ատ խոստովանութիւն եւ ապաշխարութիւն է այնմ մաքրութեան գործակից. եւ որպէս անդ յատուկ հուրն այրէ եւեթ, այլ ոչ եթէ հալէ եւ զատուցանէ զոսկին եւ զարծաթն յաղտոյ, այնպէս

life, hope of resurrection and atonement and remission of our sins:"

This passage is directed to the people admonishing them about who it is they approach and receive in communion, the holy of holies, the one more treasured than heaven and earth and all creation, the creator of all, the inaugurator of everything held in esteem. It is His *body and blood* to which we cleave. He is our Lord and Savior Jesus Christ who has saved us from Satan, freed us from enslavement to our sins and taken possession of us. In His crucifixion for us on the cross His bones remained unbroken (John 19:33), but now He is divided and distributed to us to be united to us all. *This is life* because our Lord said, "Whoever eats this bread will live for ever" (John 6:51). And it is the *hope of resurrection* since our Lord also said: "I will raise on the last day whoever eats of this" (ibid. v. 55). Not that those who do not eat of this bread do not rise, but they rise not for life, but judgement and hence that resurrection is not a gift but punishment since the Lord said, "For those who do good works there is resurrection to life, but for those who have done any evil, resurrection to judgement (John 5:29). The text implies that those who taste of His body are definitely raised and this is the *hope* with which the priest arrays the people in proclaiming: *This is life, the hope of resurrection.*

It continues *atonement and remission of our sins*; for after the baptismal font it is by approaching communion with confession and repentance that stains are cleansed. The purification of the font cleanses under the outward form of washing while communion in the mystery purges like a furnace. By immersion in the font we are transformed by its cleansing agent and acquire the properties of gold and silver which do not require subsequent rinsing but rather a crucible to erase dirt. Therefore, entering that

213

և ատ իմա ստուգապէս այրումն և ոչ սրբութիւն, առանց
խոստովանութեան և ապաշխարութեան 'ի հոգեւոր հուրն
մերձումն։ իսկ ապաշխարութեամբ մերձիլն՝ սրբութիւն հոգ-
լոյն։ Զայսպիսի գբագմօզտութիւն պարգեւի լուեալ ժողովրդոցն
'ի քահանայէն՝ վկայ լինին ամենիցն,

§160 զամէնն *աս*ելով։

§161 «Սադմոս ասացէք Աստուծոյ մերում, սադմոս ա-
սացէք բարեբար և երկնաւոր թագաւորին, որ նստի 'ի
վերայ քերովբից. սադմոս ասացէք, և գիտաս տուք Հօր
և Որդւոյ և Հոգւոյն սրբոյ, այժմ և միշտ և յաւիտեանս յաւիտենից»։

Զի թէպէտ և 'ի սեդանս տեսանի, այլ յերկինս է և 'ի քրով-
բէսն, Աստուած և Թագաւոր ամենեցունg, վասն որոյ սադմոս
ասացէք և փառս տուք նմա, և ընդ նմա՝ Հօր և Հոգւոյն
սրբոյ. զի Աստուածն և Թագաւորն՝ 'ի քերովբէս նստեալն՝
գինէն 'ի սեդանս դնէ մեզ կերակուր և ըմպելի։ Եւ եղիցի
փառաւորեալ սուրբ Երրորդութիւնն. այժմ և միշտ և
յաւիտեանս *յաւիտենից*։

*Դ*արձեալ այլ եւս յաւելադրէ սարկաւագն գնոյն, թէ

§162 «Սադմոս ասացէք Տեառն Աստուծոյ մերոյ, դը-
պիրք, ձայնիւ քաղցրութեամբ. զի նմա վայելեն սադ-
մոսք եւ երգք հոգեւորք»։

վայել է *այսպէս գմեզ սիրողին*՝ սադմոս ասել 'ի ձայն քաղց-
րութեան. քաղցր է Աստուծոյ՝ որ 'ի սուրբ սրտէ սերտ սիրով
օրհնութիւն է՝

§163 «Եւ եւս որբ հաւատով ընկալաք 'ի սուրբ եւ
յանմահ եւ յանապական եւ յաստուածային խորհրդոյս՝
գՏեառնէ գոհացարուք»։

*Վ*ասն զի այսպէս 'ի Տեառնէ վարդապետեցաք. գոհացալ նախ
քան գաւանդելն գխորհուրդն, զի այնպէս եւ մեք արասցուք։
*Ա*րդ քարոզէ սարկաւագն եւ գոհանալ հրամայէ. Եւ եւս որբ
հաւատով ընկալաք, եւ այլն. աս* է*, գոհացարուք հաւատով
ընկալեալ՝ որպէս գմարմին եւ զարիւն Աստուծոյ. քանզի գայս
յայտնէ յասելն, «'ի սուրբ յանմահ յանապական, յաստուա-

214

awesome fire effects cleansing. And as other agents are essential in refining gold and silver to remove the impurities in the fire, so confession and repentance contribute to the cleansing of the eucharist. And as in that case fire alone merely burns without melting them and separating off the impurities, on that analogy yóu are to understand approaching the spiritual fire without confession and repentance precisely as burning and not purification, but approaching with repentance is purification of the soul. Hearing from the priest the manifold advantage of the gift, the people add their testimony to it all in responding:

§160 "Amen."

§161 "Sing a psalm to our God, sing a psalm to our beneficent heavenly King who sits upon the cherubim. Sing a psalm and give glory to the Father, Son and Holy Spirit, now and ever and unto ages of ages:"[1]

Although He is visible on the altar, Christ is also in the heavens and among the cherubim as God and King of all. Therefore sing a psalm and give Him glory and with Him also the Father and the Holy Spirit. For the God and King who sits upon the cherubim places Himself upon this altar as food and drink for us. Therefore, may the Holy Trinity be glorified now and for ever and to ages of ages. Again the deacon repeats:

§162 "Clerks, sing a psalm to the Lord our God with a sweet voice: for psalms and spiritual songs are fitting for him:"

It is fitting to sing psalms to the One who loves us in a sweet voice. Praise from a pure heart with sincere love is sweet to God.

§163 "You who in faith have partaken of this holy, immortal incorrupt and divine mystery, again give thanks to the Lord:"

For so we have been taught by the Lord. He gave thanks before

ծային խորիրդոյս». զի ամենեւին սուրբ եւ առանց մահու եւ
ապականութեան Աստուած է. վասն որոյ ասէ առաքեալ. Որ
միայն ունի զանմահութիւն. իսկ այլքն զանմահութիւն եւ
զանապականութիւն ոչ 'ի բնութենէ ունին, այլ 'ի նմանէ ստա-
նան։ Գոհացարուք՝ զի սրբովն սրբէք, եւ անմահին անմա-
հայք, եւ յԱստուած մերձեցեալ աստուածանայք։

Ապա ասեն միաբան ժողովուրդն.

§164 Գոհանամք զքէն, Տէր։

§165 «Գոհանամք զքէն, Քրիստոս փրկիչ մեր, որ զայսպիսի նաշակումն բարութեան շնորհեցեր մեզ 'ի փրր-
կութիւն կենդանութեան»։

Նախ առաջին զայնմանէ գոհանայ՝ զի փրկեաց զմեզ, եւ ապա՝
զի զայսպիսի նաշակումն եւոր, յորմէ փրկութիւն եւ կենդանութիւն պարգեւի. քանզի ամենայն խարդախութիւնք
դիւացն խափանին, տեսանելով 'ի մեզ զփրկական խորհրդոյն
հաղորդութիւն. քանզի որպէս ասէ երանելի վարդապետն Յովհան,
հուր աճագին տեսանէ 'ի բերանոյ մերոց արձակեալ բան-
սարկուն՝ յորժամ 'ի խորտրղեանն վայելեալ իցեմք, եւ վասն
այնորիկ ոչ մօտ գալ 'ի խարդախել զՈրդ, այլ բացուստ 'ի բաց
փախչի, եւ մեք փրկեալք լինիմք. փրկիմք նովաւ եւ 'ի
հանդերձեալ բարկութենէն։ Կենդանանամք աստ արդարութեան,
վասն զի գործութիւն առնումք յամենայն արդարագործութիւնս.
զի որպէս մեռեալք են ամայիքն արդարութեան՝ 'ի շնորհացն
Աստուծոյ, եւ կենդանիք զոն միայն մեղացն, եւ ամենայն անդամօք զանօրէնութիւն գործեն. սոյնպէս եւ որ արժանապէս
նաշակողքն են սուրբ խորհրդոյն, շնորհօքն Աստուծոյ են լցեալք,
մեռանին ամենայն անդամօք մեղացն, եւ արդարութեանն
կենդանանան ամենեքումբք։ Քանզի աչքն յամենայն ժամ առ
Տէրն լինին ըստ գրեցելոյն, եւ զՆստուած եւ զաստուածոյան
նկատեն. եւ ականջքն ունկնդիր լինին աստուածական խրա-
տուցն. բերանն խօսի զիմաստութիւն հոգելոր, եւ լեզուն զիրա-
լունս եւ օրէնքն Աստուծոյ 'ի սիրտն հաստատեալ՝ անդայթակղ
ղզնացան հաստատուն պահէ, եւ զձեռն առաւելացուցանէ 'ի
գործ Տեառն յամենայն ժամ, եւ առ Աստուած համբառնայ

entrusting the mystery to us that we might also do so. Now the deacon exclaims, bidding us *give thanks, you who in faith have partaken* etc. *Give thanks*, having received it *in faith* as God's body and blood. This is what is expressed in the phrase *for God is* entirely *pure and without death or corruption*. Thus the apostle says, "He alone possesses immortality" (I Tim 6:16). Others do not possess immortality and incorruption by nature, but receive it from Him. *Give thanks* since you are purified by the pure one, and have become immortal through the immortal One and divine by approaching God.

Then the people say together,

§164 *"We give You thanks, Lord."*

§165 *"We give You thanks, Christ our Savior, who granted us such a taste of goodness for salvation and life:"*

First of all the text thanks Him for saving us and then for *granting us such a taste* which bestows both *salvation* and *life*. For all the demons' deceptions are thwarted seeing in us communion in the saving mystery. For as the blessed vardapet Yohan says, "The devil sees fearful fire emanating from our mouths when we taste the mystery and so he does not come near to deceive us by force, but withdraws so that we are saved." We are saved thereby also from the wrath to come. We are given *life* here to further justice, since we are given strength for all just deeds. For as those bereft of God's grace are dead to righteousness and are only alive to sin and implement all their limbs to transgress, similarly, those who worthily taste of this mystery are filled with God's grace and die to sin with all their limbs and become alive with them all to righteousness. For their eyes are towards the Lord at every hour, according to the text (Ps 25 [24]:15) and observe God and what is of God and with their ears they are attentive to divine counsels. Their mouth speaks spiritual wisdom and

217

յորդորէ, եւ յաղաչանս պահէ։ Այսպիսի կենդանութիւն աշխար-
հի՝ սրբով հաղորդութեամբն պարգեւէ, եւ ՚ի Հանդերձեալն ան-
գրաւ եւ մշտնջենաւոր կենդանութիւն, որ Քրիստոսի[29] եւ ընդ
Քրիստոսի է։

Եւ զայսանէ գրհացեալ՝ աղաչանաց սկիզբն առնէ.

§166 «Սովիմբ պահեա զմեզ սրբապէսս[30] եւ անարատս»։ մի՛ աս, տացես տեղի գտանել ՚ի մեզ չարին, եւ
աղտեղել կամ արատել զմեզ. այլ ընդ մեզ լինելով՝ սուրբս եւ
անարատս պահեա. վասն որոյ եւ յարէ ՚ի նոյն։

§167 «Եւ բանակեալ շուրջ զմբօք քոյով աստուածային
խնամօդ, հովուեա զմեզ յանդաստանի կամաց քոց սրբոց եւ
բարսիրաց»։ Հովիւ խնամակալ այսպիսի գլով, որ ՚ի քոց
անդամոց գոչխարքս կերակրես, նոյն խնամօք զմեօք շուրջ
լիցիս, եւ ՚ի գայլոյն պանեսցես, եւ ՚ի մահացու արօտէ հեռի
արածեսցես։ Եւ ո՞ւր լինիցի այն. յաջորդս յայո առնէ։
«Հովուեա զմեզ յանդաստանի կամաց քոց սրբոց եւ բարբե-
սիրաց». քանզի կամք Քրիստոսի արդարութիւն եւ բարե-
գործութիւն է, զայն ասէ ճարակել արժանի արածս. այն է
վայրն դալարւոյ զոր սաղմոսերգուն նուագէ. այն է անդաստան՝
որ ըստ Քրիստոսի կամացն է, անմտանելի գայլուն, քաղաք
որմեալ պատուիրանին ամբութեամբ, որպէս եւ ասէն.

§168 «Որով ամբացեալ յամենայն բանսարկուին ընդդի-
մութեանց»։ ընդդիմութիւն բանսարկուին այն է՝ բարւոյն
զչարն ընդդէմ դնել. խոնարհութեան՝ զհպարտութիւն, հեզու-
թեան՝ զգարկութիւն, սիրոյն՝ զատելութիւն, պարկեշտութեան՝
զանագնութիւն, զզգաստութեան՝ զպղոնկութիւն. նոյնպէս եւ
այլոցն ուղղութեանց զհակառակ չարն ընդդիմադրել։ Յայնցանէ
ասէ ամբացեալ՝

§169 «Քումդ եւեթ արժանի եղիցուք լսել ձայնի. եւ քեզ
միայն քաջայագթ եւ ճշմարիտ հովուիդ հետեւել»։ Ձայն
մադթէ գլսելութիւն, զոր Տէրն ասէ, Ոչխարք իմ ձայնի իմում
լսեն, եւ ես ճանաչեմ զնոսա, եւ զկնի իմ գան, եւ ես տան
նոցա զկեանս յաւիտենականս. զայն աղօթիցն բան հայցէ, լսել

218

their tongue justice and God's law is established in their heart and keeps their steps firm from stumbling and makes their hands abound in the Lord's work at every hour and rouses them to be uplifted to God and supports them in petitions. Such life is bestowed on the world through holy communion and in the world to come eternal life without end which is Christ and with Christ.

Having given thanks to Him, the priest begins to offer petitions:

§166 *"By this keep us pure and spotless:"*
i.e. do not allow evil to find a place in us and defile or stain us. But be with us and *keep us pure and spotless.* And so it continues:

§167 *"And encompassing us with Your divine care, shepherd us in the pasture of Your holy, benevolent will:"*
Since You are such a caring shepherd who feed the sheep with Your limbs, envelop us with the same care and protect us from the wolf and keep us far from the mortal pasture. And where might that be? The continuation makes that clear: *Shepherd us in the pasture of Your holy, benevolent will.* Since Christ's will is righteousness and good deeds, it says, make us worthy to graze on this. That is the green pasture about which the psalmist sings (Ps 23 [22]:2), the meadow which accords with Christ's *will,* impassible to the wolf, a city walled with the fortification of the commandment, as it continues:

§168 *"By which we are fortified against all the devil's assaults:"*
The devil's assault is setting evil against good, pride against humility, rage against meekness, fornication against chastity and pitting the antithetical evil against other virtues. *Fortified* by these, it says:

§169 *"May we be worthy of hearing only Your voice and*

ատէ գվարդապետութեան նորա գնայնն, եւ զկնի նորա երթալ։
Եւ այս է զկնի երթալն. ուրանալ զանձն, եւ 'ի խաչ հապատակ
միշտ կալ, եւ զայն ճանապարհ երթալ՝ զոր Տէրն եցոյց, եւ ընդ
անձուկն³¹ մտանել եւ ընդ նեղն 'ի կեանսն, եւ անդ առնուլ
զայն՝ որ Հայցէ բանիւն որ զՀետ գայ։

§170 «Եւ առ 'ի քէն ընդունել զպատրաստեալ տեղի
յարքայութեան քում»։

Ըստ իւրաքանչիւր արժանաւորութեան պատրաստեալ լինին տե-
դիքն յարքայութեանն Քրիստոսի, յորժամ լուծանէ զԹագաւո-
րութիւնս, եւ միայն Թագաւորութեան նորա կայ եւ մնայ
յաւիտեան։ Զայն օԹեւանս խնդրէ աղօԹիցս բան, եւ յաւելու 'ի
նոյն զպատճառս բարեգործուԹեան։

§171 «Աստուած մեր եւ Տէր մեր Յիսուս Քրիստոս»։

գի արարիչ ես, ասէ, եւ Տէր, որ եւ ազատեցեր զմեզ 'ի մեղաց,
եւ ընդ քով տերուԹեամբդ արժանացուցեր լինել քոյով չար-
չարանօք, որով զանապականուԹիւն ընկալաք. եւ ոչ ըստ արար-
չուԹեանդ միայն տիրես մեզ, որպէս այլոց արարածոց, այլ գի
եւ գնող գնացեր, զպատուական քո զարիւնդ փրկանս տուեալ։
Վասն որոյ 'ի փառս տան Հանգուցանէ զբանն ասելով.

§172 «Որում վայելեն փարք իշխանութիւն եւ պատիւ.
այժմ եւ միշտ եւ յաւիտեանս»։

§173 «Խաղաղութիւն ընդ ամենեսան։

§174 Անքննին, անհաս, երրեակ ինքնութեանդ, հաստիչ,
ընդունօղ եւ անրաժանելի միասնական սուրբ Երրորդութեանդ»։

Անքննին ասի՝ վասն գի չանկանի եւ ոչ միով իւիք ընդ քննու-
Թեամբ. անհաս՝ վասն գի Թէպէտ եւ յանդդնի ոք հասու լինել՝
ոչ կարէ գիտակ լինել Աստուծոյ էուԹեանն կամ մշտնջենա-
ւորուԹեանն. երրեակ է՝ ըստ առանձնաւորութեան. գի Հայր է,
եւ Որդի, եւ Հոգի սուրբ, որոշեալ դիմօք եւ միաւորեալ ա-
ռուԹեամբ. ինքնութիւն է՝ գի ոչ յումեքէ ունի զգոյու-
Թիւնն, այլ ինքնուԹեամբ է, որպէս սուրբ Լուսաւորիչն ասէ.
Տէր Աստուած՝ որ նա միայն ինքնուԹեամբ, եւ ոչ ոք յառաջ

220

following You alone, the victorious and true shepherd:"
The priest prays for the kind of hearing the Lord mentions: "My sheep hear my voice and I recognize them. They follow me and I give them eternal life" (John 10:27). The prayer implores the same, to hear the sound of His teaching and follow Him. And this is to follow, to deny oneself and always bear the cross and go on the road which the Lord mapped out and enter into life by the narrow way, there to gain what is sought in the text which follows:

§170 *"And receive from You the place prepared in Your Kingdom:"*

Places in Christ's *Kingdom* are *prepared* according to the worthiness of each, when He dissolves the *Kingdoms* and only His *Kingdom* stands for ever. The prayer seeks these dwellings and adds the reasons for good works:

§171 *"Our God and our Lord Jesus Christ:"*

For You are creator and *Lord* who freed us from sin and by Your sufferings by which we have received incorruption You made us worthy to be under Your rule. And You rule over us not only in Your capacity as creator, as over the other creatures, but as You bought us at a price, giving Your precious blood as ransom. Therefore the text concludes with the doxology:

§172 *"To whom glory, dominion and honor is fitting, now and ever and to ages of ages."*

§173 *"Peace to all."*

§174 *"To the inscrutable, incomprehensible, triune essence, founder, receiver and indivisible unitary Holy Trinity:"*

Inscrutable because it is not subject to examination in any particular. *Incomprehensible* because though someone may venture to *comprehend*, no one can grasp God's essence and eternity. It is

221

քան զնա։ Հաստիչ է՝ զի հաստատեաց զարարածս՝ յանդոյից գոյացուցեալ, եւ հաստատուն պահէ յիւրաքանչիւր կարգի։ Ընդունող է՝ վասն զի ընդունի եւ խնամէ զբոլոր յինքէնէ եղեալսն[32], եւ պատրաստէ զիւրաքանչիւրոցն պէտս, ոչ միայն Հրեշտակաց եւ մարդկան՝ այլ եւ ամենայն կենդանեաց. եւ բնաւ իսկ տայ գոյից զանձն իւր զարդ եւ զկացումն։ Չերկինս անխոնարհելի պահէ եւ պայծառ՝ լուսաւորացն շրջապնացութեամբ. զերկիր՝ ունի անսասանելի, եւ վայելչացուցանէ զանազան բուսովք եւ տնկովք եւ սերմամբ, զոր եւ առողջ անձրեւածին ամպօք միշելէ ցյացումն. այլ եւ գծով փակէ յիւրն սահմանի, զի մի՛ յատակացն սուզանիցի, կամ եզերոջն ստուումն առնուցու՝ աւելի քան զցամն։ Անգաժանելի է սուրբ Երրորդութիւնն, վասն զի թէ եւ առանձնաւորութեամբ բաժանեալ է սուրբ Երրորդութիւնն՝ այլ ըստ աստուածութեանն անբաժանելի է. մի է բնութիւն սուրբ Երրորդութեանն, մի է էութիւն, մի տէրութիւն, մի կամք, մի փառաւորութիւն։ Եւ նմա միայնոյ վայելէ երկրպագութիւն յամենայն գոյից. որպէս ասէ յետ այսորիկ.

§175 «Որում վայելէն փառք, իշխանութիւն եւ պատիւ. այժմ եւ միշտ եւ յաւիտեանս»։

ՅՈՐԴՈՐԱԿ[33]

Շնորհիւն Աստուծոյ յայտնաբանութիւն արարեալ եկեղեցական կարգադրութեանց՝ ըստ իւրաքանչիւր ժամուց 'ի կատարումն Հասուցաք. ոչ որչափ ունէր խորհրդածութիւն քարոզացն եւ աղօթիցն բանք, այլ որչափ Հասողութիւն մեր բաւեաց՝ Համառօտեցաք։ Եւ թէպէտ եւ բազում են եկեղեցականացն կարգաց զանազանութիւնք, քարոզաց եւ աղօթից եւ պատարագամատուցաց, եւ են որք ըստ Մարտիրոսաց յիշատակի, եւ են որք ըստ տէրունական տօնից՝ ծննդեանն եւ յարութեանն, եւ է որ չնորհատուութիւն կարգեալք. այսինքն՝ 'ի մկրտութիւն, 'ի ձեռնադրութիւն եւ յօրհնութիւն պսակի, եւ 'ի թաղումն մեռելոց, եւ 'ի սեղան Հաստատել, եւ սպաս եկե-

222

triune according to the persons, for it is Father, Son and Holy Spirit, distinct in hypostases but united in divinity. It is *Essence* since it does not derive its existence from anything, but subsists by its essence, as the holy Illuminator says, "Only the Lord God exists in essence,"[1] and there is none before Him. He is *founder* because He founded creation, bringing creatures to existence from non-existence and keeps them firmly in each one's genus. He is *receiver* because He receives and cares for everything which came into being through Him and cares for the needs of each, not only angels and men, but also other animals and gives Himself as an embellishment and support to all that exists. He sustains the sky from falling and keeps it illumined by the orbit of the luminaries. He maintains the earth unshaken and beautifies it with various plants, shrubs and seeds which He irrigates to satiety with rain-bearing clouds. He also confines the sea within its limit, so as not to sink beneath its depths or extend its shores beyond measure. The *Holy Trinity* is *indivisible* since, though the hypostases are distinguished in the *Holy Trinity*, it is *indivisble* in its divinity. The nature of the *Holy Trinity* is one, one essence, one rule, one will, one glory. To it alone is fitting worship by all beings, as it. says after this:

> §175 *"To whom is fit glory, dominion and honor, now and ever and to ages of ages."*

Afterword

By God's grace we have brought to completion our exposition of the ecclesiastical rites for each hour. The bounds of our interpretation were determined by the limitation of our understanding rather than the profundity of thought contained in the text of these proclamations and prayers. Moreover, the diversity of these rites is so vast that not only would we not countenance subjecting them all to detailed scrutiny, but readers would not tolerate listen-

դեցլոյ օրհնել, եւ զջուր սրբել 'ի յայտնութեան Տեառն, եւ
խաչ օրհնել, եւ 'ի յօրհնել գաեր՞մն, զկալ, զզուարակ, զաղ,
զշատ, եւ որ այլ եւս են չնորշաբարշխութիւնք, եւ որ վասն ճա-
նապարհորդաց եւ հիւանդաց, եւ վասն այլ ինչ սովյապխսաց,
զորս բովանդակ բան առ բան ընդ քննութեամբ արկանել, ոչ
միայն մեք գրելոյն չլինեաք հանդուրժող, այլ եւ ոչ ըն-
թերցողքն՝ լսելութեան։ Բայց եթէ հատատութեամբ ոք միտ
դնէ այսոցիկ՝ որ ասացաս, բաւականապէս առ այլսն ամենեսին
միտս ստանայ։ Եւ գի՞նչ աստմք թէ ամենեքումբք գրիցելովլքս
առ բովանդակ թողեալ կարողանայ իմաստից, այլ թէ եւ
մասին ինչ ի ստցանէ հասանէ մտաց՝ բաւականանայ առ ամենայն լրումն եկեղեցական կարգաւորութեանց։

Վասն որոյ ապաչեմ՝ մի' վարկպարազի գործ համարել
գմտածութիւն աստուածեղէն բանից, մանաւանդ զքարոզութեանց
եւ զաղօթից, զորմէ մեր փրկութիւն կախեալ կայ. եւ ոչ միայն
մերն՝ այլ որոց մեք պարտապան իցեմք, եթէ կենդանեաց եւ
եթէ մեռելոց։ Զի ոչ եթէ լեզու որ ընդ օդն բախէն՝ առանց
մտացն զնեստ երթալոյ՝ օգուտ ինչ գործէ. զի սրտագէտն
Աստուած 'ի սիրտն եւ 'ի միտսն եւ ոչ ի բերանն հայի։ Վասն
որոյ արթուն մտօք եւ անգրագ խորհրդով եւ կատարեալիմաստ
հոգւով՝ զաղօթսն հատուսցուք Աստուծոյ, զի գմեզ եւ զայլս
օգտեցուսցուք. եւ մեք յայլոցն աղօթից՝ շահեալ լիցուք։ Քանգի
թէ սրտի մտօք վասն ամենայն հաւատացելոց աղօթս արաս-
ցուք՝ 'ի բոլոր աղօթից հաւատացելոց օգուտ մեզ արասցուք.
քանգի որով չափով չափեմք՝ չափեալ մեզ լինի։ Յաղագս որոյ
նախ անձինս՝ ապա այլոց ամենեցունց տամ զգուշութիւն, հոգ
անձին ունել, եւ յԱստուծոյ օգնութիւն հայցել, զի կարասցուք
ըստ հանջիցն Աստուծոյ մատուցանել նմա զաղօթս մեր։

Եւս առաւել զգուշալի է առաջնորդաց եկեղեցլոյ, որք փոխանակ բովանդակ եկեղեցլոյ՝ զճնոս առ Աստուած ամբառնան,
եւ զամենեցուն Հայցուածն՝ Աստուծոյ պատգամաւորեն։

Որոց հարկ է՝ զի այնպիսի վարս ստանայցեն, որ համար-
ձակութիւն տացեն նոցա առ աստուածխոսութիւն. զի որպէս
Մովսէս՝ յԱստուծոյ տեսութիւնն՝ ողլովքն արժանացին, եւ որ-

224

ing to what we wrote. Among other things they comprise the regular proclamations, prayers and liturgy as well as the variable provisions for martyrs' commemoration, the dominical feasts of Nativity and Resurrection, the sacraments of baptism, ordination, blessing of the marriage crown, burial of the dead and sacramentals for erecting an altar, blessing church vessels, purifying the water at the Lord's Epiphany, blessing the cross, the seed, threshing floor, bull, salt and corn, in addition to prayers for travellers and the sick etc. However, if one applies one's mind with firmness of purpose to those dealt with here, one will gain sufficient grounding to grasp the import of all the rest. Now what is the point we are making? If by building on all those commented upon here one can comprehend the sense of all those omitted, even by penetrating the thought of one part of these, one can cope with all the remaining ecclesiastical rites.

Therefore, I beg you not to regard it a superfluous task to contemplate these divine texts, especially those of the proclamations and prayers, on which our salvation depends, and not only ours but those to whom we are obligated, whether alive or dead. For if the tongue strikes the air without thought following it, it produces no benefit. For God who knows the heart looks at the heart and mind and not the tongue. Therefore, let us render prayer to God with alert mind, undistracted thoughts and soul fully-aware, to be of benefit to ourselves and others and thus gain from others' prayers. For if we pray earnestly for all believers, we will gain a benefit from all the prayers of believers, since the measure by which we measure will be measured to us (Matth 7:2, MK 4:24). Therefore, I admonish first myself and then everyone else to have concern for yourself and seek God's help to enable us to offer Him our prayers as is pleasing to Him.

Prelates of the church should show even greater care since they

պէս երեւմամբ՝ օժական իւրեանց առօթից գնախագնաց զսուլբան ունիցին, եւ նորոք գժողովլրդոյն պատդամմ՝ Աստուծոյ մատուցցեն: Եւ զի ասացի նմանել Մովսիսի մի՛ ինչ անտեղի համարեցցի քո. քանզի որ եւուն գբահանայութիւն մեզ առաքեալքն՝ զԱՀարոն եւ զՄովսէս մեզ ցուցին. եւ այնպիսիք լեալէ ապա ՚ի պաշտօնն մատչել Հրամայեցին: Իսկ եթէ մեզ յօրինականն այնց վերջացեալք եմք՝ այս զի խստուծոյ զՀաւանելն լուաք, այլ զի զանձանց խնդրեմք եւ ոչ զքրիստոսի. զի Քրիստոսա եւ օրինացն նմանելովն՝ շարար աբքայութեանն աբժանի մոից. եւ զայս ոչ առ քանանայս եւեթ օրինադրեաց, այլ Հասարակաց ամենեցունց. քանզի ամենեցուն խմբեալ կուտիցն արանց եւ կանանց, որ յայնժամ մերձ էին՝ սկզբնաւորեաց գբանն. զի յայղ լիցէ՝ թէ նոյն առ յապա Հաւատացելոց՝ այս կանոնեացի սաՀման: Եւ զի՞նչ գոր ասացն. Եթէ ոչ առաւելուգու արդարութիւնն ձեր՝ քան գդպրացն եւ գփարիսեցլողն՝ ոչ մտանէք յարքայութիւնն Աստուծոյ. եւ թէ առ բոլորս ասէ գայս, քանի՞ն է առ քանանայան առաւելութեան խնդիր: Եւ յաւետ յիրաւի. զի նոցա որ ըստ օրինացն էին քանանայք, անասնոց արեամբ քանանայագործութիւն էր. զի ստուերն էին պաշ-տօնեայք, գորոգ ասէ Պաւղոս, թէ առակաւ օրինական երկնա-լորագն էր պաշտօն. իսկ որ շնորՀացս եւ ճշմարտութեանս քանայացան՝ Որդւոյն Աստուծոյ արեանն սպասաւորեալ կարգե-ցան. եւ այս է գոր Պաւղոս երկնաւոր ասաց, եւ առակ սոցա եւ օրինակ լինել ասաց գգՀինն գամենայն: Չի թէպետ եւ յերկրի կատարի՝ այլ ոչ եթէ երկրային նուիրօք, այլ Հացիւն՝ որ իջանէ յերկնից, եւ կեանս տայ աշխարՀի. վասն որոյ եւ դարձեալ իսկ ասէ Պաւղոս երանելին, ՚ի յիշել գորինական պատարագն, թէ վասն որոյ Հարկ էր օրինաւորացն այնպիսեքն սրբել, եւ բուն իսկ երկնաւորացն առաւել եւս պատարագօք քան գնոյնս: Տեսանե՞ս, զի ոչ միայն զպատարագն երկնաւոր կոչէ, այլ եւ զմեզ՝ որք երկնաւոր պատարագին Հաղորդեցաք: Եւ դարձեալ եւս յայտնագոյնս՝ յորժամ ասէ. Եղբարք սուրբք, երկնաւոր կոչմանն բաժանորդք. եւ գերկնաւորն մատուցանեմք պատարագ:

raise their hands to God on behalf of the whole church and convey to Him the petitions of all.

They should attain such a way of life that gives them boldness in addressing God. They should be worthy of seeing God in the spirit like Moses and, as in a vision, have the saints who went before them as helpers in their prayers as the medium by which to communicate the people's words to God. Let no one consider it out of place that I spoke of emulating Moses since the apostles who entrusted us the priesthood revealed to us Aaron and Moses. Only after becoming like them did they rule that one might advance to the office. But if we have fallen short of these models, this is because, although we have heard from God about pleasing Him, we seek to please ourselves and not Christ. For it was not even by conforming to the law that Christ made us worthy of entering the kingdom and he established the following precept not only for priests, but all ordinary believers. Gathering all who were close to Him then in groups of men and women, He inaugurated the teaching to demonstrate that this same canon was fixed for subsequent believers.

And what did He say? "If your righteousness does not exceed that of the scribes and pharisees, you will not enter the kingdom of God" (Matth 5:20). And if He says this to everyone, how much more does this apply to priests. And this is true for all time. Since those who were priests according to the law exercised their priestly functions with the blood of animals, they were ministers of the shadow, whose cult Paul describes as "an image and type of the heavenly" (Heb 8:5). But those who became priest of grace and truth were ordained to offer the blood of the Son of God. This is the heavenly reality to which Paul alluded, stating that all the old order was their image and type.

Although it is celebrated on earth, yet not with earthly gifts,

Ապա կարի յոյժ առաւելուլ պարտիմք՝ քան որք 'ի Հնումն
ստուերապաշտօնքն. զի որում շատ տուաւ՝ շատ խնդրի, Տէրն
ասաց: Վասն որոյ զկատարեալ առաքինութեանցն բուռն հարցուք 'ի կատարելութեանս. եւ զանձինս եւ զիշխեցեալան ապրե-
ցուցանցուք, եւ զայլս բազումս: Եւ հասարակաց ամենեցուն Տէրն
Քրիստոս՝ հասարակաց օգնական լիցի յամենայնի, եւ զանուն
իւր սուրբ փառաւորեսցէ 'ի մեզ որում միշտ փառք. ամէն:

Համարձակեցայ առ այս յանդգնաբար՝ 'ի հարկէ, եւ ոչ զի
անձին փառս ստացայց. այլ զի զեպիսկոպոսութիւն վիճակեցայ,
եւ 'ի վիճակէն՝ տգիտութիւն 'ի յոլովան վարկայ, եւ բանիւ
ամենայն ումեք զրովանդակ զայս ծանուցանել՝ անհնար գիտա-
ցի, պատշաճ համարեցայ 'ի գրի հարկանել. զի թերեւս այսպէս
դիւրին առ ուսանել արաբից կամողաց: Յաղագս որոյ եւ որք
հանդիպին այսոցիկ լսելութեան՝ աղօթս վասն մեր փրկութեան
արասցեն, սուղ աշխատութեանս փոխահատոյց լինել առ 'ի
Քրիստոսէ զնորա ողորմութեանցն պարգեւս: Որում լիցի ամենեցուն մեզ հանդիպել յերկրի եւ յերկինս, եւ փառա վե-
րառաքել Հօր եւ Որդւոյ եւ Հոգւոյն սրբոյ, այժմ եւ միշտ եւ
յաւիտեանս:

228

but with the bread that descends from heaven (John 6:41, 51) and gives life to the world. Moreover, the blessed Paul returns to this again mentioning the sacrifices of the law, affirming "it was necessary for those under the law to be cleansed by even greater sacrifices" (Heb 9:23). Do you see? Not only does he call the sacrifice heavenly, but also us who have communicated of the heavenly sacrifice. And again even more explicitly he calls us "holy brothers, sharers in the heavenly calling" (Heb 3:1) and "heavenly" (cf. Heb 9:23) the sacrifice we offer.

Consequently, we ought greatly to exceed those shadow-ministers of the old dispensation for "to whom much is given, from him much is sought" (Lk 12:48), as the Lord said. Hence, let us match the perfection of our worship by attaining perfect virtue and thus save ourselves and those under our authority and many others. And may Christ, the Lord of all, be the helper of all and may He glorify His holy name in us, to whom be glory for ever. Amen.

I ventured upon this boldly out of necessity and not to win myself renown. It fell to my lot to become bishop and, on taking office, I perceived ignorance was rampant in everyone and, realizing the impossibility of communicating all this to everybody verbally, I deemed it appropriate to commit it to writing to alleviate the task of those eager to learn. And so I ask those who happen to hear this being read to pray for our salvation, to receive from Christ His gifts of mercy in return for this brief composition. Indeed, may all of us receive them on earth and in heaven, and send up glory to Father, Son and Holy Spirit, now and ever and unto ages of ages.

ՅԻՇԱՏԱԿԱՐԱՆ

Շնորհիւն Աստուծոյ եղեւ մեկնութիւն այսմ գրոց՝ 'ի ձեռն Խոսրովայ Անձեւացեաց եպիսկոպոսի, յոյժ հետեւողի պատուիրանացն Աստուծոյ. զոր մեզ եւ դովել անձառ է, զի մի՛ զար—թակղեսչիք 'ի նոյն, վասն դոլոյ նորուն հայր իմ լաս մարմնոյ. որոյ չեմ արժանի կոչիլ որդի եւ ոչ վարձկան, լաս գրեցելումն. այլ 'ի գրելոցդ լինիցին հասու խնդրողքն վասն նորա, որք սրտի մտոք ունկն դնիցեն. որք եւ աղօթիւք փոխադարձել պարտին ընդ տուիցելոյս. եւ հասարակացն տուօղն Աստուած եւ ձեզ հայ—ցողացդ ճիրեացէ զիւրականն պարդեւ: Այլ յոյժ ամաչեցեալ եւ տարակույս դոանիմ ես Դրիդոր, պարտաւոր պատուիրանաց սուրբ դրոց:

Արդ առաջին սուրբ դրոցս այսորիկ դծադրութիւն՝ եղեւ ձեռամբ Սահակայ որդլոյ տեառն Խոսրովու՝ սոյն սուրբ դրոցս մեկնողի, յերեք հարիւր իննսուն եւ ինն Թուականութեանս Հայոց:

Scribal Colophon

By God's grace this commentary was composed by Xosrov, bishop of Anjewac'ik', a man who followed closely God's commandments. For us to praise him is unseemly, so as not to scandalize you, since he is my father according to the flesh. I am not worthy to call myself his son nor his hired help, according to the text (cf. Lk 15:19). But may those who pray for him and pay earnest attention understand what he wrote. After all, they are bound to offer supplication in return for what has been given them here and may God who gives all to all bestow on you who intercede for him His very own gift. But I, Grigor, am very ashamed and perturbed, a defaulter from the commandments of scripture.

Now the first copy of this holy book was made by Sahak, son of bishop Xosrov, the commentator, in the year 399 of the Armenian era (= A.D. 950).

Notes on the Armenian Text

1 Another Ms. reads Քարոզ զկնի աւետարանին:
2 Another Ms. reads մարդասիրութիւնս:
3 Another Ms. reads տկարութեան:
4 Another Ms reads ՛ի բացեալ:
5 Another Ms. reads առաջի մտեալ մեր է հարցումն ՛ի նմանէ ընկալեալ:
6 Another Ms. reads զլեղին զոր ճաշակեաց:
7 Another Ms. reads զքեզ ընդ Հօր եւ ընդ սուրբ Հոգւոյդ:
8 Another Ms. reads լսելով:
9 Another Ms. reads քան սիրոյն, եւ խոտորեա ՛ի չարէն:
10 Another Ms. reads յարդարութեան:
11 Another Ms. reads գործէս:
12 Another Ms. reads միայն ցոյց զվէրսն. չէ յօտարաց:
13 Another Ms. reads պատարագ:
14 Another Ms. reads յապաշխարողաց եւ անմաքրից:
15 Another Ms. adds ՛ի Հօրէ:
16 իմա' անշփոթ միաւորեալ աստուածութեամբ եւ մարդկութեամբ:
17 Another Ms. reads լինէին:
18 Հօր եւ Որդւոյ եւ is ommited by several Mss.
19 One Ms. reads ՛ի քարտռսն: And another ՛ի կուսէն:
20 Thus in Mss.
21 Another Ms. reads մարդ:
22 Other Mss. read չհամարձակիմք:
23 The Mss. read պակասումն:
24 Thus in Mss.
25 Another Ms. reads համողք:
26 Another Ms. reads քո միածնաւ որդւովդ առնու զանունն:
27 Another Ms. reads զբնութեան:
28 The recent Mss. read ՛ի սուրբ ՛ի սուրբ:
29 The more recent Mss. read Քրիստոսիւ:
30 Another Ms. reads սուրբս:
31 Other Mss. read ընդ արձակն:
32 The oldest Ms. reads եղեալսս:
33 This superscription and the text are not represented in the text.

Notes on the English Translation

1)   For an examination of some of the unique features of the Armenian creed see G. Winkler, "Eine bemerkenswerte Stelle im armenischen Glaubensbekenntnis: 'Credimus et in Sanctum Spiritum qui descendit in Jordanem proclamavit missum'", *Or Chr* 63 (1969) pp. 130-162. With regard to the location of the creed one might cite the letter of Vrt'anēs k'erdoł to the Georgian catholicos Kyrion of the turn of the seventh century to the effect that "in orthodox churches all over the world after reading the holy gospel we confess the holy faith defined at Nicaea" (Girk' t'łt'oc', p. 139).

§1, 1   Armenian theologians perceived in their term for deity an etymological support for the doctrine of divine creation, deriving the form *astuac* from the elements *ast* ('here') and *acel* ('to bring') which would connote God's bringing everything into existence. See *ArmB*, vol. 1, 1971, p. 280 from which it appears that Xosrov is the first extant author to attest this view. For its use by the influential thirteenth century scholar Vardan Arewelc'i see M. E. Prud'homme, "Extraits du livre intitulé: Solutions de passages de l'Ecriture Sainte, écrites à la demande de Hethoum Ier . . ." *JA* ser. 6, 9 (1867), p. 170.

§15, 1   More recent manuscripts add here:
> The people says "Amen."
> The priest says, "Blessed be our Lord Jesus Christ."
> The people says, "Amen."
> The priest turns to the people. He bids catechumens depart saying, "May the Lord bless you all."
> The deacon [says] "Sing psalms to the Lord, our God."

Then the hagiody is sung as appointed for the day.

This can hardly originate with Xosrov since it alludes to the hagiody which is otherwise unknown to him as to Nersēs. Moreover, as some of the other passages of this nature, it comments on material the author has already treated. It also pays far more attention to rubrics than does Xosrov. For the various hagiodies see Nersoyan, *Divine Liturgy*, p. 55, 129-211.

§16, 1   The *bema* refers to the raised sanctuary area which is uniquely high in Armenian churches.

2   What follows is in fact a sermon against those ostensibly professing such views.

3   In composing the canons of the confraternity (primarily of young men) of Erznka in 1280 the vardapet Yovhannēs was particularly exercised to institutionalize such acts of piety and social welfare for the benefit of the whole Armenian community. For the critical edition see E. M. Bałdasaryan, *Hovhannes Erznkac'in ev nra xratakan arjakě* [Yovhannēs Erznkac'i and His Paraenetic Prose] Erevan, Armenian Academy of Sciences: 1977, pp. 220-228.

§17, 1   The Armenian term *eraxay* underwent an interesting evolution. Originally meaning catechumen, it was later applied to young children when they became the most common candidates for baptism. See *ArmB*, vol. 2, 1973, p. 35.

2   The *textus receptus* adds a fourth category of worshippers who must leave at this point ('the unclean').

§17, 3   Some manuscripts contain the following addition at this
point:

"The dominical body and salvific blood stand before
us, the heavenly hosts sing immaterially and say
with incessant utterance, "Holy, holy, holy, Lord
of Hosts." Thereafter the catechumens are first
bid to leave who have come to faith, but have not
yet undergone the cleansing of the baptismal font
and are called *of weak faith* because of their incomplete formation, since they are not perfect in faith.
Then follow the penitents who were involved in
serious sin but turned to contrition and came to
confession, but have not yet concluded their term
of penance. Then come the unclean who suffer
from unclean spirits.

Until this point these three groups are intermin-
gled with pure believers to benefit from seeing the
high priest who, formed in the likeness of Christ,
revealed his incomparable love to mankind.
Moreover, the readings from the prophets and
gospel act as a cautionary injunction and suste-
nance in their incomplete state.

But now that Christ the king is about to enter
the sacrament with His beloved and faithful servants who comprise the priestly ranks, it is not
right for any who are imperfect to be present, but
only those made perfect in Christ. The subdeacons
escort them outside and stay by the doors; for they
instruct them and nourish them on the milk of the
Old and New Testaments.

The secondary nature of this material is obvious from the inclusion of the hymn of the great entrance not otherwise referred to by our author as well as the mention of the category of the unclean who, as we saw in the previous note, are unknown to Xosrov.

§22, 1   This citation closely parallels several injunctions of the Holiness Code in Leviticus in general terms. With this we may compare Xosrov's comment in §33 about approaching "the holy mystery with all holiness."

§42, 1   Here the *textus receptus* adds "let us stand well" adopted from the Liturgy of St. John Chrysostom (Trempelas, *Three Liturgies*, p. 95).

§46, 1   For a detailed examination of this passage see R. Taft, "The Dialogue before the Anaphora in the Byzantine Eucharistic Liturgy I: The Opening Greeting," *OCP* 52 (1986), pp. 299-324.

§47, 1   The formula Xosrov adduces here is highly unusual. It does not recur elsewhere in his text, nor is it paralleled by Nersēs or the *textus receptus*.

§48, 1   For a detailed examination of this passage of great antiquity see R. Taft, "The Dialogue before the Anaphora in the Byzantine Eucharistic Liturgy II: The *Sursum corda*," *OCP* 54 (1988), pp. 47-77.

§50, 1   For the background to this passage see R. Taft, "The Dialogue before the Anaphora in the Byzantine Eucharistic Liturgy III: 'Let us give thanks to the Lord—It is fitting and right,'" OCP 55 (1989), pp. 63-74 (esp. p. 66 for the Armenian addition).

§52, 1   As witnessed by Xosrov, the prayer of the preface begins with an invocation to the trinity and then turns fairly abruptly to address the Father.   By Nersēs' time this difficult transition was obviated by eliminating the trinitarian phraseology and directing the whole prayer to the Father.   With minor variations the revised form is preserved in the *textus receptus* (Nersoyan, *Divine Liturgy*, pp. 64-65).

§61, 1   Xosrov's explication elaborates the etymology of the terms *zuart'un* ('angel') and *zuart'* ('joyful').   From the basic sense of brightness of mood *zuart'un* derives the more specific connotation of alertness and vigilance in which sense it renders the angelic 'watcher' of Dan 4:10 and hence becomes a variant of the standard *hreštak* ('messenger, angel').   See *ArmB*, vol. 2, 1973, p. 107.

2   Subsequently the attempt was made to parallel Ps. Dionysius' distinction of nine angelic ranks by an equal number of ecclesiastical offices for the clergy.   For a discussion of how this affected Armeno-Byzantine relations see Cowe, "Job Fragment."

§68, 1   Xosrov here adduces a repetition of the previous refrain where Nersēs reflects the semitic form (*ovsanna*) of the gospel passage.

2   The reference to the Spirit's descent at Christ's baptism in the Jordan and upon the apostles at Pentecost derives from the

237

Armenian form of the creed (Nersoyan, *Divine Liturgy*, pp. 48-49).

§74, 1 For the significance of these figures see R. W. Thomson, "Number Symbolism and Patristic Exegesis in Some Early Armenian Writers," *HA* 90 (1976), cols. 117-138.

§82, 1 By Nersēs' time this phrase had been embellished by the addition of the epithets "divine, immortal, spotless" (Gat'rčean/Tašean, *Pataragamatoyc'k'*, p. 544).

§84, 1 The phrase was later expanded by the insertion of the epithets "holy and seated," witnessed by Nersēs (ibid.).

§85, 2 Although the reference to 'all' is still found in Nersēs (ibid.), it is absent from the *textus receptus* (Nersoyan, *Divine Liturgy*, pp. 66-67).

3 By Nersēs' time the text concluded with the phrase "for the atonement and remission of sins" (Gat'rčean/Tašean, *Pataragamatoyc'k'*, p. 544).

§85, 1 Nersēs witnesses here the plus "He wiped" (*srbeac'*) (ibid.) along with some manuscripts of the missal. Others read "He drank" (*ēarb*, a post-classical form; see Meillet, *Elementarbuch*, p. 94) which became the *textus receptus* (Nersoyan, *Divine Liturgy*, pp. 68-69). The former reading would seem to imply the latter: i. e. Christ wiped the cup before passing it to the disciples, having already drunk from it Himself.

2 As in §84, 1, Nersēs adduces the qualification of the

238

disciples as "holy and seated."

3   Although still witnessed by Nersēs (Gat'rčean/Tašean, *Pataragamatoyc'k'*, p. 544), the first imperative fell out of the *textus receptus* (Nersoyan, *Divine Liturgy*, p. 69), perhaps under the influence of Matth 26:27.

4   As in §84, 3 Nersēs and the *textus receptus* witness here also the variant on the theme ("for the remission of sin").

§89, 1 By Nersēs' time the text had been altered to state that Christ demonstrated the Father was "true God, the God of the living and the dead" (Gat'rčean/Tašean, *Pataragamatoyc'k'*, p. 545), a reading also accepted into the *textus receptus* in abbreviated form.

§95, 1 Nersēs adduces a further phrase relating to Christ's sitting at the right hand of the Father (Gat'rčean/Tašean, *Pataragamatoyc'k'*, p. 545) which parallels Byzantine usage. See Trempelas, *Three Liturgies*, p. 109.

§101, 1 This reference seems to allude to a passage in the homily on the church, confirming the editor's attribution of the piece to Catholicos Yovhannēs (Ōjnec'i, *Matenagrut'iwnk'*, p. 154). There too, the coherence, as well as contrast, between the earthly and heavenly aspects of the sacrifice are discussed.

§102, 1 More recent manuscripts add here:

>People: And with your spirit.
>Deacon: Let us bow before God.

239

People: Before you, Lord:
The priest bows, kisses the altar and says this prayer:

One must realize that all the text of the prayer uttered by the priest to this point is analogous to that of a prince's friend who wishes to reconcile him to a servant he is angry with on account of some misdemeanor. First he implores him to be reconciled and accept the sweetener the servant has offered and, when the other takes it, he perceives the reconciliation has been effected. Next he thanks him and is then emboldened to make further petitions. So now the priest as an intermediary rehearses all Christ's economy as if it had all been accomplished today and he had presented offerings to the Father. Then when the Father was pleased to accept them, he gives thanks to Him. Now therefore he is emboldened to ask Him for other petitions. And what is the petition? It is as follows:

Although this commentary is very much in Xosrov's character, making the analogy between relations with God and those with a secular prince and yet there are a number of difficulties in accepting its authenticity. As we have seen, Xosrov rarely mentions rubrics concerning the priest's actions as here. Moreover, the passage does not dovetail well into the present context but rather overlaps with some of its material (see *let us bow before God* and §103 *Then the priest says*).

§104, 1 This *epiclesis* formula recurs in Nersēs but differs from the *textus receptus*. The latter not only blesses the elements separately, but also together, like the liturgy of St. John Chrysostom with which it also shares the phrase relating to the Spirit's transforming operation (Trempelas, *Three Liturgies*, p. 115). At the same time, the *textus receptus* is unusual in performing thrice each of the three blessings, which is clearly a further example of its powerful trinitarian focus.

2   This verb represents the traditional Armenian formulation of the union of Godhead and manhood in Christ. See R. W. Thomson, *The Teaching of St. Gregory: An Early Armenian Catechism*, Cambridge, MA, Harvard University Press: 1970, pp. 19-21.

§105, 1 More recent manuscripts add here:
> And the priest kisses the altar and then lowers his hands to the level of the gifts and, fixing his gaze upon them, he says the silent prayer.
> Thereafter, he beseeches the Father through the visible gifts; for at the descent of the Holy Spirit upon the gifts the dead material [became] alive and the inanimate became animate. It truly became a type and was transformed in reality into a symbol of Christ's body and blood. Therefore, directing his supplication to God, he appeals as follows:

This treatment appears dependent on Nersēs' commentary *ad loc*. Once more it gives greater attention to rubrics than is normal for Xosrov.

§106, 1 Xosrov does not adduce the petition "for the whole world" which precedes that for the church in Nersēs and the *tex-*

tus receptus. See also Trempelas, *Three Liturgies*, p. 124.

§111, 1 In the ordering familiar to Nersēs apostles preceded prophets and this in turn was preceded by 'holy patriarchs.' The *textus receptus* goes one step further in prefixing 'forefathers' to the list in keeping with the Liturgy of St. John Chrysostom (Trempelas, *Three Liturgies*, p. 115).

2   As Xosrov explains, *uxt* ('covenant') refers here to the clergy. For a discussion of the term's semantic range see R. W. Thomson, *Ełishē: History of Vardan and the Armenian War*, Cambridge, MA, Harvard University Press: 1982, pp. 9-11.

§113, 1 More recent manuscripts add here the following commentary:

> Someone may ask, "How can it be that the priest commemorates the righteous also as in need, although we look to their intercession? This is to be understood in the following way. Although they have been glorified and are at rest, they have not attained to full perfection. Rather they hunger from day to day and seek growth; for there is no fulfilment to the incorporeal glory to which they have attained, since its wisdom is spiritual and knowledge divine. Hence, if there can be no limit to our earthly science, how much more to that which is purely intelligible and divine. On the contrary, they ascend daily from glory to glory as the angels. Each day they receive new knowledge and understanding from God as the saints.
> Thus, first [the priest] implores Christ's mercy

on them and then he commemorates the others in order. But note, you who are wise and prudent, that in the order of prayers you offer you commemorate first the living and then the departed. From this you are to learn precisely that the divine sacrifice is firstly for the salvation of the living and then of the dead. The childish view that there is no need to commemorate the living in the liturgy has no basis. Are not kings alive, along with princes, bishops and priests, wayfarers and sailors, the sick and all the others? If you want to know the truth, the sacrifice you offer is not only for one person, as some people think, but for the whole world, as the text of the prayer makes clear.

But if anyone gives you a donation in faith and asks you to commemorate him or someone else either living or dead during the liturgy, you should first examine his way of life to determine whether he is worthy of commemoration before the fearful mystery or could be dissolute, a fornicator, adulterer or drunkard, oppressor or criminal. If you were to accept something from someone like that and sacrifice Christ, you would be an accessory to his wrongdoing and would abuse not only the petitions but also your priestly order. However, if the person making a donation in faith to commemorate him in the liturgy you offer is reverent and pious, then though you offer the liturgy for the whole world, the donor would be blessed in return according to his hope not only through the liturgy you offered him but from everywhere in the world where

Christ is sacrificed in orthodox churches, a hundredfold in this life and in the life to come would inherit eternal life. The Lord is one and there is a single mystery of His body and blood which is fulfilled throughout the universe.

Similarly, when you offer the liturgy on behalf of the dead, inquire whether they had performed good deeds before they left the world or again sinned and had remorse and made an acceptable confession and penance and proved their worthiness through tears and almsgiving. But those not like that who were found to be unremorseful and heedless and not even worthy of repentance at their last hour, it is not right to commemorate at the liturgy.

But be even more ready in your own soul to be completely pure and free from every stain of sin, especially from the passions of rapacity and vanity; for then you would be peddling Christ, which is worse than what Judas did.

This section can hardly belong to Xosrov since the text commented upon is not that with which our author was familiar (e.g. the reference to sailors in the diptychs as well as to prayers for the whole world). It also appears that the main issue of contention over whether the liturgy could be offered on behalf of the living arose in the period after Xosrov when it became common to honor the major benefactors of a church or monastery with an annual liturgy in perpetuity. The rectitude of offering the liturgy on behalf of the living was upheld in the third canon of the Council of Sis in 1203 (Mxit'areanc', *Patmut'iwn xołovoc'*, p. 119).

§117, 1 In this paragraph Xosrov outlines the advantages of

brevity and conciseness in matters of faith. The origin of this approach can be traced to the Armenian rendering of the compound form ὀρθοτομοῦντα in 2 Tim 2:1 by *uṙiṙ hamaṙotel*, interpreting the verbal component in terms of συντέμνειν ('to talk succinctly'). This basic equivalency was retained in translating the liturgy. The phrase with which Xosrov was familiar is introduced by the metaphor of straight steps characteristic of the psalter (37 [36]:23, 60 [59]:10 etc.). By Nersēs' time this was replaced by the more direct expression 'with right teaching' (Gat'rčean/Tašean, *Pataragamatoyc'k'*, p. 548) which reappears in the later form of the petition for the local bishop.

§129, 1 As in §106 Xosrov has no acquaintance with the petition for the whole world.

§130, 1 This petition is unattested by Nersēs and the *textus receptus*, both of which in diverse language evince a prayer for kings and princes. In view of the almost continual hostilities in which the Cilician realm was embroiled, Nersēs adduces a further petition for the release of brethren in captivity (Gat'rčean/Tašean, *Pataragamatoyc'k'*, p. 548).

§136, 1 See G. Zarbhanalean, *Matenadaran haykakan t'argmanut'eanc' naxneac'* (dar d-žg) [Library of Early Armenian Translations: fourth-thirteenth centuries] Venice, Mxit'arist Press: 1889, p. 364 for the Armenian version of St. Gregory of Nyssa's commentary on the Lord's Prayer and p. 582 for St. John Chrysostom's commentary on St. Matthew's gospel where he treats the same text.

§145, 1 Strangely Nersēs does not appear to adduce the *embolis*

(Gat'rčean/Tašean, *Pataragamatoyc'k'*, pp. 550-551). The form preserved by the *textus receptus* has been expanded at this point by the reverential phrases "King everlasting, creator of all creatures" (Nersoyan, *Divine Liturgy*, pp. 82-83).

§147, 1 The more recent manuscripts add here:

> The priest bestows the peace.
> People: And with your spirit.
> Deacon: Let us bow before God.
> People: Before You.
> This completes the prayer to the Father. Now focus is directed to the divine mystery. Thus, first the priest gives the peace and the deacon bids them [the congregation] bow so as not to be negligent or inadvertent in witnessing this great mystery. Also when they bend to make a prostration, as they witness it, the priest bows his head like the people and prays to the Holy Spirit since, as we have said, every bestowal of grace is from the Holy Spirit. First the Holy Spirit divinized the symbols and so now the priest prays to the Holy Spirit on behalf of the people.

Once again it appears that these comments devote more attention to rubrics than Xosrov tends to allow. His coverage passes directly from the *embolis* to the prayer of inclination, and yet it is clear from the text of the latter that the deacon has admonished the people to bow their heads. Consequently, this section is not so alien to its context as some of the others we have considered.

§150, 1 For this dialectical variant see *ArmB* vol. 1, 1971, p. 152.

§154, 1 The more recent manuscripts add here:

The deacon says in a loud voice, *Prosxumē* (let us attend). This Greek word means pay attention or look upwards. The priest elevates the host above his head and says, "For the sanctification of the saints."

The people is moved by the deacon's exclamation, "Look up in fear," and when they have heard and seen the object of their desire, the priest says "This is sanctification," but sanctification of the saints and those who have been purified and have cleansed themselves of sin by confession and tears.

The clerks sing in unison, "You alone are holy, You alone are Lord, Jesus Christ, to the glory of God the Father. Amen."

From excess of joy they confess their indebtedness, saying, "Our Lord is priest. What is the source of our sanctification when we live according to flesh and blood? Only the Holy of Holies is holy who alone is Lord of heaven and earth—our Lord Jesus Christ to the glory of the Father who is glorified [with Him]."

Holding the host in both hands, the priest says:
"Blessed is the holy Father, the true God."
"The clerk says, "Amen."
"Blessed is the holy Son, the true God."
The clerk: "Amen."
"Blessed is the Holy Spirit, the true God."
The clerk: "Amen. Praise and glory to the Father, Son and Holy Spirit. Since the priest received this great grace from the trinity, he offers

Him the song of thanksgiving and the clerks repeat the same as the priest.

The priest bows again, prays and says: "Lord Jesus Christ, look down from Your holiness and the glorious throne of Your kingdom." This demonstrates the Son's infinite divinity.

"Come to purify and save us, You who sit with the Father and are sacrificed here."

Christ is the sanctification and vivification of everyone. Though indivisibly with the Father, He is constantly sacrificed on the altar.

"Make us worthy to partake of Your stainless body and precious blood and all the people at our hand. For by our deeds we have no boldness to approach You. In Your mercy make us worthy and through us all the people."

Saying this, he kisses the altar. Taking the holy body, he dips it whole into the incorrupt blood and raises it to be visible to the people and says [that prayer]. Firstly, he kissed the altar when he came before it at the beginning of the liturgy; then when he implored the Spirit to descend and perform the sacrifice and now he kisses it a third time.

As when a messenger comes into the presence of the king he first makes obeisance and then delivers his message, this is symbolic of the priest's first bow. As when someone receives a favor from the king he bows and thanks him, so [the priest] bowed and gave thanks when he received the Spirit. Similarly, now he gives thanks on receiving the other petitions and says the following prayer.

Once again the rubrics in this passage are much more developed than those of Xosrov's time, as is the rite it presents. In particular, it adduces the hymn and prayer of the elevation which entered the Armenian liturgy from the Byzantine ordo probably in the late eleventh or twelfth century and are first witnessed by Nersēs. However, the structure outlined here seems even more advanced than this: whereas Nersēs describes the people as singing the hymn, here it has already been assigned to the clerks who later echo the priest's blessings to the holy trinity in the hymn of the doxology, an element not yet elaborated in Nersēs' time (Gat'rčean/Tašean, *Pataragamatoyc'k'*, pp. 551-552). Nevertheless, most of the rubrics are a close approximation to what we find in Nersēs whose order of the sections is also preserved. Hence, in contrast to the later *textus receptus*, the prayer of elevation follows the blessings to the trinity rather than preceding it according to current practice (Nersoyan, *Divine Liturgy*, pp. 84-87). The contextual rendering of the Greek diaconal proclamation πρόσχωμεν as 'look upwards' suggests the author did not share Xosrov's interest in Greek philology and etymology.

§155, 1 Although the prayer of intinction in the *textus receptus* largely preserves the format of Xosrov's period, the opening of the later first prayer before communion (Nersoyan *Divine Liturgy*, pp. 88-89) commencing with the phrase "Holy Father" is a better reflection of Xosrov's data than the current introduction "O Lord our God" (ibid., pp. 86-87).

§159, 1 In the exhortation for communion by Xosrov there is an ellipse of the verb of partaking which is supplied in Nersēs' text *čašakesc'uk'*, 'let us taste' (Gat'rčean/Tašean, *Pataragamatoyc'k'*, p. 552). Strikingly, the later text also alludes to Christ's body and blood descending from heaven (cf. Jn 6:50-51). This would seem to imply that by this period the influence of Yovhannēs Mayragomec'i and his aphthartodocetist disciples had largely been overcome, so that such language would no longer be misinterpreted as undermining the reality of the incarnation.

§161, 1 Neither Nersēs nor the *textus receptus* witnesses the third repetition of the exhortation with doxology.

§170, 1 The reference is to a statement of St. Gregory in his preliminary exhortations which is then repeated at the outset of his teaching as documented by the hagiographer Agathangelos who probably wrote in the 460's. For the text see G. Tēr-Mkrtč'ean and St. Kanayeanc' (eds.), *Agat'angełay patmut'iwn hayoc'* [Agathangelos' History of the Armenians] Tiflis, Martiroseanc': 1909, §254, p. 131 (cf. §259, p. 134) and for an English translation R. W. Thomson *Agathangelos History of the Armenians* Albany, State University of New York Press: 1976, p. 253.

Bibliography

i *Abbreviations*

AJ	*Acta Jutlandica*
AnjB	H. Ačaŕean, *Hayoc' anjnanunneri baŕaran* [Armenian Prosopographical Dictionary] Beirut, Sewan Press: 5 vols. 1972.
ArmB	H. Ačaŕyan, *Hayeren armatakan baŕaran* [Armenian Etymological Dictionary] Erevan, Erevan State University: 4 vols. 1971-79.
ASIMHB	*Armenian Studies in Memoriam Haïg Berbérian*, D. Kouymjian (ed.), Lisboa, Calouste Gulbenkian Foundation: 1986.
BMat	*Banber Matenadarani* [Library Herald]
CA	*Cahiers archéologiques*
CSCO	Corpus Scriptorum Christianorum Orientalium
DOS	Dumbarton Oaks Studies
ECR	*Eastern Churches Review*
EO	*Echos d'Orient*
HA	*Handēs amsōreay*
JA	*Journal Asiatique*
JSAS	*Journal of the Society for Armenian Studies*
JTS	*Journal of Theological Studies*
Mus	*Le Muséon*
NBH	*Nor baŕgirk' haykazean lezui* [New Dictionary of the

251

Armenian Language] Venice, St. Lazar's Press 2 vols. 1836-7.

OCA	Orientalia Christiana Analecta
OCP	*Orientalia Christiana Periodica*
Or Chr	*Oriens Christianus*
PBH	*Patmabanasirakan Handes* [Historico-philological Journal]
PG	*Patrologia Graeca*
REA	*Revue des études arméniennes*
RHE	*Revue d'histoire ecclésiastique*
RHR	*Revue de l'histoire des religions*
UPATS	University of Pennsylvania Armenian Texts and Studies

ii *Editions of Armenian Texts*

Anania Mokac'i, "Letters"
> G. Tēr-Mkrtč'ean (ed.), *"Teařn Anania hayoc' kat'ořikosi jaŧags apstambut'ean tann Ałuanic'"* [Concerning the Revolt of the House of Albania by the Lord Anania, Catholicos of the Armenians] etc. *Ararat* (1897), pp. 129-144, 275-288.

Gat'rčean/Tašean, *Pataragamatoyc'k'*
> Y. Gat'rčean and Y. Tašean, *Srbazan pataragamatoyc'k' hayoc'* [Armenian Holy Missals] Vienna, Mxit'arist Press: 1897.

Girk' t'łt'oc' [Book of Letters] Tiflis, 1901.

Kirakos, *Patmut'iwn*
> Kirakos Ganjakec'i, *Hamařōt patmut'iwn* [Brief History] Venice, Mxit'arist Press: 1865.

Mandakuni, *Čaṙk'*

Teaṙn Yovhannu Mandakunwoy hayoc' hayrapeti čaṙk' [Homilies of the Lord Yovhan Mandakuni, Catholicos of the Armenians] 2nd ed., Venice, St. Lazar's Press: 1860.

Nersēs, *Meknut'iwn*

Xorhrdacut'iwnk' i kargs ekełec'woy ew meknut'iwn xorhrdoy pataragin [Meditations on Church Order and Commentary on the Mystery of the Liturgy] Venice, St. Lazar's Press: 1847.

ōjnec'i, *Matenagrut'iwnk'*

Yovhannu Imastasiri Awjnec'woy Matenagrut'iwnk' [Complete Works of Yovhannēs ōjnec'i the Philosopher] Venice, St. Lazar's Press: 1953.

Xosrov, *Meknut'iwn*

Xosrov Anjewac'eac' episkoposi meknut'iwn ałotic' pataragin [Xosrov bishop of Anjewac'ik''s Commentary on the Prayers of the Liturgy] Venice, St. Lazar's Press: 1869.

Yovsep'eanc', *Yišatakarank'*

G. Yovsep'eanc', Yišatakarank' jeṙagrac' [Manuscript Colophons] Antelias: 1951.

iii *Secondary Studies*

Anasyan, *Matenagitut'yun*

H. Anasyan, Haykakan matenagitut'yun [Armenian Bibliography] Erevan, Armenian Academy of Science, vol. 1, 1959.

Baumstark, "Denkmäler"

A. Baumstark, "Denkmäler altarmenischer Messliturgie 3. Die armenische Rezension der Jakobusliturgie," Or Chr n. ser. vii (1918), pp. 1-32.

Beck, *Kirche*

> H.-G. Beck, *Kirche und theologische Literatur im byzantinischen Reich*, Munich, Beck: 1959.

Bogharian, *Hay grotner*

> N. Bogharian, *Hay grotner* [Armenian Writers] Jerusalem, St. James Press: 1971.

Bogharian, *Mayr c'uc'ak*

> N. Bogharian, *Mayr c'uc'ak jeragrac' srboc' Yakovbeanc'* [Grand Catalogue of the St. James Manuscripts] Jerusalem, St. James Press, vols. 1-9, 1966-79.

Conybeare, *Rituale*

> F. C. Conybeare, *Rituale Armenorum*, Oxford, Clarendon Press: 1905.

Cowe, "Job Fragment"

> S. P. Cowe, "An Armenian Job Fragment from Sinai and Its Implications," *Or Chr* 76(1992).

Cowe, *Daniel*

> S. P. Cowe, *The Armenian Version of Daniel*, UPSATS Atlanta, GA, Scholars Press [in press].

Engberding, *Hochgebet*

> H. Engberding, *Das eucharistische Hochgebet des Basileios-liturgie. Textgeschichtliche Untersuchungen und kritische Ausgabe*, Münster, 1931.

Hage, *Syrisch-jakobitische Kirche*

> *Die syrisch-jakobitische Kirche in frühislamischer Zeit* Wiesbaden, Harrassowitz: 1966.

Kolandjian, "Uxtanēs"

> S. E. Kolandjian, "The Tenth Century Armenian Historian

Uxtanēs: Was He Bishop of Sebastia or Edessa?" *ASIMHB*, pp. 397-413.

Mathews/Sanjian, *Armenian Gospel*
>T. F. Mathews and A. K. Sanjian, *Armenian Gospel Iconography* DOS XXIX Washington, D. C.: 1991.

Mécérian, *Livre de prières*
>I. Kechichian, *Grégoire de Narek Le livre de prières avec une preface de J. Mécérian, S. J.*, Paris, Cerf: 1961, pp. 7-25.

Meillet, *Elementarbuch*
>A. Meillet, *Altarmenisches Elementarbuch*, Heidelberg, Carl Winters Universitäts-Buchhandlung: 1913.

Meyendorff, *St. Germanos*
>P. Meyendorff, *St. Germanos of Constantinople on the Divine Liturgy*, Crestwood, NY, St. Vladimir's Seminary Press: 1984.

Mxit'areanc', *Patmut'iwn žołovoc'*
>A. Mxit'areanc', *Patmut'iwn žołovoc' hayastaneayc' ekełec'woy* [History of the Councils of the Armenian Church] Vałaršapat, Catholicate Press: 1874.

Nersessian, *Tondrakian Movement*
>V. Nersessian, *The Tondrakian Movement: Religious Movements in the Armenian Church from the Fourth to the Tenth Centuries* London, Kahn and Averill: 1987.

Nersoyan, *Divine Liturgy*
>T. Nersoyan, *Divine Liturgy of the Armenian Apostolic Orthodox Church* New York, Delphic Press: 1950.

Salaville, "Consécràtion"
>S. Salaville, "Consécration et epiclèse dans l'église arménienne au xiie siècle. Témoignage de S. Nerses de Lampron," *EO LXVI*

(1913), pp. 28-31.

Salaville, "Explication"

S. Salaville, "L'explication de la Messe de l'arménien Chosrov (950). Théologie et liturgie," EO XXXIX (1940), pp. 349-382.

Taft, *Beyond East and West*

R. Taft, *Beyond East and West: Problems in Theological Understanding*, Washington, D. C., Pastoral Press: 1984.

Taft, *The Great Entrance*

R. Taft, *The Great Entrance: A History of the Transfer of Gifts and Other Preanaphoral Rites of the Liturgy of St. John Chrysostom*, OCA 200 Rome: 1975

Trempelas, *Three Liturgies*

P. Trempelas, Αι τρεῖς λειτουργίαι κατὰ τοὺς 'ἐν 'Αθήναις κώδικας Athens, Verlag der Byzantinisch-neugriechischen Jahrbücher, 1935.

Vetter, *Explicatio*

P. Vetter, *Chosroae magni episcopi monophysitici explicatio precum missae* Freiburg-im-Breisgau, Herder: 1880.

Yarnley, "Armenian Philhellenes"

C. Yarnley, "The Armenian Philhellenes. A Study in the Spread of Byzantine Religious and Cultural Ideas Among the Armenians in the Tenth and Eleventh Centuries," ECR VIII (1976), pp. 45-53.

Index of Scriptural Citations and Allusions

General Index

3) Modern Scholars

Nersessian, V., 17, 84.

Nersoyan,T., 29, 42, 43, 45-47, 49, 50, 93, 234, 237, 238, 246, 249.

Renoux, A., 41.

Robinson, N. F., 15.

Rücker, A., 41, 43.

Sahakyan, A. S., 18.

šahnazareanc', K., 16, 83.

Salaville, S., 82-84, 90.

Sanjian, A. K., 62, 63, 92.

Shrikian, G., 45.

Siwrmæean, A., 86.

Spinks, B. D., 49.

Taft, R., 44-50, 92, 236.

Tašean, Y., 41-45, 47, 49, 238, 239, 245, 246, 249.

Tēr-Mik'ayelean, A., 18.

Tēr-Mkrtč'ean, G., 250.

Thomson, R. W., 41, 63, 86, 238, 241, 242, 250.

Trempelas, P., 49, 50, 236, 239, 241, 242.

Vetter, P., 83, 84.

Walter, C., 18.

Ware, K. T., 16.

Wawryk, M., 15.

Winkler, G., 42, 49, 233.

Xač'ikyan, L., 44.

Yarnley, C., 82, 84.

Yuzbašyan, K. N., 84.

Zarbhanalean, G., 245.

4) Toponyms

Albania, 4, 8.

Alexandria, 52.

Ałt'amar, 18, 82.

Amida, 6.

Ani, 9, 39, 77.

Anjewac'ik', 4, 5, 9-11, 231.

Antioch, 22, 52, 59.

Arcn, 77.

Argina, 18.

Armenia, 5, 6, 9, 19, 24, 50, 53, 76.

Babel, 60.

Byzantium, 7.

Caesarea, 19.

Cappadocia, 19, 39, 48, 69.

Chalcedon, 5.

Cilicia, 21, 47.

Constantinople, 32, 33, 50, 51, 64 (see also Byzantium).

Duin, 16, 31, 78, 85.

Edessa, 19.

Egypt, 153.

Erevan, 44.

Georgia, 5.

Gethsemane, 76.

Glajor, 3, 63.

Hałbat, 3.

Hawuc' Tař, 21.

Hogeac' Vank', 4.

Iran, 19.

Jerusalem, 12, 21, 27, 78, 111, 151, 189.

Jordan, river, 151, 237.
Kars, 18, 39.
Lyon, 22.
Melitene, 6, 86.
Moscow, 17.
Munich, 45.
Narek, 4.
Nicaea, 28, 233.
Part'aw, 8, 17.
Rome, 22, 43.
Sanahin, 3, 68.
Sebastia, 7, 15, 19, 69.
Sinai, 48, 60.
Sion, 27.
Širakavan, 5.
Sis, 244.
Siwnik', 5, 8, 9, 15.
Sodom, 153.
Tarōn, 6.
Tarson, 87.
Tat'ew, 3, 63.
Trebizond, 39, 82.
Varag, 4.
Vaspurakan, 4, 6, 9, 23, 39, 68.
Venice, 23.
Xoranašat, 23.
Xorin Anapat, 22.

5) Subject Index

Anagogy, 53.
Anamnesis, 33, 57, 70, 93.

Anathematization, 10.
Angels, 12, 26, 30, 62, 73, 74, 105, 127, 137, 145, 147, 149, 151, 153, 155, 217, 236, 243.
Apophatic theology, 74, 141, 143, 223.
Apostolic Constitutions, 30.
Bema, 32, 111, 234.
Byzantium, 6-9, 16-18, 25, 30, 35, 36, 39-41, 44, 59, 68, 69, 71, 72, 239, 249.
Catechumens, 24, 25, 30, 31, 48, 74, 119, 234.
Catholicos, prerogatives of, 5, 8, 9, 12, 13.
Chalcedon, Council of, 5, 6, 9, 68-71, 73, 84.
Chalcedonians, 7, 21, 42.
Cherubicon, 31, 32, 48.
Christology, 5, 9, 58-61, 68-71, 73, 76, 77, 135, 137, 141, 143, 145, 153, 155, 157, 159, 161, 169, 171, 173, 177, 179, 197, 199, 211, 213, 219, 235.
Clerk (dpir), 28, 37, 215, 249.
Creation, 56, 57, 60, 74, 97, 99, 125, 127, 143, 161, 163, 177, 223, 233.
Creed, 26, 28, 39, 54, 69, 72, 77, 78, 97, 123, 233.
Cross, blessing of, 7, 12, 16, 225.
Demoniacs, 109, 111.
Dictation, 4, 51.
Diptychs, 34, 94, 244.
Dismissal, 24, 29, 38, 111.